W9-CCM-992

Prentice Hall

MATHEMATICS
Course 2

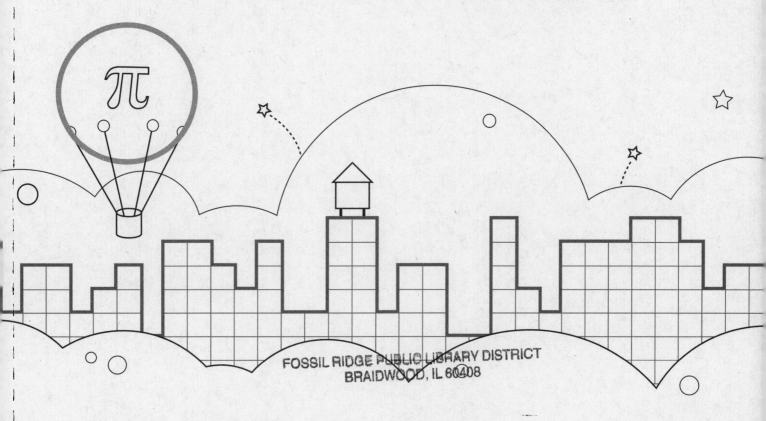

FOSSIL RIDGE PUBLIC LIBRARY DISTRICT
BRAIDWOOD, IL 60408

ALL-IN-ONE
Student Workbook

VERSION A

PEARSON

Boston, Massachusetts • Chandler, Arizona • Glenview, Illinois • Upper Saddle River, New Jersey

ISBN-13: 978-0-13-372144-7
ISBN-10: 0-13-372144-2

14 15 16 17 V011 17 16 15 14

Daily Notetaking Guide

Daily Notetaking Guide (continued)

Chapter 5: Ratios, Rates, and Proportions

Chapter 6: Percents

Chapter 7: Geometry

Chapter 8: Measurement

Chapter 9: Patterns and Rules

Chapter 10: Graphing in the Coordinate Plane

Chapter 11: Displaying and Analyzing Data

Chapter 12: Using Probability

A Note to the Student:

This section of your workbook contains notetaking pages for each lesson in your student edition. They are structured to help you take effective notes in class. They will also serve as a study guide as you prepare for tests and quizzes.

Lesson 1-1

Using Estimation Strategies

Lesson Objective	NAEP 2005 Strand: Number Properties and Operations
To estimate using rounding, front-end estimation, and compatible numbers	**Topic:** Estimation
	Local Standards: _____

Vocabulary

Compatible numbers are _____

_____

Example

❶ **Estimating by Rounding** At the zoo, you see a Colombian black spider monkey. The length of its body is 58.31 cm. The length of its tail is 78.96 cm. To the nearest centimeter, estimate the total length of the monkey's body and tail.

$78.96 + 58.31 \approx$ [   ] + [   ] ← **Round to the nearest whole number.**

             $=$ [   ] ← **Add.**

The total length is about [   ] cm.

Quick Check

1. Estimate. First round to the nearest whole number.

  a. $1.75 + 0.92$

  [   ]

  b. $14.34 - 7.8$

  [   ]

  c. 4.90×6.25

  [   ]

Examples

❷ Estimating by Front-End Estimation At a snack shop, you order a taco that costs $3.79, a juice that costs $.89, and a yogurt that costs $1.39. Estimate the total cost of your order.

Step 1 Add the front-end digits.

$\$\boxed{}.79$

$\$\boxed{}.39$

$+\$\boxed{}.89$

$\$\boxed{}.$

Step 2 Estimate the total amount of cents to the nearest dollar.

$\$3.\boxed{}$

$\$1.\boxed{}$ ⎫ ← about $\$\boxed{}$

$\$0.\boxed{}$ ← about $\$\boxed{}$

$+$ $\$\boxed{} = \$\boxed{}$

The total cost is about $\$\boxed{}$.

Check Round each cost to the nearest whole dollar.

$\boxed{} + \$1 + \boxed{} = \boxed{}$

The answer checks.

❸ Estimating Using Compatible Numbers Suppose you save $61.80. About how many CDs can you buy if each costs $15.95?

$61.8 \div 15.95$ ← **Use division.**

$64 \div 16$ ← **Choose compatible numbers such as 64 and 16.**

$\boxed{}$ ← **Simplify.**

You can buy about $\boxed{}$ CDs.

Quick Check

2. Estimate to the nearest dollar the total cost of a dog collar for $5.79, a dog toy for $2.48, and a dog dish for $5.99.

_____

3. Your friend says that you can buy about twice as many CDs priced at $7.95 each as CDs priced at $15.95 each. Is your friend correct? Explain.

_____

Lesson 1-2

Adding and Subtracting Decimals

Lesson Objective	NAEP 2005 Strand: Number Properties and Operations
To add and subtract decimals and to do mental math using the properties of addition	**Topic:** Number Operations
	Local Standards: _____

Key Concepts

Properties of Addition

Identity Property of Addition _____

Arithmetic	**Algebra**
$5.6 + \boxed{} = 5.6$	$a + \boxed{} = a$

Commutative Property of Addition _____

_____

Arithmetic	**Algebra**
$1.2 + 3.4 = \boxed{}$	$\boxed{} = b + a$

Associative Property of Addition _____

_____

Arithmetic	**Algebra**
$(2.5 + 6) + 4 = 2.5 + \boxed{}$	$(a + b) + c = a + \boxed{}$

Example

❶ Adding Decimals Find $2.15 + 7.632 + 16.5$.

Estimate $2.15 + 7.632 + 16.5 \approx \boxed{} + \boxed{} + \boxed{}$, or $\boxed{}$

Align the decimal points. →

$$
\begin{array}{r}
2.150 \\
7.632 \\
+16.500 \\
\hline
\boxed{}
\end{array}
$$

← Insert zeros so each addend has the same number of decimal places.

Check for Reasonableness Since $\boxed{}$ is close to $\boxed{}$, the answer is reasonable.

Quick Check

1. Find $9.75 + 14.851 + 2$.

Examples

❷ Subtracting Decimals You have 5.08 min left on a CD. How much time will you have left after you record a 2.5-minute song?

   5.08 ← **Align the decimal points.**

  −2.50 ← **Insert a zero.**

             4 10

         5̷.0̷8 ← **Regroup.**

       −2.50 ← **Subtract.**

You will have [   ] min left on the CD.

❸ Using Properties of Addition Use mental math to find 0.2 + 15.7 + 3.8.

What you think

I should look for compatible numbers. The sum of [   ] and [   ] is 4.

Then add [   ] and 15.7 for a total of [   ].

Why it works

$$0.2 + 15.7 + 3.8 = 0.2 + 3.8 + 15.7 \quad ← \boxed{} \textbf{ Property of Addition}$$

$$= (0.2 + 3.8) + 15.7 \quad ← \boxed{} \textbf{ Property of Addition}$$

$$= \boxed{} + 15.7 \quad ← \textbf{ Add within parentheses.}$$

$$= \boxed{} \quad ← \textbf{ Simplify.}$$

Quick Check

2. Find 26.7 − 14.81.

3. Use mental math to find 4.4 + 5.3 + 0.6.

Lesson 1-3

Multiplying Decimals

Lesson Objective	**NAEP 2005 Strand:** Number Properties and Operations
To multiply decimals and to do mental math using the properties of multiplication	**Topic:** Number Operations
	Local Standards: _____

Key Concepts

Properties of Multiplication

Identity Property of Multiplication _____

        Arithmetic $5 \cdot \boxed{} = 5$ **Algebra** $a \cdot \boxed{} = a$

                    $\boxed{} \cdot 5 = 5$ $\boxed{} \cdot a = a$

Zero Property _____

        Arithmetic $5 \cdot \boxed{} = 0$ **Algebra** $a \cdot \boxed{} = 0$

                    $\boxed{} \cdot 5 = 0$ $\boxed{} \cdot a = 0$

Commutative Property of Multiplication _____

_____

        Arithmetic $5 \cdot 2 = 2 \cdot \boxed{}$ **Algebra** $a \cdot 2 = 2 \cdot \boxed{}$

Associative Property of Multiplication _____

_____

        Arithmetic $(3 \cdot 2) \cdot 5 = 3 \cdot \boxed{}$ **Algebra** $(a \cdot b) \cdot c = a \cdot \boxed{}$

Examples

❶ Multiplying Decimals Estimate 11.4×3.6. Then find the product.

Estimate $11.4 \times 3.6 \approx \boxed{} \times \boxed{} = \boxed{}$

Step 1 Multiply as if the numbers are whole numbers.

Step 2 Locate the decimal point in the product by adding the decimal places of the factors.

$$
\begin{array}{r}
1\ 1\ 4 \\
\times \quad 3\ 6 \\
\hline
\boxed{\ }\ \boxed{\ }\ \boxed{\ } \\
\boxed{\ }\ \boxed{\ } \\
\hline
\boxed{\ }\ \boxed{\ }\ \boxed{\ }\ \boxed{\ }
\end{array}
$$

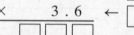

$$
\begin{array}{r}
1\ 1\ .\ 4 \\
\times \quad 3\ .\ 6 \\
\hline
\boxed{\ }\ \boxed{\ }\ \boxed{\ } \\
\boxed{\ }\ \boxed{\ } \\
\hline
\boxed{\ }\ \boxed{\ }\ .\ \boxed{\ }\ \boxed{\ }
\end{array}
$$

← $\boxed{}$ decimal place (tenths)

← $\boxed{}$ decimal place (tenths)

← tenths × tenths = hundredths

Use $\boxed{}$ decimal places.

The product of 11.4 and 3.6 is $\boxed{}$.

Check for Reasonableness The product $\boxed{}$ is close to the estimate of $\boxed{}$. The answer is reasonable.

❷ Using Multiplication Properties Use mental math to find $2 \cdot 4.097 \cdot 0.5$.

What you think

I should look for compatible numbers. The product of ☐ and 0.5 is 1.

Then the product of 1 and 4.097 is [   ]

Why it works

$2 \cdot 4.097 \cdot 0.5 = 2 \cdot 0.5 \cdot 4.097$ ← [   ] **Property of Multiplication**

$= (2 \cdot 0.5) \cdot 4.097$ ← [   ] **Property of Multiplication**

$= 1 \cdot 4.097$ ← **Simplify.**

$=$ [   ] ← [   ] **Property of Multiplication**

Quick Check

1. Estimate, then find each product.

a. 3.7×9

b. 14.3×0.81

c. 8.73×5.4

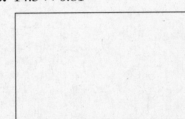
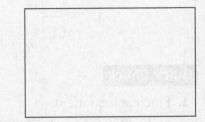

2. Use mental math to find $2.5 \cdot 6.3 \cdot 4$.

Lesson 1-4

Dividing Decimals

Lesson Objectives	NAEP 2005 Strand: Number Properties and Operations
To divide decimals and to solve problems by dividing decimals	**Topic:** Number Operations
	Local Standards: _____

Example

1 **Dividing a Decimal by a Decimal** Find $1.512 \div 0.36$.

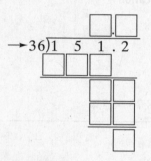   ← Multiply the divisor and the dividend by 100 to make the divisor a whole number.

   ← Place the decimal point in the quotient above the decimal point in the dividend.

Quick Check

1. Find each quotient.

a. $12.42 \div 5.4$

b. $67.84 \div 0.64$

c. $144.06 \div 9.8$

Example

❷ Annexing Zeros to Divide In a restaurant, one serving of coleslaw weighs 3.5 oz. The owner buys coleslaw in cans that weigh 98 oz each. How many servings are in one can?

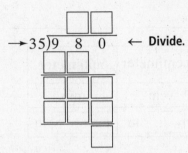

3.5)98.0   ← **Annex the zero in the dividend. Multiply the divisor and dividend by 10 to make the divisor a whole number.**

→ 35)9 8 0   ← **Divide.**

The quotient is ⬚ . There are ⬚ servings in a 98-oz can of coleslaw.

Quick Check

2. You use 0.6 lb of bananas in each smoothie. How many smoothies can you make with 3.12 lb of bananas?

Lesson 1-5

Measuring in Metric Units

Lesson Objective	NAEP 2005 Strand: Measurement
To use and convert metric units of measure	Topic: Systems of Measurement
	Local Standards: _____

Key Concepts

Unit	kilometer	hecto-meter	deca-meter	meter	deci-meter	centimeter	millimeter
Symbol	km	hm	dam	m	dm	cm	mm
Value	☐ m	100 m	10 m	☐ m	0.1 m	☐ m	☐ m

Example

❶ Choosing a Reasonable Estimate Choose a reasonable estimate. Explain your choice.

a. length of a pencil: 19 mm   19 cm   19 m

_____

_____

_____

b. capacity of a bucket: 12 ml   12 L   12 kL

_____

_____

Quick Check

1. Choose a reasonable estimate. Explain your choice.

a. capacity of a soup bowl: 180 mL   180 L   180 kL

_____

b. mass of a butterfly: 500 mg   500 g   500 kg

_____

Examples

❷ **Multiplying to Change Units** Change 871 centimeters to meters.

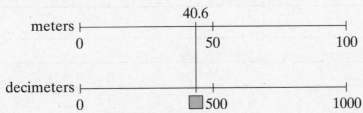

$$871 \text{ cm} = \boxed{} \text{ m}$$

$1 \text{ cm} = \boxed{} \text{ m} \leftarrow$ **You are starting with centimeters. Complete the relationship 1 cm = $\boxed{}$ m.**

$871 \cdot \boxed{} = \boxed{} \text{ m} \leftarrow$ **To change centimeters to meters, multiply by $\boxed{}$.**

$871 \text{ cm equals } \boxed{} \text{ m.}$

❸ **Multiplying to Change Units** Change 40.6 meters to decimeters.

$$40.6 \text{ m} = \boxed{} \text{ dm}$$

$1 \text{ m} = \boxed{} \text{ dm} \leftarrow$ **You are starting with meters. Complete the relationship 1 m = $\boxed{}$ dm.**

$40.6 \cdot \boxed{} = \boxed{} \leftarrow$ **To change meters to decimeters, multiply by $\boxed{}$.**

$40.6 \text{ meters equals } \boxed{} \text{ decimeters.}$

Quick Check

2. Change 34 liters to milliliters.

3. Change 4,690 grams to kilograms.

Lesson 1-6

Comparing and Ordering Integers

Lesson Objective To compare and order integers and to find absolute values	**NAEP 2005 Strand:** Number Properties and Operations **Topic:** Number Sense **Local Standards:** _____

Vocabulary

Integers are _____

_____

_____

Two numbers are opposites if _____

_____

_____

The absolute value of a number is _____

_____

_____

Example

❶ **Finding an Opposite** Find the opposite of 2.

The opposite of 2 is ⬜, because 2 and ⬜ are each ⬜ units from ⬜, but in ⬜ directions.

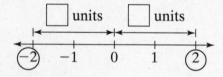

⬜ units   ⬜ units

Quick Check

1. Find the opposite of each number.

a. −8

b. 13

c. −22

Examples

❷ **Finding Absolute Value** Find $|-5|$ and $|5|$.

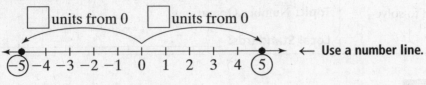

$\boxed{}$ units from 0 $\boxed{}$ units from 0

← **Use a number line.**

$|-5| = \boxed{}$ and $|5| = \boxed{}$.

❸ **Comparing Integers** Compare 3 and -8 using $<$, $=$, or $>$.

3 is $\boxed{}$ units to the right of 0.

-8 is $\boxed{}$ units to the left of 0.

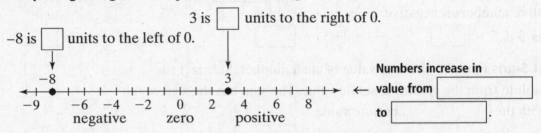

← **Numbers increase in** value from $\boxed{}$ to $\boxed{}$.

Since 3 is to the $\boxed{}$ of -8 on the number line, 3 $\boxed{}$ -8.

Quick Check

2. Find $|-8|$.

3. Compare -8 and -2 using $<$, $=$, or $>$.

4. Order the numbers 3, -1, -4, and 2 from least to greatest.

Lesson 1-7   **Adding and Subtracting Integers**

Lesson Objective	NAEP 2005 Strand: Number Properties and Operations
To add and subtract integers and to solve problems involving integers	**Topic:** Number Operations
	Local Standards: _____

Vocabulary and Key Concepts

Adding Integers

Same Sign The sum of two positive numbers is [   ]. The sum of two negative numbers is negative.

Examples $3 + 5 =$ [   ] $-3 + (-5) =$ [   ]

Different Signs Find the absolute value of each number. Subtract the lesser absolute from the greater absolute value. The sum has the sign of the integer with the [   ] absolute value.

Examples $-3 + 5 =$ [   ] $3 + (-5) =$ [   ]

Subtracting Integers

To subtract an integer, add its [   ].

Examples $3 - 5 = 3 + ($[   ]$) =$ [   ] $-3 - 5 = -3 + ($[   ]$) =$ [   ]

Two numbers are additive inverses if _____

_____

Example

① **Adding Integers With a Number Line** Use a number line to find the sum $-4 + (-2)$.

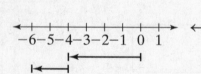

Start at [   ]. Move 4 units [   ].

Then move another 2 units [   ].

The sum is [   ].

Quick Check

1. Use a number line to find each sum.

$-8\ -7\ -6\ -5\ -4\ -3\ -2\ -1\ \ \ 0$

   a. $-8 + 1$ **b.** $-1 + (-7)$ **c.** $-6 + 6$

Examples

② Adding Integers Find $24 + (-6)$.

$|24| = \boxed{}$ and $|^-6| = \boxed{}$ ← **Find the absolute value of each integer.**

$24 - \boxed{} = \boxed{}$ ← **Subtract** $\boxed{}$ **from 24 because** $|-6|\ \boxed{}\ |24|$.

$24 + (-6) = \boxed{}$ ← **The sum has the same sign as** $\boxed{}$.

③ Subtracting Integers Find $-7 - 2$.

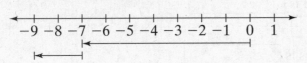

Start at $\boxed{}$. **Move 7 units left.**

← **Then** $\boxed{}$ **the opposite of 2,**

which is $\boxed{}$.

$-7 - 2 = -7\ \boxed{}\ (-2) = \boxed{}$

④ Application: Weather Recorded temperatures at Amundsen-Scott Station in Antarctica have ranged from a low of $-89°F$ to a high of $-13°F$. Find the difference in temperatures.

Subtract to find the difference.

$-13 - (-89) = -13 + \boxed{}$ ← **Add the** $\boxed{}$ **of −89, which is** $\boxed{}$.

$= \boxed{}$ ← **Simplify.**

The difference in temperatures is $\boxed{}$.

Quick Check

2. Find each sum.

a. $-97 + (-65)$

b. $21 + (-39)$

c. $22 + (-22)$

3. Find $-6 - 1$.

4. During the biggest drop of the Mean Streak roller coaster in Ohio, your altitude changes by -155 ft. The Texas Giant™ in Texas has a -137 ft change. How much farther do you drop on the Mean Streak?

Lesson 1-8

Multiplying and Dividing Integers

Lesson Objective	**NAEP 2005 Strand:** Number Properties and Operations
To multiply and divide integers and to solve problems involving integers	**Topic:** Number Operations
	Local Standards: _____

Key Concepts

Multiplying Integers

The product of two integers with the same sign is [   ].

Examples $3(2) =$ [   ] $-3(-2) =$ [   ]

The product of two integers with different signs is [   ].

Examples $-3(2) =$ [   ] $3(-2) =$ [   ]

Dividing Integers

The quotient of two integers with the same sign is [   ].

Examples $10 \div 2 =$ [   ] $-10 \div (-2) =$ [   ]

The quotient of two integers with different signs is [   ].

Examples $-10 \div 2 =$ [   ] $10 \div (-2) =$ [   ]

Example

1 Multiplying Integers Find each product.

a. $3(7) =$ [   ] ← [   ] signs; [   ] product. → **b.** $-3(-7) =$ [   ]

c. $3(-7) =$ [   ] ← [   ] signs; [   ] product. → **d.** $-3(7) =$ [   ]

Quick Check

1. Simplify the expression $-4(-7)$.

[   ]

Daily Notetaking Guide

Example

❷ **Dividing Integers** You are riding your bicycle at a speed of 12 ft/s. Four seconds later, you come to a complete stop. Find the acceleration of your bicycle.

$$\text{acceleration} = \frac{\text{final velocity} - \text{initial velocity}}{\text{time}}$$

$$= \frac{\boxed{} - \boxed{}}{\boxed{}}$$ ← Substitute $\boxed{}$ for final velocity, $\boxed{}$ for initial velocity, and $\boxed{}$ for time.

$$= \frac{\boxed{}}{\boxed{}} = \boxed{}$$ ← Simplify. The $\boxed{}$ sign means the bicycle is slowing.

The bicycle's acceleration is $\boxed{}$ ft/s per second.

Quick Check

2. Suppose you are running at the rate of 24 ft/s in a 40-yd dash. It takes you 4 s to slow to a stop. Find your acceleration.

Lesson 1-9

Lesson Objective	NAEP 2005 Strand: Number Properties and Operations
To simplify numerical expressions involving order of operations	**Topics:** Number Operations and Properties of Numbers and Operations
	Local Standards: _____

Key Concepts

Order of Operations

1. Work inside grouping symbols.

2. [ ] and [ ] in order from left to right.

3. [ ] and [ ] in order from left to right.

Distributive Property

Arithmetic

$9(4 + 5) = \boxed{}(4) + \boxed{}(5)$

$5(8 - 2) = 5(\boxed{}) - 5(\boxed{})$

Algebra

$a(b + c) = \boxed{}(b) + \boxed{}(c)$

$a(b - c) = a(\boxed{}) - a(\boxed{})$

Example

1 Using the Order of Operations Find the value of each expression.

a. $9 + 3 \cdot 5 - 1$

[ ]   ← **Multiply.**

23   ← **Add and subtract.**

b. $9 + 3 \cdot (5 - 1)$

[ ]   ← **Work inside grouping symbols.**

[ ]   ← **Multiply.**

21   ← **Add.**

Quick Check

1. Find the value of each expression.

a. $7(-4 + 2) - 1$

b. $\dfrac{-40}{4} + 2 \cdot 5$

c. $\dfrac{8 + 4}{6} - 11$

Name _____ Class _____ Date _____

Examples

❷ **Application: Shopping** You want to buy four CDs at a price of $11.95 each and two DVDs at a price of $18.75 each. What is the total cost of the items?

Words ☐ CDs + ☐ DVDs

Expression ☐ × 11.95 + ☐ × ☐ = ☐ + 37.50 ← **First multiply.**

= ☐ ← **Then add.**

The total cost is $☐ .

❸ **The Distributive Property in Mental Math** Use the Distributive Property to find 4(4.8).

What you think
If I think of 4.8 as (5.0 − 0.2), then, 4(4.8) is the same as

4(☐ − ☐).

I know that 4(5.0) − 4(0.2) = ☐ − ☐ = ☐.

Why it works
4(4.8) = 4(5.0 − 0.2)

= 4(5.0) − 4(0.2) ← **Use the ☐ Property.**

= ☐ − ☐ ← **Multiply.**

= ☐ ← **Subtract.**

Quick Check

2. What is the total cost of one CD at a price of $11.95 and three DVDs at a price of $18.75 each?

3. Use the Distributive Property and mental math to find 9(14).

Lesson 1-10

Mean, Median, Mode, and Range

Lesson Objective To describe data using mean, median, mode, and range	**NAEP 2005 Strand:** Data Analysis and Probability **Topic:** Characteristics of Data Sets **Local Standards:** _____

Vocabulary

The mean of a data set is _____

_____

An outlier is a data item that _____

_____

The median of a data set is _____

_____

The mode of a data set is _____

_____

The range of a data set is _____

_____

Examples

❶ Finding the Mean Find the mean of 502, 477, 593, 481, 735, and 614.

$$\frac{502 + 477 + 593 + 481 + 735 + 614}{\boxed{}}$$ ← **Divide the sum by the number of items.**

$$\frac{\boxed{}}{\boxed{}} = \boxed{}$$ ← **Simplify.**

❷ Finding the Median Find the median of the data in the chart. First write the data in order from least to greatest.

18 Responses to "How many pets do you have?"					
2	0	1	2	4	2
1	0	3	2	0	8
0	1	2	3	0	1

_____

The two middle values are $\boxed{}$ and $\boxed{}$.

Find the mean of the two $\boxed{}$ values.

$$\frac{\boxed{} + \boxed{} = \boxed{}}{\boxed{}}$$

The median is $\boxed{}$.

Quick Check

1. Find the mean of 216, 230, 198, and 252. [_____]

2. Find the median in this data set: −5 −1 3 −18 −2 2

[_____]

 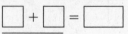

Examples

❸ **Finding the Mode** Find the mode of the data in the chart. Make a table to organize the data.

Peppers	Onions	Mushrooms	Sausage

The mode is [   ] .

Favorite Pizza Topping of Twelve People Surveyed

peppers	onions	mushrooms
onions	sausage	peppers
onions	peppers	mushrooms
onions	sausage	onions

❹ **Geography** Elevations in California range from −282 ft (or 282 ft below sea level) at Badwater in Death Valley to 14,495 ft at the top of Mt. Whitney. Find the elevation range in California.

$14{,}495 - (-282) = 14{,}495 +$ [   ] ← Add the [   ] of −282, which is [   ] .

$=$ [   ] ← Simplify.

The elevation range in California is [   ] ft.

Quick Check

3. Find the modes.
   a. 17 16 18 17 16 17

   [   ]

   b. 3.2 3.7 3.5 3.7 3.5 3.2

   [   ]

   c. pen, pencil, marker, marker, pen, pen, pen, pencil, marker

   [   ]

4. Record temperatures in Texas set in the 1930s were a low of −23°F and a high of 120°F. Find the temperature range.

   [   ]

Lesson 2-1

Lesson Objective	NAEP 2005 Strand: Number Properties and Operations
To write and simplify expressions with exponents	**Topic:** Number Operations
	Local Standards: _____

Vocabulary and Key Concepts

Order of Operations

1. Do all operations within [   ] first.

2. Evaluate any term(s) with [   ].

3. [   ] and [   ] in order from left to right.

4. [   ] and [   ] in order from left to right.

An exponent _____

_____

exponent ——→

value of the expression ——↓

$5\,\square = \underbrace{5 \cdot 5 \cdot 5}_{} = \boxed{}$

base ——→

↑ The base is used as a factor three times.

A power is _____

_____

Example

❶ Writing Expressions Using Exponents Write $7 \cdot 7 \cdot 7 \cdot 7$ using an exponent.

$7 \cdot 7 \cdot 7 \cdot 7 = \boxed{}$ ← [   ] is the base.

[   ] is the exponent.

Quick Check

1. Write each product using exponents.

a. $44 \cdot 44 \cdot 44 \cdot 44$

b. $(-2) \cdot (-2)$

Examples

❷ **Geography** A seaside village has an area of 1.3^2 km². Find the value of 1.3^2.

Method 1

$$(1.3)^2 = \left(\boxed{}\right)\left(\boxed{}\right) \qquad \leftarrow \textbf{Write as a product of repeated factors.}$$

$$= \boxed{} \qquad \leftarrow \textbf{Multiply.}$$

Method 2

Use a calculator.

$$1.3 \;\boxed{}\; \blacksquare \;\boxed{} \qquad \leftarrow \textbf{Use the } \boxed{} \textbf{ key to square numbers.}$$

The area of the village is $\boxed{}$ km².

❸ **Simplify Using Order of Operations** Simplify $2^3 \cdot (9 - 3)^2$.

$$2^3 \cdot (9 - 3)^2 = 2^3 \cdot \boxed{}^2 \qquad \leftarrow \textbf{Do operations in parentheses.}$$

$$= \boxed{} \cdot \boxed{} \qquad \leftarrow \textbf{Find the values of the powers.}$$

$$= \boxed{} \qquad \leftarrow \textbf{Multiply.}$$

Quick Check

2. Simplify. Use paper and pencil, a model, or a calculator.

   a. 3^5 **b.** 10^9 **c.** 3.1^2

3. Simplify.

   a. $(-2)^3$ **b.** -2^3 **c.** $(3 + 5)^2 - 2$

Lesson 2-2

Prime Factorization

Lesson Objective To find multiples and factors and to use prime factorization	**NAEP 2005 Strand:** Number Properties and Operations **Topic:** Properties of Number and Operations **Local Standards:** _____

Vocabulary

A multiple of a number is _____

_____

The least common multiple (LCM) of two or more numbers is _____

_____

A factor is _____

_____

A composite number is _____

_____

A prime number is _____

_____

Prime factorization is _____

_____

The greatest common factor (GCF) of two or more numbers is _____

_____

Example

❶ **Finding the LCM** Dan goes to the health club every 4 days. His sister Neesa goes there every 6 days. Dan and Neesa both went to the health club today. When will they both go there on the same day again?

Find the least common multiple of 4 and 6.

Multiples of 4: 4, 8, ☐, ☐, ☐, ... ⎫
                                        ⎬ ← List the first several
Multiples of 6: 6, 12, ☐, ☐, ... ⎭   multiples of 4 and 6.

The LCM of 4 and 6 is ☐. Both will go to the health club again in ☐ days.

Quick Check

1. Find the LCM of each pair of numbers.

a. 4, 10   **b.** 5, 7   **c.** 12, 15

Examples

② **Prime Numbers and Composite Numbers** Determine whether each number is prime or composite.

a. 17   Factors: [   ]   17 is a [   ] number.

b. 22   Factors: [   ]   22 is a [   ] number.

③ **Writing Prime Factorization** Use a factor tree to write the prime factorization of 90.

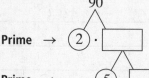

90

Prime → ②·[   ]   ← **Write 90 as the product of any two of its factors.**

Prime → ⑤·[   ]   ← **Write [   ] as the product of two factors.**

Prime → ③·[   ]   ← **Write [   ] as the product of two factors.**

$90 = $ [   ]. Using exponents, you can write $90 = 2 \cdot$ [   ] $\cdot 5$.

④ **Finding the GCF** Find the GCF of 32 and 48.

$32 = $ [   ]

$48 = $ [   ]   ← **Write the prime factorizations.**

$GCF = $ [   ] $=$ [   ]   ← **Find the product of the common factors.**

The GCF of 32 and 48 is [   ].

Quick Check

2. Is 15 prime or composite? Explain.

[   ]

3. Write the prime factorization of 72. Use exponents where possible.

[   ]

4. Find the GCF of 16 and 24.

[   ]

Lesson 2-3

Lesson Objective	**NAEP 2005 Strand:** Number Properties and Operations
To write equivalent fractions and to simplify fractions	**Topic:** Number Operations
	Local Standards: _____

Vocabulary

Equivalent fractions are _____

_____

A fraction is written in simplest form when _____

_____

Examples

① **Using Multiples** Use a table of multiples to write three fractions equivalent to $\frac{3}{7}$.

	× 2	× 3	× 4
3			
7			

← Multiples in the same column form fractions equivalent to $\frac{3}{7}$.

Three fractions equivalent to $\frac{3}{7}$ are $\frac{\boxed{}}{\boxed{}}$, $\frac{\boxed{}}{\boxed{}}$, and $\frac{\boxed{}}{\boxed{}}$.

② **Using Factors** Find three fractions equivalent to $\frac{16}{24}$.

Factors of 16: [   ]
Factors of 24: [   ]

} ← List the factors of each number. Look for common factors.

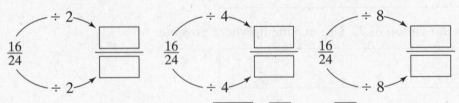

Three fractions equivalent to $\frac{16}{24}$ are $\frac{\boxed{}}{\boxed{}}$, $\frac{\boxed{}}{\boxed{}}$, and $\frac{\boxed{}}{\boxed{}}$.

Name _____ Class _____ Date _____

Examples

❸ Simplify by Dividing Write $\frac{12}{30}$ in simplest form.

$$\frac{12 \div 3}{30 \div 3} = \frac{\boxed{}}{\boxed{}}$$ ← **Divide the numerator and denominator by a common factor.**

$$\frac{4 \div \boxed{}}{10 \div \boxed{}} = \frac{\boxed{}}{\boxed{}}$$ ← **If necessary, divide again by another common factor.**

In simplest form, $\frac{12}{30}$ is $\dfrac{\boxed{}}{\boxed{}}$.

❹ Using the GCF to Simplify a Fraction There are 28 students in Mai's homeroom. Of these, 20 students have a pet. What fraction of the students have a pet? Write your answer in simplest form.

$$\frac{20}{28} = \frac{20 \div \boxed{}}{28 \div \boxed{}} = \frac{\boxed{}}{\boxed{}}$$ ← **Divide both numerator and denominator by the GCF, $\boxed{}$.**

The fraction of students that have a pet is $\dfrac{\boxed{}}{\boxed{}}$.

Quick Check

1. Use multiples to write two fractions equivalent to $\frac{4}{5}$.

2. Use common factors to write two fractions equivalent to $\frac{18}{30}$

3. Write $\frac{8}{12}$ in simplest form.

4. Your class ordered 45 calculators. Of these, 18 were solar powered. What fraction of the calculators were solar powered?

Lesson 2-4

Comparing and Ordering Fractions

Lesson Objective	NAEP 2005 Strand: Number Properties and Operations
To compare and order fractions	**Topic:** Number Sense
	Local Standards: _____

Vocabulary

A least common denominator (LCD) of two or more fractions is _____

_____

Example

1 Comparing Fractions Compare $\frac{7}{12}$ and $\frac{5}{9}$.

The denominators are 12 and 9. Their LCM is [ ]. So [.] is their LCD.

$$\frac{7}{12} = \frac{7 \times 3}{12 \times 3} = \frac{\boxed{}}{\boxed{}}$$

$$\frac{5}{9} = \frac{5 \times 4}{9 \times 4} = \frac{\boxed{}}{\boxed{}}$$

← Write equivalent fractions with a denominator of [ ].

$$\frac{\boxed{}}{\boxed{}} > \frac{\boxed{}}{\boxed{}}$$

← Compare the numerators.

So $\frac{7}{12}$ [ ] $\frac{5}{9}$.

Quick Check

1. Compare each pair of fractions. Use $<$, $=$, or $>$.

a. $\frac{3}{4}$ [ ] $\frac{5}{6}$

b. $\frac{1}{6}$ [ ] $\frac{2}{9}$

c. $\frac{4}{10}$ [ ] $\frac{3}{8}$

Example

❷ **Multiple Choice** Giselda wants to paint her room. She found $\frac{3}{5}$ gal of yellow paint, $\frac{2}{3}$ gal of blue paint, and $\frac{1}{2}$ gal of green paint. Which list shows these fractions in order from least to greatest?

A. $\frac{1}{2}, \frac{2}{3}, \frac{3}{5}$ **B.** $\frac{3}{5}, \frac{2}{3}, \frac{1}{2}$ **C.** $\frac{1}{2}, \frac{3}{5}, \frac{2}{3}$ **D.** $\frac{2}{3}, \frac{3}{5}, \frac{1}{2}$

Order $\frac{3}{5}, \frac{2}{3}$, and $\frac{1}{2}$. The LCM of 5, 3, and 2 is $\boxed{}$. So $\boxed{}$ is the LCD.

Yellow → $\dfrac{3}{5} = \dfrac{3 \times \boxed{}}{5 \times \boxed{}} = \dfrac{\boxed{}}{\boxed{}}$

← Write equivalent fractions with a denominator of $\boxed{}$.

Blue → $\dfrac{2}{3} = \dfrac{2 \times \boxed{}}{3 \times \boxed{}} = \dfrac{\boxed{}}{\boxed{}}$

Green → $\dfrac{1}{2} = \dfrac{1 \times \boxed{}}{2 \times \boxed{}} = \dfrac{\boxed{}}{\boxed{}}$

$\dfrac{\boxed{}}{\boxed{}} < \dfrac{\boxed{}}{\boxed{}} < \dfrac{\boxed{}}{\boxed{}}$. So, $\dfrac{\boxed{}}{\boxed{}}$ gal $< \dfrac{\boxed{}}{\boxed{}}$ gal $< \dfrac{\boxed{}}{\boxed{}}$ gal. ← Compare the numerators.

So the order is $\dfrac{\boxed{}}{\boxed{}}, \dfrac{\boxed{}}{\boxed{}}, \dfrac{\boxed{}}{\boxed{}}$. The correct answer is choice $\boxed{}$.

Quick Check

2. A carpenter uses four screws with diameters of $\frac{1}{4}$ in., $\frac{3}{8}$ in., $\frac{5}{16}$ in., and $\frac{5}{32}$ in. Order the diameters from least to greatest.

Lesson 2-5

Mixed Numbers and Improper Fractions

Lesson Objective	**NAEP 2005 Strand:** Number Properties and Operations
To write a mixed numbers and improper fractions	**Topic:** Number Operations
	Local Standards: _____

Vocabulary

An improper fraction has _____

_____

A mixed number is _____

_____

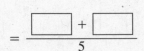

$$1\frac{2}{3} \qquad\qquad \frac{5}{3}$$

Examples

❶ Writing an Improper Fraction Write $3\frac{2}{5}$ as an improper fraction.

Method 1 Using Addition

$3\frac{2}{5} = 3 + \frac{2}{5}$　　　　← **Write the mixed number as a sum.**

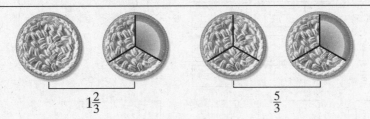

$= \dfrac{\boxed{}}{\boxed{}} + \dfrac{2}{5}$　　← **Change 3 to a fraction with the same denominator as $\frac{2}{5}$.**

　　　　　　　　　Substitute $3 = 3 \times \dfrac{\boxed{}}{\boxed{}} = \dfrac{\boxed{}}{\boxed{}}$.

$= \dfrac{\boxed{} + \boxed{}}{5}$　　← **Add the numerators.**

$= \dfrac{\boxed{}}{\boxed{}}$　　← **Simplify.**

Method 2 Using Multiplication

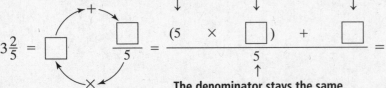

Multiply the denominator by the whole number.　Add the numerator.

$3\frac{2}{5} = \boxed{}\quad \dfrac{\boxed{}}{5} = \dfrac{(5 \;\times\; \boxed{}) \;+\; \boxed{}}{5} = \dfrac{\boxed{}}{\boxed{}}.$

The denominator stays the same.

❷ **Writing a Mixed Number** Karl needs $\frac{18}{4}$ cups of milk to make several loaves of bread. Express the amount of milk as a mixed number in simplest form.

                 □ ← whole number

denominator → 4)18

         −16

           □ ← remainder

$4\frac{\Box}{4} = \Box\frac{\Box}{\Box}$ ← Write the remainder as a fraction, $\frac{remainder}{denominator}$. Simplify.

Karl needs $\Box\frac{\Box}{\Box}$ cups of milk.

Quick Check

1. **Choose a Method** Write $2\frac{5}{8}$ as an improper fraction.

2. A bakery sells a jumbo pie with 12 slices. If you need 30 slices, how many jumbo pies should you buy?

Lesson 2-6

Fractions and Decimals

Lesson Objective	NAEP 2005 Strand: Number Properties and Operations
To convert between fractions and decimals	**Topic:** Number Operations
	Local Standards: _____

Vocabulary

A terminating decimal is _____
_____

A repeating decimal is _____
_____

Examples

❶ Writing a Terminating Decimal The total amount of rainfall yesterday was reported as $\frac{1}{4}$ in. Write this fraction as a decimal.

$\frac{1}{4}$ or $1 \div 4 = 4\overline{)1.0\ 0}$ ← **quotient**

$-\boxed{}$

$\ \ \ 2\ 0$

$-2\ 0$

$\ \ \ \ \ 0$ ← **The remainder is 0.**

So $\frac{1}{4} = \boxed{}$. The total amount of rainfall as a decimal is $\boxed{}$ in.

❷ Writing a Repeating Decimal Write $\frac{7}{15}$ as a decimal.

Method 1: Paper and Pencil

$\frac{7}{15}$ or $7 \div 15 = 15\overline{)7.0000}$ ← The digit 6 repeats.

$\ \ -6\ 0$

$\ \ \ \ 1\ 0\ 0$

$\ \ -\ 9\ 0$

$\boxed{}$ ← There will always be a remainder of $\boxed{}$.

So $\frac{7}{15} = \boxed{}$.

Method 2: Calculator

7 ⊟ 15 ⊟ $\boxed{}$

❸ Writing a Decimal as a Fraction Write 4.105 as a fraction in simplest form

Since $0.105 = \frac{105}{1000}$, $4.105 = \boxed{}\dfrac{\boxed{}}{\boxed{}}$.

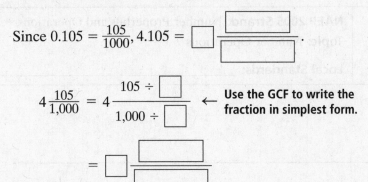

$$4\frac{105}{1{,}000} = 4\,\frac{105 \div \boxed{}}{1{,}000 \div \boxed{}} \quad \leftarrow \quad \text{Use the GCF to write the fraction in simplest form.}$$

$$= \boxed{}\,\frac{\boxed{}}{\boxed{}}$$

❹ Application: Surveys In a survey of next year's seventh-grade students, 0.25 said they will come to school by bus, $\frac{5}{24}$ said they will walk, 0.375 said they will come in a car, and $\frac{1}{16}$ said they will ride their bicycles. Order the means of transportation from most used to least used.

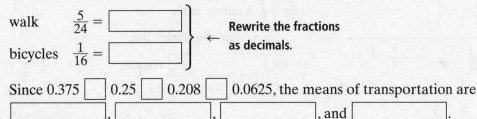

walk $\quad \frac{5}{24} = \boxed{}$

bicycles $\quad \frac{1}{16} = \boxed{}$ $\quad \leftarrow$ Rewrite the fractions as decimals.

Since $0.375 \boxed{} 0.25 \boxed{} 0.208 \boxed{} 0.0625$, the means of transportation are $\boxed{}$, $\boxed{}$, $\boxed{}$, and $\boxed{}$.

Quick Check

1. The fraction of nitrogen in a chemical sample is $\frac{5}{8}$. Write the fraction as a decimal.

2. Write $\frac{5}{9}$ as a decimal.

3. Write each decimal as a mixed number with a fraction in simplest form.

a. 1.364

b. 2.48

c. 3.6

3. In a survey about pets, $\frac{2}{5}$ of the students prefer cats, 0.33 prefer dogs, $\frac{3}{25}$ prefer birds, and 0.15 prefer fish. List the choices in order of preference.

Lesson 2-7

Rational Numbers

Lesson Objective	NAEP 2005 Strand: Number Properties and Operations
To compare and order rational numbers	**Topic:** Number Operations
	Local Standards: _____

Vocabulary

A rational number is _____

_____

Example

1 Comparing Rational Numbers Compare $-\frac{1}{4}$ and $-\frac{3}{8}$.

Method 1

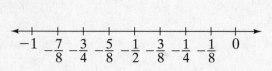

Since $-\frac{3}{8}$ is farther to the

⟵ [____] on the number line,

it is the [____] number.

So, $-\frac{1}{4}$ ☐ $-\frac{3}{8}$.

Method 2

$-\frac{1}{4} = \frac{-1}{4}$ ⟵ Rewrite $-\frac{1}{4}$ with −1 in the numerator.

$= \frac{-1 \times \boxed{}}{4 \times \boxed{}}$ ⟵ The LCD is ☐. Write an equivalent fraction.

$= \frac{-2}{8} = -\frac{2}{8}$ ⟵ The fraction $-\frac{2}{8}$ is equivalent to $\frac{-2}{8}$.

Since $-\frac{2}{8}$ ☐ $-\frac{3}{8}$, $-\frac{1}{4}$ ☐ $-\frac{3}{8}$.

Quick Check

1. Compare $-\frac{2}{3}$ and $-\frac{1}{6}$. Use <, = or >.

Examples

❷ Comparing Decimals Compare. Use <, = , or >.

a. 8.7 and 8.1

8.7 $\boxed{}$ 8.1   ← **Both numbers are positive. Compare the digits.**

b. −8.7 and 8.1

−8.7 $\boxed{}$ 8.1 ← **Any negative number is less than a positive number.**

c. −8.7 and −8.1

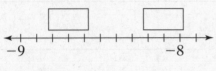

← **Place the decimals on a number line and compare their locations.**

−8.7 $\boxed{}$ −8.1

❸ Ordering Rational Numbers Which list shows the numbers $-\frac{3}{5}, 0.625, \frac{2}{3}$, and −0.5 listed in order from least to greatest?

A. $-\frac{3}{5}, -0.5, 0.625, \frac{2}{3}$ **B.** $-0.5, -\frac{3}{5}, 0.625, \frac{2}{3}$ **C.** $-0.5, \frac{2}{3}, -\frac{3}{5}, 0.625$ **D.** $-\frac{3}{5}, \frac{2}{3}, 0.625, -0.5$

$-\frac{3}{5}, = -3 \div 5 = -0.6$ ← **Write as a decimal.**

$\frac{2}{3} = 2 \div 3 = 0.66666\ldots = 0.\overline{6}$ ← **Write as a repeating decimal.**

$-0.6 \boxed{} -0.5 \boxed{} 0.625 \boxed{} 0.\overline{6}$ ← **Compare the decimals.**

From least to greatest, the numbers are $\boxed{}$, $\boxed{}$, $\boxed{}$, $\boxed{}$.
The correct answer is choice $\boxed{}$.

Quick Check

2. Compare −4.2 and −4.9. Use <, = , or >.

3. The following temperatures were recorded during a science project: $12\frac{1}{2}°C$, −4°C, 6.55°C, and $-6\frac{1}{4}°C$. Order the temperatures from least to greatest.

$\frac{3}{5}$

Lesson 2-8

Scientific Notation

Lesson Objective	**NAEP 2005 Strand:** Number Properties and Operations
To write numbers in both scientific notation and standard form	**Topic:** Number Sense
	Local Standards: _____

Vocabulary and Key Concepts

Scientific Notation

A number in scientific notation is _____

_____

_____

$$7{,}500{,}000{,}000{,}000 \qquad = \qquad 7.5 \qquad \times \qquad 10^{12}$$

First factor is greater than or equal to 1, but less than 10.

Second factor is a power of 10.

Example

❶ **Writing in Scientific Notation** The mean distance from Mars to the sun is about 141,750,000 mi. Write this number in scientific notation.

1.41,750,000.   ←   Move the decimal point to get a factor greater than 1 but less than 10.

141,750,000 = ⬚ × ⬚   ← Write as a product of two factors.

= ⬚ × ⬚   ← Write 100,000,000 as a power of 10.

The mean distance from Mars to the sun is about ⬚ mi.

Quick Check

1. NASA's Hubble Telescope took pictures of a supernova that is 169,000 light years away. Write this number in scientific notation.

⬚

Name _____ Class _____ Date _____

Example

② **Writing in Standard Form** Light from the sun reaches Earth in about
4.99012×10^2 s. Write this number in standard form.

Method 1

$4.99012 \times 10^2 =$ [ ] $\times$ [ ]   ← **Write as a product of 2 factors.**

$=$ [ ]   ← **Multiply the factors.**

Method 2

$4.99012 \times 10^2 =$ [ ]   ← **The exponent is 2. Move the decimal point 2 places to the right.**

Light from the sun reaches Earth in about [ ] s.

Quick Check

2. A large telescope gathers about 6.4×10^5 times the amount of light your eye receives. Write this number in standard form.

[ ]

Lesson 3-1

Estimating With Fractions and Mixed Numbers

Lesson Objective	**NAEP 2005 Strand:** Number Properties and Operations
To estimate sums, differences, products, and quotients of fractions	**Topic:** Estimation
	Local Standards: _____

Vocabulary

A benchmark is _____

_____

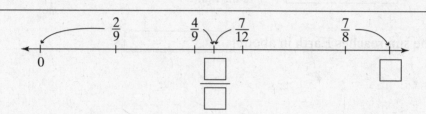

Examples

1 **Using Benchmarks With Fractions** Use benchmarks to estimate $\frac{4}{7} + \frac{4}{5}$.

$$\frac{4}{7} \quad + \quad \frac{4}{5}$$
$$\downarrow \qquad\qquad \downarrow$$

$\frac{\Box}{\Box} + \Box = 1\frac{1}{2}$ ← Use $\boxed{}$ to estimate each fraction. Then add.

2 **Estimating With Mixed Numbers** Estimate $5\frac{1}{9} - 2\frac{5}{6}$.

$$5\frac{1}{9} \quad - \quad 2\frac{5}{6}$$
$$\downarrow \qquad\qquad \downarrow$$

$\Box - \Box = \Box$ ← Round each mixed number. Then subtract.

Quick Check

1. Use benchmarks to estimate $\frac{3}{5} - \frac{1}{8}$.

2. Science For your experiment in plant growth, you record the height of a plant every day. On Monday, the plant was $5\frac{1}{4}$ in. tall. A week later, it was $10\frac{7}{8}$ in. tall. About how many inches did the plant grow?

Examples

❸ Estimating With Mixed Numbers Estimate the product $6\frac{1}{8} \cdot 6\frac{5}{8}$.

$$6\frac{1}{8} \cdot 6\frac{5}{8}$$
$$\downarrow \qquad \downarrow$$
$$\boxed{} \cdot \boxed{} = 42 \quad \leftarrow \quad \text{Round each mixed number. Then multiply.}$$

❹ Estimating With Compatible Numbers Estimate the quotient $26\frac{1}{4} \div 8\frac{2}{3}$.

$$26\frac{1}{4} \div 8\frac{2}{3}$$
$$\downarrow \qquad \downarrow$$
$$\boxed{} \div \boxed{} = 3 \quad \leftarrow \quad \text{Use } \boxed{} \text{ numbers.}$$
$$26\frac{1}{4} \approx \boxed{} \text{ and } 8\frac{2}{3} \approx \boxed{}$$

Quick Check

3. Use rounding to estimate each product.

a. $3\frac{5}{6} \cdot 5\frac{1}{8}$

b. $8\frac{1}{8} \cdot 5\frac{11}{12}$

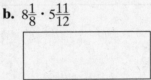

c. $7\frac{1}{3} \cdot 1\frac{13}{16}$

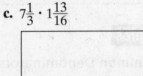

4. Use compatible numbers to estimate each quotient.

a. $35\frac{3}{4} \div 5\frac{11}{12}$

b. $22\frac{7}{8} \div 3\frac{5}{6}$

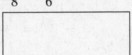

c. $46\frac{2}{5} \div 5\frac{1}{10}$

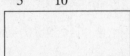

Lesson 3-2

Adding and Subtracting Fractions

Lesson Objective	**NAEP 2005 Strand:** Number Properties and Operations
To add and subtract fractions and to solve problems involving fractions	**Topic:** Number Operations
	Local Standards: _____

Key Concepts

Adding and Subtracting Fractions

You can use models to add or subtract fractions with different denominators. The models below show

$\frac{1}{4} + \frac{1}{3} = \frac{\Box}{\Box}$ and $\frac{1}{2} - \frac{1}{3} = \frac{\Box}{\Box}$.

Examples

❶ Common Denominators Find $\frac{2}{7} + \frac{3}{7}$.

Estimate $\frac{2}{7} + \frac{3}{7} \approx \Box + \frac{\Box}{\Box}$, or $\frac{1}{2}$.

$\frac{2}{7} + \frac{3}{7} = \frac{\Box + \Box}{\Box}$ ← Keep the denominator the same.

$= \frac{\Box}{\Box}$ ← Add the numerators. The answer is close to the estimate.

❷ Different Denominators Find $\frac{5}{9} + \frac{1}{6}$.

Estimate $\frac{5}{9} + \frac{1}{6} \approx \frac{\Box}{\Box} + \Box$, or $\frac{1}{2}$.

$\frac{5}{9} = \frac{5 \cdot \Box}{9 \cdot \Box} = \frac{\Box}{\Box}$ ← The LCD is $\Box$. Write an equivalent fraction.

$+ \frac{1}{6} = \frac{1 \cdot \Box}{6 \cdot \Box} = + \frac{\Box}{\Box}$ ← Write an equivalent fraction.

$\frac{\Box}{\Box}$ ← Add the numerators. The answer is close to the estimate.

❸ Carpentry A carpenter begins with a board that is $\frac{3}{4}$ in. thick. She removes $\frac{1}{16}$ in. from its thickness. How thick is the board now?

Estimate $\frac{3}{4} - \frac{1}{16} \approx \dfrac{\boxed{}}{\boxed{}} - \boxed{}$, or $\frac{3}{4}$.

$\dfrac{3}{4} = \dfrac{3 \cdot \boxed{}}{4 \cdot \boxed{}} = \dfrac{\boxed{}}{\boxed{}}$ ← The LCD is $\boxed{}$. Write an equivalent fraction.

$-\dfrac{1}{16} = -\dfrac{\boxed{}}{\boxed{}} = -\dfrac{\boxed{}}{\boxed{}}$ ← Write an equivalent fraction.

$\dfrac{\boxed{}}{\boxed{}}$ ← Subtract the numerators.

The board is now $\dfrac{\boxed{}}{\boxed{}}$ in. thick.

Check for Reasonableness The answer $\dfrac{\boxed{}}{\boxed{}}$ is close to the estimate $\dfrac{\boxed{}}{\boxed{}}$.

Quick Check

1. Find each sum or difference.

a. $\frac{3}{5} + \frac{1}{5}$

b. $\frac{13}{16} - \frac{9}{16}$

c. $\frac{1}{4} + \frac{3}{4}$

2. a. Find $\frac{3}{4} - \frac{1}{6}$.

b. Find $\frac{3}{7} + \frac{5}{14}$.

3. You hiked $\frac{5}{8}$ mi and $\frac{1}{4}$ mi in the afternoon. How far did you hike?

Lesson 3-3

Adding and Subtracting Mixed Numbers

Lesson Objective	NAEP 2005 Strand: Number Properties and Operations
To add and subtract mixed numbers and to solve problems involving mixed numbers	**Topic:** Number Operations
	Local Standards: _____

Examples

❶ Cross Country You are training for a race. You run $2\frac{3}{5}$ mi in the morning and $1\frac{4}{5}$ mi in the afternoon. What is your total mileage?

$$2\frac{3}{5} + 1\frac{4}{5} = \boxed{}\frac{7}{5}$$ ← Add the fractions.
Add the whole numbers.

$$= 3 + \boxed{}\frac{\boxed{}}{\boxed{}}$$ ← Write as a sum. Write $\frac{7}{5}$ as $\boxed{}\frac{\boxed{}}{\boxed{}}$.

$$= \boxed{}\frac{\boxed{}}{\boxed{}}$$ ← Add the whole numbers.

Your total mileage is $\boxed{}\frac{\boxed{}}{\boxed{}}$ mi.

❷ Different Denominators Find $5\frac{1}{2} + 3\frac{2}{3}$.

Estimate $5\frac{1}{2} + 3\frac{2}{3} \approx 5 + 4$, or 9.

$$5\frac{1}{2} = 5\frac{\boxed{}}{\boxed{}}$$ ← The LCD is $\boxed{}$. Write an equivalent fraction.

$$+3\frac{2}{3} = +3\frac{\boxed{}}{\boxed{}}$$ ← Write an equivalent fraction.

$$= \boxed{}\frac{\boxed{}}{\boxed{}}$$ ← Add the fractions.
Add the whole numbers.

$$= 8 + \boxed{}\frac{\boxed{}}{\boxed{}}$$ ← Write the mixed number as a sum. Write $\frac{7}{6}$ as $\boxed{}\frac{\boxed{}}{\boxed{}}$.

$$= \boxed{}\frac{\boxed{}}{\boxed{}}$$ ← Add the whole numbers.

Check for Reasonableness The answer $\boxed{}\frac{\boxed{}}{\boxed{}}$ is close to the estimate 9. The answer is reasonable.

Name _____ Class _____ Date _____

❸ Subtracting With Renaming You bought $6\frac{1}{4}$ ft of rope and used $4\frac{3}{8}$ ft. How many feet of rope did you have left?

A. $10\frac{5}{8}$ **B.** $2\frac{1}{8}$ **C.** $1\frac{7}{8}$ **D.** $1\frac{1}{8}$

Find $6\frac{1}{4} \ \square \ 4\frac{3}{8}$.

$6\frac{1}{4} \ = \ 6\frac{\square}{\square}$ ← Write an equivalent fraction using the LCD, $\square$.

$-4\frac{3}{8} \ = \ -4 \ \frac{3}{8}$ ← Write an equivalent fraction.

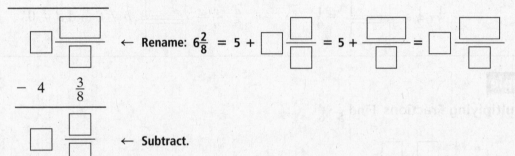

← Rename: $6\frac{2}{8} = 5 + \square\frac{\square}{\square} = 5 + \frac{\square}{\square} = \square\frac{\square}{\square}$

$- \ 4 \quad \frac{3}{8}$

$\square\frac{\square}{\square}$ ← Subtract.

You have $\square\frac{\square}{\square}$ feet of rope left. The correct answer choice is $\square$.

Quick Check

1. Find each sum or difference.

a. $1\frac{2}{3} + 2\frac{2}{3}$ **b.** $1\frac{2}{5} + 3\frac{2}{5}$ **c.** $5\frac{1}{2} - 4\frac{1}{2}$

2.

a. $2\frac{3}{4} - 1\frac{3}{4}$ **b.** $3\frac{1}{6} + 8\frac{7}{8}$ **c.** $6\frac{1}{2} - 2\frac{1}{5}$

3. Your friend bought $4\frac{1}{3}$ ft of gift-wrap and used $2\frac{5}{6}$ ft to wrap a gift. How many feet of gift-wrap did your friend have left?

Lesson 3-4   Multiplying Fractions and Mixed Numbers

Lesson Objective	NAEP 2005 Strand: Number Properties and Operations
To multiply fractions and mixed numbers and to solve problems by multiplying	Topic: Number Operations
	Local Standards: _____

Key Concepts

Multiplying Fractions

Arithmetic

$$\frac{1}{3} \cdot \frac{1}{2} = \frac{\boxed{}}{\boxed{}} = \frac{1}{6}$$

Algebra

$$\frac{a}{b} \cdot \frac{c}{d} = \frac{\boxed{}}{\boxed{}}, b \neq 0 \text{ and } d \neq 0.$$

Example

1 Multiplying Fractions Find $\frac{3}{5} \cdot \frac{5}{6}$.

$$\frac{3}{5} \cdot \frac{5}{6} = \frac{\boxed{} \cdot \boxed{}}{5 \cdot 6}$$ ← Multiply the numerators. Multiply the denominators.

$$= \frac{\boxed{}}{\boxed{}}$$ ← Find the two products.

$$= \frac{\boxed{}}{\boxed{}}$$ ← Simplify.

Quick Check

1. Find each product.

  a. $\frac{3}{5} \cdot \frac{1}{4}$ **b.** $\frac{5}{6} \cdot \frac{4}{5}$ **c.** $\frac{2}{3} \cdot \frac{4}{5}$

Name _____ Class _____ Date _____

Examples

❷ Multiplying by a Whole Number Ebony biked 12 miles on Saturday,
Kate biked $\frac{2}{3}$ of Ebony's distance. How far did Kate bike?
Find $\frac{2}{3}$ of 12 miles, or $\frac{2}{3} \cdot 12$.

$\frac{2}{3} \cdot 12 = \frac{2}{3} \cdot \frac{12}{\boxed{}}$ ← Write 12 as $\frac{12}{1}$.

$= \boxed{} \frac{2}{\cancel{3}} \cdot \frac{\cancel{12}}{1} \boxed{}$ ← Simplify before multiplying.

$= \frac{8}{1}$ ← Multiply the numerators. Multiply the denominators.

$= \boxed{}$ ← Simplify. Kate biked $\boxed{}$ miles.

❸ Multiplying Mixed Numbers Find $5\frac{1}{2} \cdot 3\frac{1}{3}$.

Estimate $5\frac{1}{2} \cdot 3\frac{1}{3} \approx \boxed{} \cdot \boxed{}$, or $\boxed{}$.

$5\frac{1}{2} \cdot 3\frac{1}{3} = \dfrac{\boxed{}}{2} \cdot \dfrac{\boxed{}}{3}$ ← Write the mixed numbers as improper fractions.

$= \dfrac{\boxed{} \cdot \boxed{}}{2 \cdot 3}$ ← Multiply the numerators.
Multiply the denominators.

$= \dfrac{\boxed{}}{\boxed{}}$ ← Simplify.

$= \dfrac{\boxed{}}{\boxed{}}$ ← Simplify.

$= \boxed{}\dfrac{\boxed{}}{\boxed{}}$ ← Write as a mixed number.

Check for Reasonableness $\boxed{}\dfrac{\boxed{}}{\boxed{}}$ is close to the estimate $\boxed{}$.

Quick Check

2. There are 168 members in an orchestra, and $\frac{3}{8}$ of them play the violin. How
many members play the violin?

\
\

3. Find each product.

a. $2\frac{1}{3} \cdot 4\frac{5}{8}$ **b.** $3\frac{3}{5} \cdot 1\frac{3}{10}$ **c.** $5\frac{3}{4} \cdot 2\frac{5}{8}$

Lesson 3-5

Dividing Fractions and Mixed Numbers

Lesson Objective	**NAEP 2005 Strand:** Number Properties and Operations
To divide fractions and mixed numbers and to solve problems by dividing	**Topic:** Number Operations
	Local Standards: _____

Vocabulary and Key Concepts

Dividing Fractions

Arithmetic	**Algebra**
$3 \div \frac{3}{4} = 3 \cdot \dfrac{\square}{\square} = 4$	$\dfrac{a}{b} \div \dfrac{c}{d} = \dfrac{a}{b} \cdot \dfrac{\square}{\square}$ for b, c and $d \neq 0$.

Two numbers are reciprocals if _____

_____

Examples

1 Dividing Mixed Numbers Find $4\frac{2}{3} \div 1\frac{3}{4}$.

$4\frac{2}{3} \div 1\frac{3}{4} = \dfrac{\square}{\square} \div \dfrac{\square}{\square}$ ← **Write the mixed numbers as improper fractions.**

$= \dfrac{14}{3} \cdot \dfrac{\square}{\square}$ ← **Multiply by** $\dfrac{\square}{\square}$, **the** $\boxed{}$ **of** $\frac{7}{4}$.

$= \dfrac{14 \cdot 4}{3 \cdot 7}$ ← **Divide 14 and 7 by their GCF,** $\square$.

$= \dfrac{\square}{\square}$ ← **Multiply.**

$= \square\dfrac{\square}{\square}$ ← **Write as a mixed number.**

❷ You have a piece of fabric that is $12\frac{1}{2}$ ft long. You need to cut it into strips that are $1\frac{1}{4}$ ft long. How many strips will you have?

To find how many $1\frac{1}{4}$-ft long strips are in $12\frac{1}{2}$ ft, divide $\boxed{}\frac{\boxed{}}{\boxed{}}$

by $\boxed{}\frac{\boxed{}}{\boxed{}}$.

Estimate $12\frac{1}{2} \div 1\frac{1}{4} \approx \boxed{} \div \boxed{}$, or $\boxed{}$.

$12\frac{1}{2} \div 1\frac{1}{4} = \dfrac{\boxed{}}{\boxed{}} \div \dfrac{\boxed{}}{\boxed{}}$ ← Write the mixed numbers as improper fractions.

$= \dfrac{25}{2} \cdot \dfrac{\boxed{}}{\boxed{}}$ ← Multiply by $\dfrac{\boxed{}}{\boxed{}}$, the reciprocal of $\dfrac{5}{4}$.

$= \dfrac{\boxed{}\boxed{}}{\boxed{}\boxed{}}\; \dfrac{25 \cdot 4}{2 \cdot 5}$ ← Divide 25 and 5 by their GCF, $\boxed{}$. Divide 4 and 2 by their GCF, $\boxed{}$.

$= \dfrac{\boxed{}}{\boxed{}} = \boxed{}$ ← Simplify.

There are $\boxed{}$ $1\frac{1}{4}$-ft strips of fabric in $12\frac{1}{2}$ ft.

Check for Reasonableness $\boxed{}$ is close to $\boxed{}$. The answer is reasonable.

Quick Check

1. Find each quotient.

   a. $5\frac{3}{4} \div 3\frac{2}{3}$

   b. $4\frac{1}{8} \div 5\frac{1}{2}$

   c. $3\frac{9}{16} \div 3$

   $\boxed{}$ $\boxed{}$ $\boxed{}$

2. One can of iced tea holds 12 fl oz. A 2-liter bottle holds $67\frac{3}{5}$ fl oz. How many cans of iced tea will you need to fill a 2-liter bottle?

   $\boxed{}$

Lesson 3-6

Changing Units in the Customary System

Lesson Objective	NAEP 2005 Strand: Measurement
To change units of length, capacity, and weight in the customary system	Topic: Systems of Measurement
	Local Standards: _____

Key Concepts

Customary Units of Measure

Type	Length	Capacity	Weight
Unit	inch (in.) foot (ft) yard (yd) mile (mi)	fluid ounce (fl oz) cup (c) pint (pt) quart (qt) gallon (gal)	ounce (oz) pound (lb) ton (t)
Equivalents	1 ft = ☐ in. 1 yd = ☐ ft 1 mi = ☐ ft	1 c = ☐ fl oz 1 pt = ☐ c 1 qt = ☐ pt 1 gal = ☐ qt	1 lb = ☐ oz 1 t = ☐ lb

Examples

① **Changing Units of Length** A carpenter cuts a 4 ft 10 in. piece from an 8-ft board. What is the length in feet of the remaining piece?

You need to subtract ☐ from ☐ ft.

$$4 \text{ ft } 10 \text{ in.} = 4\frac{\Box}{\Box} \text{ ft} = 4\frac{\Box}{\Box} \text{ ft} \qquad \leftarrow \textbf{Write 10 in. as a fraction of a foot.}$$

$$8 - 4\frac{\Box}{\Box} = 7\frac{\Box}{\Box} - 4\frac{\Box}{\Box} \qquad \leftarrow \textbf{Rename 8 as } 7\frac{\Box}{\Box}.$$

$$= \Box\frac{\Box}{\Box} \qquad \leftarrow \textbf{Subtract.}$$

The remaining piece is ☐ $\frac{\Box}{\Box}$ ft long.

❷ Multiple Choice How many 2-cup servings are in a
36-fluid-ounce sports drink bottle?

A. $1\frac{1}{8}$ **B.** $2\frac{1}{4}$ **C.** $2\frac{1}{2}$ **D.** $4\frac{1}{2}$

First find the number of fluid ounces in 2 cups. Since there are 8 fluid
ounces in 1 cup, you know there are ☐ ounces in 2 cups.

$36 \div 16 = $ ☐ $= $ ☐ $\frac{☐}{☐}$ ← **Divide 36 by 16. Write as a mixed number.**

There are ☐ $\frac{☐}{☐}$ servings in a 36-fl oz of sports drink bottle. The correct answer choice is ☐.

❸ Changing Units of Weight Which weighs more, a $1\frac{3}{4}$-lb book or a 24-oz catalog?

Think of the relationship between pounds and ☐ . 1 lb = ☐ oz

To change $1\frac{3}{4}$ lb to ounces, multiply $1\frac{3}{4}$ by ☐ . $\left(\times\right.$ ☐ $\left.\right)$

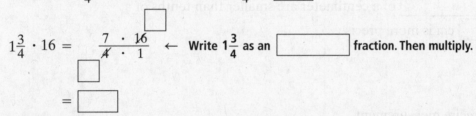

$1\frac{3}{4} \cdot 16 = \dfrac{7 \cdot \overset{☐}{\cancel{16}}}{\cancel{4} \cdot 1}$ ← **Write $1\frac{3}{4}$ as an** ☐ **fraction. Then multiply.**

$= $ ☐

The $1\frac{3}{4}$-lb book weighs ☐ oz. It is ☐ than the 24-oz catalog.

Quick Check

1. How much shorter than a board 10 ft long is a board 8 ft 5 in. long?

2. How many 1-cup servings are in 50 fluid ounces of juice?

3. Find the number of ounces in $4\frac{5}{8}$ lb.

Name _____ Class _____ Date _____

Lesson 3-7

Precision

Lesson Objective	NAEP 2005 Strand: Measurement
To find and compare the precision of measurements	Topic: Systems of Measurement
	Local Standards: _____

Vocabulary

The precision of a measurement _____

_____

Example

① **Precision in Measurement** Choose the more precise measurement:
3.6 cm or 9.15 cm.

Since [　　　　　　　　] of a centimeter are smaller than tenths of a

centimeter, [　　　　] cm is more precise.

Quick Check

1. Choose the more precise measurement.

a. 2 ft, 13 in.   **b.** 12.5 g, 11 g   **c.** $3\frac{1}{2}$ mi, $10\frac{1}{5}$ mi

All rights reserved.

© Pearson Education, Inc., publishing as Pearson Prentice Hall.

50 •••••••••• *Course 2 Lesson 3-7*   Daily Notetaking Guide

Examples

❷ **Finding Precision** What is the greatest precision possible with a digital clock that shows the hour and minutes?

The clock shows both [_____] and [_____].

Measurements are precise to the nearest [_____].

❸ **Precision and Rounding** Find: $7 \text{ mi} - 2\frac{3}{4}$ mi. Round your answer appropriately.

$7 \text{ mi} - 2\frac{3}{4}$ mi

$7 - 2\frac{3}{4} = \boxed{}\dfrac{\boxed{}}{\boxed{}}$

Since 7 is [_____] precise than $2\frac{3}{4}$, round to the nearest

[_____].

The difference is $\boxed{}$ mi.

Quick Check

2. What is the greatest precision possible with each ruler below?

   a.   **b.**

   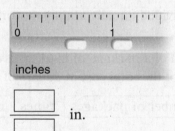

   $\dfrac{\boxed{}}{\boxed{}}$ in. $\dfrac{\boxed{}}{\boxed{}}$ in.

3. Find each sum or difference. Round your answer appropriately.

   a. 11.4 g + 2.65 g   **b.** 45 m − 0.9 m

Lesson 4-1

Evaluating and Writing Algebraic Expressions

Lesson Objective	**NAEP 2005 Strand:** Algebra
To write and evaluate algebraic expressions	**Topic:** Variables, Expressions, and Operations
	Local Standards: _____

Vocabulary

A variable is _____

_____

An algebraic expression is _____

_____

Examples

❶ Writing Algebraic Expressions Write an algebraic expression for each word phrase.

a. 6 less than d dollars [   ]

b. the sum of s students and 9 students [   ]

c. 12 times b boxes [   ]

d. 20 hours of work divided equally among w workers [   ]

❷ Art Supplies The cost of a package of markers is d dollars. Write an algebraic expression for the total cost in dollars of 7 packages of markers.

Words

| number of packages | times | cost per package |

Let d = cost per package.

Expression [   ] · [   ]

An algebraic expression for the total cost in dollars is [   ].

❸ Writing Word Phrases Write three different word phrases for $2y$.

_____

_____

_____

④ Evaluating Algebraic Expressions Evaluate each expression.
Use the values $r = 8$, $s = 1$, and $t = 3$.

a. $6(t - 1)$

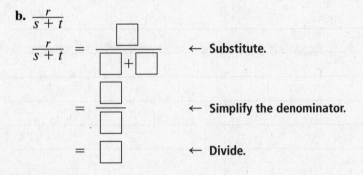

$6(t - 1) = 6\left(\boxed{} - 1\right)$ ← **Substitute.**

$= 6\left(\boxed{}\right)$ ← **Subtract.**

$= \boxed{}$ ← **Multiply.**

b. $\dfrac{r}{s + t}$

$\dfrac{r}{s + t} = \dfrac{\boxed{}}{\boxed{} + \boxed{}}$ ← **Substitute.**

$= \dfrac{\boxed{}}{\boxed{}}$ ← **Simplify the denominator.**

$= \boxed{}$ ← **Divide.**

Quick Check

1. Write an algebraic expression for a price p decreased by 16.

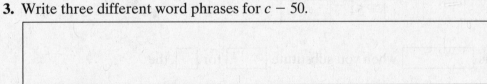

2. Nine students will hang t posters each. Write an algebraic
expression for the total number of posters the students will hang.

3. Write three different word phrases for $c - 50$.

4. Use the values $n = 3$, $t = 5$, and $y = 7$ to evaluate $(n + t) \cdot y$.

Lesson 4-2

Using Number Sense to Solve Equations

Lesson Objective To solve one-step equations using substitution, mental math, and estimation	**NAEP 2005 Strand:** Algebra **Topic:** Equations and Inequalities **Local Standards:** _____

Vocabulary

An equation is _____

_____

An open sentence is _____

_____

A solution of an equation is _____

_____

Example

❶ Solving Equations Using Substitution Find the solution of $h - 18 = 54$ from the numbers 3, 36, 62, and 72. You can test each number by substituting for h in the equation.

$3 - 18 \stackrel{?}{=} 54$ $36 - 18 \stackrel{?}{=} 54$

$\boxed{} = 54$ False $18 = 54$ $\boxed{}$

$62 - 18 \stackrel{?}{=} 54$ $72 - 18 \stackrel{?}{=} 54$

$\boxed{} = 54$ $\boxed{}$ $\boxed{} = 54$ $\boxed{}$

Since the equation is $\boxed{}$ when you substitute $\boxed{}$ for $\boxed{}$, the solution is $\boxed{}$.

Quick Check

1. Find the solution of each equation from the given numbers.

   a. $24n = 120$; 3, 5, or 11

   $\boxed{}$

   b. $124p = 992$; 4, 6, or 8

   $\boxed{}$

Examples

❷ Solving Equations Using Mental Math Use mental math to solve each equation.

a. $s - 9 = 5$

What you think

What number minus $\boxed{}$ equals $\boxed{}$?

Since $\boxed{} - 9 = 5$,

$s = \boxed{}$.

b. $4z = 28$

What you think

What number times $\boxed{}$ equals $\boxed{}$?

Since $4 \cdot \boxed{} = 28$,

$z = \boxed{}$.

❸ Estimating Solutions The weight of a packing crate is 14.65 lb. The crate and its contents together weigh 85.21 lb. Which is the best estimate of the weight of the contents?

A. about 70 lb   **B.** about 80 lb

C. about 100 lb   **D.** about 110 lb

Words $\boxed{\text{crate's weight}}$ plus $\boxed{\text{contents' weight}}$ equals $\boxed{\text{total weight}}$

Let c = the weight of the contents.

Equation $\boxed{} + \boxed{} = \boxed{}$

$14.65 + c = 85.21$

$14.65 \approx 15 \quad 85.21 \approx 85$ ← **Choose compatible numbers.**

$15 + c = 85$ ← **What number added to 15 is 85?**

$c = 70$ ← **Use mental math.**

The contents of the crate weigh about $\boxed{}$ lb. The correct answer is choice $\boxed{}$.

Quick Check

2. Use mental math to solve each equation.

a. $t - 3 = 7$ $\boxed{}$ **b.** $n + 6 = -10.1$ $\boxed{}$

c. $\dfrac{h}{4} = 2.2$ $\boxed{}$ **d.** $7x = -63$ $\boxed{}$

3. A box of machine parts weighs 14.7 lb. A forklift has a maximum weight limit of 390 lb. About how many boxes of parts can the forklift carry at one time?

$\boxed{}$

Lesson 4-3

Solving Equations by Adding or Subtracting

Lesson Objective	**NAEP 2005 Strand:** Algebra
To solve equations by adding or subtracting	**Topic:** Equations and Inequalities
	Local Standards: _____

Vocabulary and Key Concepts

Properties of Equality

Addition Property of Equality

If you ☐ the same value to each side of an equation, the two sides remain ☐.

Arithmetic

$\frac{20}{2} = 10$,

so $\frac{20}{2} + 3 = 10 + $ ☐.

Algebra

If $a = b$,

then $a + c = b + $ ☐.

Subtraction Property of Equality

If you ☐ the same value from each side of an equation, the two sides remain ☐.

Arithmetic

$\frac{12}{2} = 6$,

so $\frac{12}{2} - 4 = 6 - $ ☐.

Algebra

If $a = b$,

then $a - c = b - $ ☐.

Inverse operations are _____

Examples

① **Solving Equations by Adding** Solve $t - 58 = 71$. Check your solution.

$t - 58 = 71$

$t - 58 + $ ☐ $= 71 + 58$ ← ☐ **Property of Equality:** Add ☐ to each side.

$t + $ ☐ $= 129$ ← The numbers 58 and -58 are ☐.

$t = 129$ ← ☐ **Property**

Check ☐ ← Check the solution in the original equation.

☐ $- 58 \stackrel{?}{=} 71$ ← Substitute 129 for t.

☐ $= 71$ ← Subtract.

Daily Notetaking Guide

② **Solving Equations by Subtracting** Your friend purchased a DVD and a CD. The DVD cost $6 more than the CD. The DVD cost $22. How much did the CD cost?

Words [ ] is $6 more than [ ].

Let c = the cost of the CD.

Equation

$$[\quad] \;=\; 6 \;+\; [\quad]$$

$$22 \;=\; 6 + c$$

$$22 - [\quad] \;=\; 6 - [\quad] + c \qquad \leftarrow \text{Subtract } [\quad] \text{ from each side.}$$

$$[\quad] \;=\; c \qquad \leftarrow \text{Simplify.}$$

The CD cost [ ].

Quick Check

1. Solve the equation $x - 104 = 64$.

[   ]

2. A hardcover book costs $19 more than its paperback edition. The hardcover book costs $26.95. How much does the paperback cost?

[   ]

Lesson 4-4

Solving Equations by Multiplying or Dividing

Lesson Objective	NAEP 2005 Strand: Algebra
To solve equations by multiplying or dividing	**Topic:** Equations and Inequalities
	Local Standards: _____

Key Concepts

Division Property of Equality

If you [_____] each side of an equation by the same nonzero

number, the two sides remain [_____].

Arithmetic

Since $3(2) = 6$,

$$\frac{3(2)}{2} = \frac{6}{\boxed{}}.$$

Algebra

If $a = b$ and $c \neq 0$

then $\dfrac{a}{c} = \dfrac{b}{\boxed{}}$.

Multiplication Property of Equality

If you [_____] each side of an equation by the same number, the two

sides remain [_____].

Arithmetic

$$\frac{12}{2} = 6,$$

so $\dfrac{12}{2} \cdot 2 = 6 \cdot \boxed{}.$

Algebra

If $a = b$,

then $a \cdot c = b \cdot \boxed{}$.

Examples

1 Solving Equations by Dividing Solve $-3j = 44.7$. Check your solution.

$-3j = 44.7$ ← Notice j is being [_____] by -3.

$\dfrac{-3j}{\boxed{}} = \dfrac{44.7}{\boxed{}}$ ← [_____] each side by [___] to get j alone.

$j = \boxed{}$ ← Simplify.

Check $\boxed{}$ ← Check your solution in the original equation.

$-3\left(\boxed{}\right) \overset{?}{=} 44.7$ ← Replace j with $\boxed{}$.

$\boxed{} = 44.7\checkmark$ ← The solution checks.

❷ Supplies The Art Club must buy 84 pieces of poster board. There are 6 pieces of poster board in a package. How many packages of poster board must the Art Club buy?

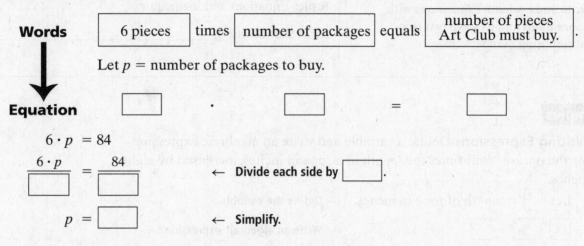

Words

| 6 pieces | times | number of packages | equals | number of pieces Art Club must buy. |

Let p = number of packages to buy.

Equation

$\boxed{} \cdot \boxed{} = \boxed{}$

$6 \cdot p = 84$

$\dfrac{6 \cdot p}{\boxed{}} = \dfrac{84}{\boxed{}}$ ← **Divide each side by** $\boxed{}$.

$p = \boxed{}$ ← **Simplify.**

The Art Club must buy $\boxed{}$ packages of poster board.

❸ Solving Equations by Multiplying Solve $\frac{m}{-3} = 27$.

$\dfrac{m}{-3} = 27$ ← **Notice that m is** $\boxed{}$ **by** -3.

$\boxed{} \cdot \dfrac{m}{-3} = \boxed{} \cdot 27$ ← $\boxed{}$ **each side by** $\boxed{}$.

$m = -81$ ← **Simplify.**

Quick Check

1. Solve each equation. Check your answer.

a. $3x = -21.6$

b. $-12y = -108$

c. $104x = 312$

2. Suppose you and four friends go to a baseball game. The total cost for five tickets is $110. Write and solve an equation to find the cost of one ticket.

3. Solve the equation $\frac{w}{26} = -15$. Check your answer.

Lesson 4-5

Exploring Two-Step Problems

Lesson Objective	NAEP 2005 Strand: Algebra
To write and evaluate expressions with two operations and to solve two-step equations using number sense	**Topic:** Equations and Inequalities
	Local Standards: _____

Examples

1 Writing Expressions Define a variable and write an algebraic expression for the phrase "four times the length of a rope in inches, increased by eight inches."

Let ☐ = length of rope in inches.   ← **Define the variable.**

☐ · ☐ + ☐   ← **Write an algebraic expression.**

☐ + 8   ← **Rewrite** $4 \cdot \ell$ **as** ☐ .

2 Evaluating Expressions Evaluate the expression if the length of a rope is 9 inches.

$4\ell + 8$

$4 \cdot$ ☐ $+ 8$ ← **Evaluate the expression for a rope length of** ☐ .

☐ $+ 8$ ← **Multiply.**

☐   ← **Simplify.**

3 Using Number Sense Solve $3n - 4 = 14$ by using number sense.

$3n - 4 = 14$

☐ $- 4 = 14$ ← **Cover 3n.** *Think:* **What number minus 4 is 14?**

Answer: ☐ .

$3n =$ ☐   ← **So** ☐ **, or 3n, must equal** ☐ .

$3 \cdot$ ☐ $=$ ☐   ← **Now cover n.** *Think:* **What number times 3 is** ☐ ?

Answer: ☐

$n =$ ☐   ← **So** ☐ **, or n, must equal** ☐ .

Check

$3n - 4 = 14$ ← **Check your solution in the original equation.**

$3(6) - 4 \stackrel{?}{=} 14$ ← **Substitute 6 for n.**

$18 - 4 \stackrel{?}{=} 14$ ← **Simplify.**

$14 = 14$ ← **The solution checks.**

❹ Shopping The Healy family wants to buy a TV that costs $200. They already have $80 saved toward the cost. How much will they have to save per month for the next six months in order to have the whole cost saved?

Words

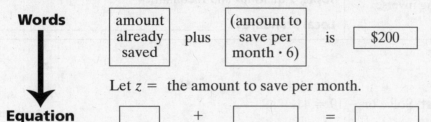

| amount already saved | plus | (amount to save per month · 6) | is | $200 |

Let $z = $ the amount to save per month.

Equation

☐ + ☐ = ☐

$80 + 6z = 200$

$80 + \blacksquare = 200$ ← **Cover 6z. Think: What number added to 80 is 200?**

Answer: ☐ .

$6z = $ ☐ ← **So** ☐ **, or 6z, must equal** ☐ .

$6 \cdot \blacksquare = 120$ ← **Now cover z. Think: What number times 6 is** ☐ ?

Answer: ☐

$z = $ ☐ ← **So** ☐ **, or z, must equal** ☐ .

They will have to save ☐ per month.

Quick Check

1. Define a variable and write an algebraic expression for "a man is two years younger than three times his son's age."

2. Evaluate the expression to find the man's age if his son is 13.

3. Solve each equation using number sense.

   a. $3m + 9 = 21$

   b. $8d + 5 = 45$

   c. $4y - 11 = 33$

4. **Basketball** During the first half of a game you scored 8 points. In the second half you made only 3-point baskets. You finished the game with 23 points. Write and solve an equation to find how many 3-point baskets you made.

Lesson 4-6

Solving Two-Step Equations

Lesson Objective	**NAEP 2005 Strand:** Algebra
To solve two-step equations using inverse operations	**Topic:** Equations and Inequalities
	Local Standards: _____

Examples

❶ Undoing Subtraction First Solve $6r - 19 = 41$.

$$6r - 19 = 41$$

$$6r - 19 + \boxed{} = 41 + \boxed{} \quad \leftarrow \text{To undo } \boxed{}, \text{ add } \boxed{} \text{ to each side.}$$

$$6r = 60 \quad \leftarrow \text{Simplify.}$$

$$\frac{6r}{\boxed{}} = \frac{60}{\boxed{}} \quad \leftarrow \text{To undo } \boxed{}, \text{ divide each side by } \boxed{}.$$

$$r = \boxed{} \quad \leftarrow \text{Simplify.}$$

Check $6r - 19 = 41 \quad \leftarrow$ Check your solution with the original equation.

$$6(\boxed{}) - 19 \stackrel{?}{=} 41 \quad \leftarrow \text{Substitute } \boxed{} \text{ for } r.$$

$$\boxed{} - 19 \stackrel{?}{=} 41 \quad \leftarrow \text{Simplify.}$$

$$\boxed{} = 41 ✔ \quad \leftarrow \text{The solution checks.}$$

❷ Undoing Addition First Solve $\frac{a}{5} + 4 = 10$.

$$\frac{a}{5} + 4 = 10$$

$$\frac{a}{5} + 4 \boxed{} 4 = 10 \boxed{} 4 \quad \leftarrow \text{To undo addition, } \boxed{} \text{ 4 from each side.}$$

$$\frac{a}{5} = 6 \quad \leftarrow \text{Simplify.}$$

$$(\boxed{})\left(\frac{a}{5}\right) = (\boxed{})(6) \quad \leftarrow \text{To undo division, multiply each side by } \boxed{}.$$

$$a = \boxed{} \quad \leftarrow \text{Simplify.}$$

Daily Notetaking Guide

❸ Solving Two-Step Equations An amusement park charges $15.00 for admission and $.50 for each ride. You spend $27.00 total. How many rides did you go on?

A. 54 **B.** 43 **C.** 24 **D.** 6

Words [ ] times [the number of rides] plus [ ] is 27.

Let n = number of rides you went on.

Equation [ ] · n + [ ] = 27

[ ] · n + [ ] = 27

[ ] · n + [ ] − 15 = 27 − 15   ← **Subtract 15 from each side.**

[ ] · n = 12   ← **Simplify.**

$\frac{0.50n}{0.50} = \frac{12}{0.50}$ ← **Divide each side by** [ ].

n = [ ]   ← **Simplify.**

You went on [ ] rides. The correct answer is choice [ ].

Quick Check

1. Solve the equation $-8y - 28 = -36$. Check your answer.

2. Solve the equation $\frac{x}{5} + 35 = 75$. Check your answer.

3. Solomon decides to make posters for the student council election. He bought markers that cost $.79 each and a poster board that cost $1.25. The total cost was $7.57. Write and solve an equation to find the number of markers that Solomon bought.

Lesson 4-7

Graphing and Writing Inequalities

Lesson Objective	NAEP 2005 Strand: Algebra
To graph and write algebraic inequalities	Topic: Equations and Inequalities
	Local Standards: _____

Vocabulary

An inequality is _____

_____

A solution of an inequality is _____

_____

Examples

1 Identifying Solutions of an Inequality Find whether each number is a solution of $k > -6$; $-8, -6, 0, 3, 7$.

Test each value by replacing the variable and evaluating the sentence.

$-8 > -6$ ← -8 is greater than -6; false.

$-6 > -6$ ← -6 is greater than -6; [ ].

$0 > -6$ ← 0 is greater than -6; [ ].

$3 > -6$ ← 3 is [ ] than -6; [ ].

$7 > -6$ ← 7 is [ ] than -6; [ ].

The numbers [ ], [ ], and [ ] are solutions of $k > -6$.

The numbers [ ] and [ ] are not solutions of $k > -6$.

2 Graphing Inequalities Graph the solution of each inequality on a number line.

a. $r \leq 2$

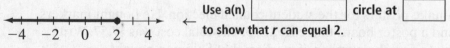

← Use a(n) [ ] circle at [ ] to show that r can equal 2.

b. $m > -5$

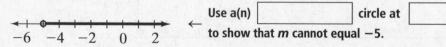

← Use a(n) [ ] circle at [ ] to show that m cannot equal -5.

Daily Notetaking Guide

❸ Writing Inequalities Write an inequality for the graph.

Since the circle at 1 is closed,

1 [_____] a solution.

y [____] 1   ← Since the graph shows values [_____] or [_____] 1, use [____].

❹ Social Studies You must be at least 18 years of age to vote in a presidential election in the United States. Write an inequality for this requirement.

Words [____] is [_____] [_____]

Let $\boxed{a}$ = age in years.

Inequality [_____]   [_____]   [_____]

The inequality is [_____].

Quick Check

1. Which numbers are solutions of the inequality $m \geq -3$; $-8, -2, 1.4$?

[_____]

2. Graph the solution of the inequality $w < -3$.

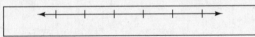

3. Write an inequality for the graph.

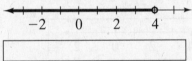

[_____]

4. Write an inequality for "To qualify for the race, your time can be at most 62 seconds."

[_____]

Lesson 4-8

Solving Inequalities by Adding or Subtracting

Lesson Objective	NAEP 2005 Strand: Algebra
To solve inequalities by adding or subtracting	Topic: Equations and Inequalities
	Local Standards: _____

Key Concepts

Addition Property of Inequality

You can ☐ the same value to each side of an inequality.

Arithmetic

Since $7 > 3, 7 + 4 > 3 + $ ☐.

Since $1 < 3, 1 + $ ☐ $< 3 + 4$.

Algebra

If $a > b$, then $a + $ ☐ $> b + c$.

If $a < b$, then $a + c < b + $ ☐.

Subtraction Property of Inequality

You can ☐ the same value from each side of an inequality.

Arithmetic

Since $9 > 6, 9 - 3 > 6 - $ ☐.

Since $15 < 20, 15 - $ ☐ $< 20 - 4$.

Algebra

If $a > b$, then $a - $ ☐ $> b - c$.

If $a < b$, then $a - c < b - $ ☐.

Example

❶ Solving Inequalities by Adding Solve $q - 2 \geq -6$. Graph the solution.

$q - 2 \geq -6$

$q - 2 + $ ☐ $\geq -6 + $ ☐ ← Add ☐ to each side.

$q \geq $ ☐ ← Simplify.

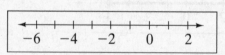

Quick Check

1. Solve $y - 3 < 4$. Graph the solution.

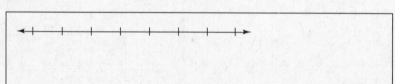

Examples

❷ Solving Inequalities by Subtracting Solve $d + 9 < 8$.
Graph the solution.

$$d + 9 < 8$$

$$d + 9 - \boxed{} < 8 - \boxed{} \quad \leftarrow \text{Subtract } \boxed{} \text{ from each side.}$$

$$d < \boxed{} \quad \leftarrow \text{Simplify.}$$

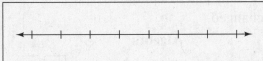

❸ Budget The Drama Club can spend no more than $120 for costumes. They already spent $79. How much more can they spend for costumes?

Words

| amount spent already | plus | amount spent on costumes | is at most | $120. |

Let c = amount the Drama Club can spend on costumes.

Inequality $\boxed{} + \boxed{} \quad \boxed{} \quad 120$

$$79 + c \le 120$$

$$79 - \boxed{} + c \le 120 - \boxed{} \quad \leftarrow \text{Subtract } \boxed{} \text{ from each side.}$$

$$c \le \boxed{} \quad \leftarrow \text{Simplify.}$$

They can spend at most $\boxed{}$.

Quick Check

2. Solve each inequality. Graph the solution.

a. $x + 9 > 5$

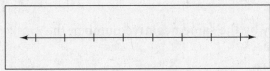

b. $y + 3 < 4$

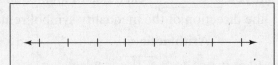

c. $w + 4 \le -5$

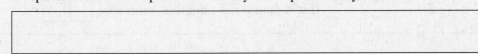

3. To get an A, you need more than 200 points on a two-part test. You score 109 points on the first part. How many more points do you need?

Lesson 4-9

Solving Inequalities by Multiplying or Dividing

Lesson Objective	**NAEP 2005 Strand:** Algebra
To solve inequalities by multiplying or dividing	**Topic:** Equations and Inequalities
	Local Standards: _____

Key Concepts

Division Property of Inequality

If you [_____] each side of an inequality by the same positive number, the direction of the inequality symbol remains unchanged.

Arithmetic

$9 > 6$, so $\dfrac{9}{3}$ [__] $\dfrac{6}{3}$

$15 < 20$, so $\dfrac{15}{5}$ [__] $\dfrac{[\ ]}{[\ ]}$

Algebra

If $a > b$, and c is positive, then $\dfrac{a}{c}$ [__] $\dfrac{b}{c}$.

If $a < b$, and c is positive, then $\dfrac{a}{c}$ [__] $\dfrac{[\ ]}{[\ ]}$.

If you [_____] each side of an inequality by the same negative number, the direction of the inequality symbol is reversed.

Arithmetic

$16 > 12$, so $\dfrac{16}{-4}$ [__] $\dfrac{12}{-4}$

$10 < 18$, so $\dfrac{10}{-2}$ [__] $\dfrac{[\ ]}{[\ ]}$

Algebra

If $a > b$, and c is negative, then $\dfrac{a}{c}$ [__] $\dfrac{b}{c}$.

If $a < b$, and c is negative, then $\dfrac{a}{c}$ [__] $\dfrac{[\ ]}{[\ ]}$.

Multiplication Property of Inequality

If you [_____] each side of an inequality by the same positive number, the direction of the inequality symbol remains unchanged.

Arithmetic

$12 > 8$, so $12 \cdot 2$ [__] [__] $\cdot 2$

$3 < 6$, so $3 \cdot 4$ [__] [__] $\cdot 4$

Algebra

If $a > b$, and c is positive, then $a \cdot c$ [__] [__] $\cdot c$.

If $a < b$, and c is positive, then $a \cdot c$ [__] [__] $\cdot c$.

If you [_____] each side of an inequality by the same negative number, the direction of the inequality symbol is reversed.

Arithmetic

$6 > 2$, so $6(-3)$ [__] [__] (-3)

$3 < 5$, so $3(-2)$ [__] [__] (-2)

Algebra

If $a > b$, and c is negative, then $a \cdot c$ [__] [__] $\cdot c$.

If $a < b$, and c is negative, then $a \cdot c$ [__] [__] $\cdot c$.

Name _____ Class _____ Date _____

Examples

1 Business A woodworker makes a profit of $30 on each picture frame that is sold. Write an inequality to describe the number of frames the woodworker must sell to make a profit of at least $500.

Words

| number of frames | times | profit on each frame | is at least | $500 |

Let f = the number of frames.

Inequality ☐ · ☐ ☐ ☐

$30f \geq 500$

$\dfrac{30f}{30} \geq \dfrac{500}{30}$ ← **Divide each side by 30.**

$f \geq 16.\overline{6}$ ← **Simplify.**

$f \geq 17$ ← **Round up to the nearest whole number.**

The woodworker must sell at least ☐ frames.

2 Solving Inequalities by Multiplying Solve $\dfrac{b}{-3} < -12$.

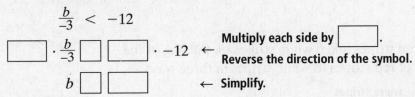

$\dfrac{b}{-3} < -12$

☐ · $\dfrac{b}{-3}$ ☐ ☐ · -12 ← **Multiply each side by ☐.**
Reverse the direction of the symbol.

b ☐ ☐ ← **Simplify.**

Quick Check

1. A long-distance telephone company is offering a special rate of $.06 per minute. Your budget for long-distance telephone calls is $25 for the month. At most how many minutes of long distance can you use for the month?

2. Solve $\dfrac{k}{-5} < -4$. Graph the solution.

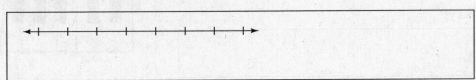

Lesson 5-1

Ratios

Lesson Objective	NAEP 2005 Strand: Number Properties and Operations
To write ratios and use them to compare quantities	**Topic:** Ratios and Proportional Reasoning
	Local Standards: _____

Vocabulary and Key Concepts

Ratio

A ratio is _____

You can write a ratio in three ways.

Arithmetic

5 to 7 ⬚ | ⬚/⬚

Algebra

⬚ | $a : b$ | ⬚/⬚ , where $b \neq 0$

Equivalent ratios are _____

Example

① **Writing Ratios** There are 7 red stripes and 6 white stripes on the flag of the United States. Write the ratio of red stripes to white stripes in three ways.

red stripes → [ ] ← white stripes

red stripes → [ ] ← white stripes

[ ] ← red stripes

[ ] ← white stripes

Quick Check

1. Write each ratio in three ways. Use the pattern of piano keys shown at the right.

   a. white keys to all keys

   [ ]

   b. black keys to white keys

   [ ]

Daily Notetaking Guide

Examples

❷ Writing Equivalent Ratios Find a ratio equivalent to $\frac{14}{4}$.

$$\frac{14 \div \square}{4 \div \square} = \frac{\square}{\square}$$ ← **Divide the numerator and denominator by 2.**

❸ Writing Equivalent Ratios Write the ratio 2 lb to 56 oz as a fraction in simplest form.

$$\frac{2\ lb}{56\ oz} = \frac{2 \times 16\ oz}{56\ oz}$$ ← **There are 16 oz in each pound.**

$$= \frac{\square\ oz}{56\ oz}$$ ← **Multiply.**

$$= \frac{\square \div \square\ oz}{56 \div \square\ oz}$$ ← **Divide by the GCF, $\square$ oz.**

$$= \frac{\square}{\square}$$ ← **Simplify.**

❹ Comparing Ratios The ratio of girls to boys enrolled at King Middle School is 15 : 16. There are 195 girls and 208 boys in Grade 8. Is the ratio of girls to boys in Grade 8 equivalent to the ratio of girls to boys in the entire school?

Entire School   **Grade 8**

$\dfrac{\square}{\square}$ ← girls → $\dfrac{\square}{\square}$

boys

$\dfrac{\square}{\square} = \boxed{}$ ← **Write as a decimal.** → $\dfrac{\square}{\square} = \boxed{}$

Since the two decimals are $\boxed{}$, the ratio of girls to boys in Grade 8 is $\boxed{}$ the ratio of girls to boys in the entire school.

Quick Check

2. Find a ratio equivalent to $\frac{7}{9}$.

3. Write the ratio 3 gal to 10 qt as a fraction in simplest form.

4. Tell whether the ratios below are *equivalent* or *not equivalent*.

   a. $7:3, 128:54$ **b.** $\frac{180}{240}, \frac{25}{34}$ **c.** 6.1 to 7, 30.5 to 35

Lesson 5-2

Unit Rates and Proportional Reasoning

Lesson Objective To find unit rates and unit costs using proportional reasoning	**NAEP 2005 Strand:** Number Properties and Operations **Topic:** Ratios and Proportional Reasoning **Local Standards:** _____

Vocabulary

A rate is _____

_____

A unit rate is _____

A unit cost is _____

Examples

❶ Finding a Unit Rate You earn $33 for 4 hours of work. Find the unit rate of dollars per hour.

dollars → $\frac{33}{4}$ = [   ] ← **Divide the first quantity by the second quantity.**
hours →

The unit rate is $\frac{}{}$, or [   ] per hour.

❷ Using Unit Cost to Find Total Cost Use the unit cost to find the total cost: 7 yd of ribbon at $.39 per yard.

Estimate $.39 · 7 ≈ $.40 · 7, or $2.80.

$.39 · 7 = [   ] ← **unit cost · number of units = total cost**

The total cost of 7 yd of ribbon is [   ] .

Check for Reasonableness The total cost of [   ] is close to the estimate of $2.80. So, [   ] is reasonable.

Quick Check

1. Find the unit rate for 210 heartbeats in 3 minutes.

[   ]

2. Dog food costs $.35/lb. How much does a 20-lb bag cost?

[   ]

Name _____ Class _____ Date _____

Example

❸ Using Unit Cost to Compare Find each unit cost. Which is the better buy?

3 lb of potatoes for $.89
5 lb of potatoes for $1.59

Divide to find the unit cost of each size.

cost → $\dfrac{\$.89}{3\,\text{lb}} \approx$ ☐

size →

cost → $\dfrac{\$1.59}{5\,\text{lb}} \approx$ ☐

size →

Since ☐ < ☐ , ☐ for ☐

is the better buy.

Quick Check

3. Which bottle of apple juice is the better buy: 48 fl oz of fruit juice for $3.05, or 64 fl oz for $3.59?

Lesson 5-3

Proportions

Lesson Objective	**NAEP 2005 Strand:** Number Properties and Operations
To test whether ratios can form a proportion by using equivalent ratios and cross products	**Topic:** Ratios and Proportional Reasoning
	Local Standards: _____

Key Concepts

Proportion

A proportion is _____

Arithmetic	**Algebra**
$\frac{1}{2} = \frac{2}{4}$	$\frac{a}{b} = \frac{c}{d}, b \neq 0, d \neq 0$

Cross Products Property

Cross products are _____

_____

If two ratios form a proportion, the cross products are equal. If two ratios have equal cross products, they form a proportion.

Arithmetic	**Algebra**
$\frac{6}{8} = \frac{9}{12}$	$\frac{a}{b} = \frac{c}{d}$
$6 \cdot 12 = 8 \cdot 9$	$ad = bc$, where $b \neq 0$, and $d \neq 0$

Example

① Writing Ratios in Simplest Form Do the ratios $\frac{42}{56}$ and $\frac{56}{64}$ form a proportion?

$$\frac{42}{56} = \frac{42 \div \boxed{}}{56 \div \boxed{}} = \frac{\boxed{}}{\boxed{}} \quad \leftarrow \text{\textbf{Divide the numerator and denominator by the GCF.}} \rightarrow \quad \frac{56}{64} = \frac{56 \div \boxed{}}{64 \div \boxed{}} = \frac{\boxed{}}{\boxed{}}$$

The ratios in simplest form are not equivalent. They $\boxed{}$ form a proportion.

Quick Check

1. Do $\frac{10}{12}$ and $\frac{40}{56}$ form a proportion?

Example

❷ Using Cross Products Do the ratios in each pair form a proportion?

a. $\frac{4}{10}, \frac{6}{15}$ **b.** $\frac{8}{6}, \frac{9}{7}$

$\frac{4}{10} \stackrel{?}{=} \frac{6}{15}$ ← **Test each pair of ratios.** → $\frac{8}{6} \stackrel{?}{=} \frac{9}{7}$

$4 \cdot \boxed{} \stackrel{?}{=} 10 \cdot \boxed{}$ ← **Write cross products.** → $8 \cdot \boxed{} \stackrel{?}{=} 6 \cdot \boxed{}$

$\boxed{} \boxed{} 60$ ← **Simplify.** → $\boxed{} \boxed{} 54$

$\boxed{}, \frac{4}{10}$ and $\frac{6}{15}$ $\boxed{}, \frac{8}{6}$ and $\frac{9}{7}$

$\boxed{}$ a proportion. $\boxed{}$ a proportion.

Quick Check

2. Determine whether the ratios form a proportion.

a. $\frac{3}{8}, \frac{6}{16}$ **b.** $\frac{6}{9}, \frac{4}{6}$ **c.** $\frac{4}{8}, \frac{5}{9}$

Lesson 5-4

Solving Proportions

Lesson Objective	**NAEP 2005 Strand:** Number Properties and Operations
To solve proportions using unit rates, mental math, and cross products	**Topic:** Ratios and Proportional Reasoning
	Local Standards: _____

Examples

❶ Using Unit Rates The cost of 4 lightbulbs is $3. Use the information to find the cost of 10 lightbulbs.

Step 1 Find the unit price.

$$\frac{3 \text{ dollars}}{4 \text{ lightbulbs}} = \$3 \div 4 \text{ lightbulbs} \quad \leftarrow \textbf{Divide to find the unit price.}$$

☐ /lightbulb

Step 2 You know the cost of one lightbulb. Multiply to find the cost of 10 lightbulbs.

☐ · ☐ = ☐ ← **Multiply the unit rate by the number of lightbulbs.**

The cost of 10 lightbulbs is ☐ .

❷ Solving Using Mental Math Solve each proportion using mental math.

a. $\frac{5}{c} = \frac{30}{42}$

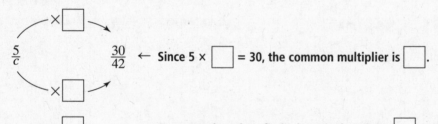

$\frac{5}{c}$ $\frac{30}{42}$ ← **Since 5 × ☐ = 30, the common multiplier is ☐ .**

$c = $ ☐   ← **Use mental math to find what number times ☐ equals 42.**

b. $\frac{9}{4} = \frac{72}{t}$

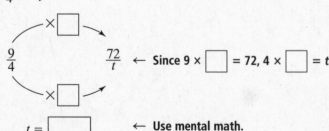

$\frac{9}{4}$ $\frac{72}{t}$ ← **Since 9 × ☐ = 72, 4 × ☐ = t.**

$t = $ ☐   ← **Use mental math.**

❸ Solving Using Cross Products Solve $\frac{6}{8} = \frac{9}{a}$ using cross products.

$$\frac{6}{8} = \frac{9}{a}$$

$6a = 8(9)$ ← **Write the cross products.**

$6a = \boxed{}$ ← **Simplify.**

$\dfrac{6a}{\boxed{}} = \dfrac{\boxed{}}{\boxed{}}$ ← **Divide each side by** $\boxed{}$.

$a = \boxed{}$ ← **Simplify.**

Quick Check

1. a. Postcards cost $2.45 for 5 cards. How much will 13 cards cost?

b. Swimming goggles cost $84.36 for 12. At this rate, how much will new goggles for 17 members of a swim team cost?

2. Solve each proportion using mental math.

a. $\frac{3}{8} = \frac{b}{24}$

b. $\frac{m}{5} = \frac{16}{40}$

c. $\frac{15}{30} = \frac{5}{p}$

3. Solve each proportion using cross products.

a. $\frac{12}{15} = \frac{x}{21}$

b. $\frac{16}{30} = \frac{d}{51}$

c. $\frac{20}{35} = \frac{110}{m}$

Lesson 5-5

Using Similar Figures

Lesson Objective	NAEP 2005 Strands: Number Properties and Operations; Measurement
To use proportions to find missing lengths in similar figures	Topics: Ratios and Proportional Reasoning; Measuring Physical Attributes
	Local Standards: _____

Vocabulary and Key Concepts

Similar Polygons

Two polygons are similar if

• corresponding angles _____

• the lengths of corresponding sides _____

A polygon is _____

Indirect measurement is _____

_____

Example

1 **Finding a Missing Measure** △ABC and △DEF are similar. Find the value of c.

$$\frac{AB}{DE} = \frac{AC}{DF}$$ ← **Write a proportion.**

$$\frac{c}{\boxed{}} = \frac{6}{\boxed{}}$$ ← **Substitute.**

$$\frac{c}{\boxed{}} = \frac{2}{\boxed{}}$$ ← **Write** $\frac{6}{\boxed{}}$ **in simplest form.**

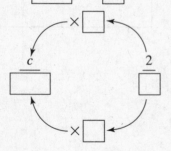

← **Find the common multiplier.**

$$c = \boxed{}$$ ← **Use mental math.**

❷ Multiple Choice A 5-ft person standing near a tree has a shadow 12 ft long. At the same time, the tree has a shadow 42 ft long. What is the height of the tree?

A. 17.5 ft   **B.** 35 ft   **C.** 49 ft   **D.** 100.8 ft

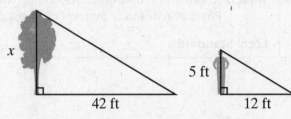

Draw a picture and let x represent the height of the tree.

$$\frac{x}{\boxed{}} = \frac{42}{\boxed{}} \quad \leftarrow \text{ Write a proportion.}$$

$$\boxed{}\, x = \boxed{} \cdot 42 \quad \leftarrow \text{ Write the cross products.}$$

$$\frac{12x}{12} = \frac{5 \cdot 42}{12} \quad \leftarrow \text{ Divide each side by 12.}$$

$$x = \boxed{} \quad \leftarrow \text{ Simplify.}$$

The height of the tree is $\boxed{}$ ft. The correct answer is choice $\boxed{}$.

Quick Check

1. The trapezoids below are similar. Find x.

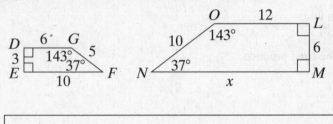

2. A 6-ft person has a shadow 5 ft long. A nearby tree has a shadow 30 ft long. What is the height of the tree?

Lesson 5-6

Maps and Scale Drawings

Lesson Objective	NAEP 2005 Strands: Number Properties and Operations; Measurement
To use proportions to solve problems involving scale	**Topics:** Ratios and Proportional Reasoning; Measuring Physical Attributes; Systems of Measurement
	Local Standards: _____

Vocabulary

A scale drawing is _____

_____

A scale is _____

_____

Example

❶ **Using a Scale Drawing** The scale of a drawing is 1 in. : 6 ft. The length of a wall is 4.5 in. on the drawing. Find the actual length of the wall.

You can write the scale of the drawing as $\frac{1 \text{ in.}}{6 \text{ ft}}$. Then write a proportion.

Let n represent the actual length.

$$\begin{array}{l} \text{drawing (in.)} \rightarrow \\ \text{actual (ft)} \rightarrow \end{array} \quad \frac{1}{6} = \frac{\boxed{}}{n} \quad \begin{array}{l} \leftarrow \text{drawing (in.)} \\ \leftarrow \text{actual (ft)} \end{array}$$

$$\boxed{} n = \boxed{} (4.5) \quad \leftarrow \text{Write the cross products.}$$

$$n = \boxed{} \quad \leftarrow \text{Simplify.}$$

The actual length is $\boxed{}$ ft.

Quick Check

1. Use the same scale as in Example 1. If an object is 2.5 in. long on the drawing, how long is the actual object?

> [blank box]

Examples

❷ Geography Find the actual distance from Asheville to Raleigh.

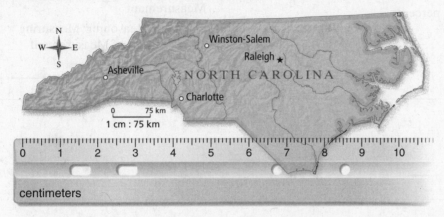

Step 1 Use a centimeter ruler to find the map distance from Asheville to Raleigh. The map distance is about 4.4 cm.

Step 2 Use a proportion to find the actual distance. Let n represent the actual distance.

$$
\begin{array}{l}
\text{map (cm)} \rightarrow \\
\text{actual (km)} \rightarrow
\end{array}
\dfrac{1}{75} = \dfrac{\boxed{}}{n}
\begin{array}{l}
\leftarrow \text{map (cm)} \\
\leftarrow \text{actual (km)}
\end{array}
\quad \leftarrow \textbf{Write a proportion.}
$$

$$
1\boxed{} = \boxed{}(4.4) \qquad \leftarrow \textbf{Write cross products.}
$$

$$
n = \boxed{} \qquad \leftarrow \textbf{Simplify.}
$$

The actual distance from Asheville to Raleigh is about $\boxed{}$ km.

❸ Finding the Scale The actual length of the wheelbase of a mountain bike is 260 cm. The length of the wheelbase in a scale drawing is 4 cm. Find the scale of the drawing.

$$
\begin{array}{l}
\text{scale length} \rightarrow \\
\text{actual length} \rightarrow
\end{array}
\dfrac{4}{260} = \dfrac{4 \div \boxed{}}{260 \div \boxed{}} = \dfrac{\boxed{}}{\boxed{}} \quad \leftarrow \textbf{Write the ratio in simplest form.}
$$

The scale is $\boxed{}$ cm : $\boxed{}$ cm.

Quick Check

2. Find the actual distance from Charlotte to Raleigh.

$\boxed{}$

3. The length of a room in an architectural drawing is 10 in. Its actual length is 160 in. What is the scale of the drawing?

$\boxed{}$

Lesson 6-1

Understanding Percents

Lesson Objective To model percents and to write percents using equivalent ratios	**NAEP 2005 Strands:** Number Properties and Operations; Measurement **Topics:** Ratios and Proportional Reasoning; Measuring Physical Attributes; Systems of Measurement **Local Standards:** _____

Vocabulary

A percent is _____

_____

Examples

1 Using Models with Percents In a floor plan of a 10 × 10 room, a chair takes up 4 spaces. Write the ratio and percent of the chair space to the total floor space.

There are ☐ grid spaces for the chair. Write as a ratio to the total number

of grid spaces, ☐ . Then write it as a percent.

$$\frac{\boxed{}}{\boxed{}} = \boxed{}\%$$

2 Using Models with Percents Model 82% in a 10 × 10 grid.

Shade ☐ of the 100 grid spaces.

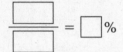

3 Finding Percents Using Models What percent does the shaded area represent?

  $$\frac{\boxed{}}{\boxed{}} = \frac{\boxed{}}{\boxed{}} = \boxed{}\%$$

❹ **Using Equivalent Ratios** Write each ratio as a percent.

a. $\frac{3}{10}$

$$\frac{3}{10} = \frac{3 \cdot \boxed{}}{10 \cdot \boxed{}}$$ ← **Multiply to get a denominator of 100.**

$$= \frac{\boxed{}}{100}$$ ← **Simplify.** →

$$= \boxed{}\%$$ ← **Write as a percent.** →

b. $\frac{4}{5}$

$$\frac{4}{5} = \frac{4 \cdot \boxed{}}{5 \cdot \boxed{}}$$

$$= \frac{\boxed{}}{100}$$

$$= \boxed{}\%$$

Quick Check

1. Write a ratio and a percent to represent the unused floor space.

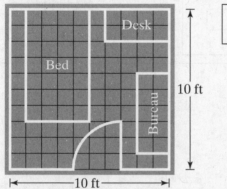

2. Model 80% on a 10 × 10 grid.

3. Write a ratio and a percent for each shaded area.

a.

b.

c.

4. A tennis team played a total of 25 games and won 20 of them. What percent of the games did the team win?

Lesson 6-2

Percents, Fractions, and Decimals

Lesson Objective	NAEP 2005 Strand: Number Properties and Operations
To convert between fractions, decimals, and percents	**Topic:** Number Sense
	Local Standards: _____

Key Concepts

Fractions, Decimals, and Percents

The model at the right shows 21 out of 100 squares shaded. You can write the shaded part of the model as a fraction, a decimal, or a percent.

Fraction	Decimal	Percent
☐ / ☐	☐	☐

Examples

❶ Writing Decimals as Percents Write 0.101 as a percent.

$0.101 = \dfrac{101}{\boxed{}}$ ← **Write as a fraction.**

$= \dfrac{\boxed{}}{\boxed{}}$ ← **Write an equivalent fraction with** $\boxed{}$ **in the denominator.**

$= \boxed{}$ ← **Write as a percent.**

❷ Writing Percents as Decimals Write 6.4% as a decimal.

$6.4\% = \dfrac{\boxed{}}{\boxed{}}$ ← **Write the percent as a fraction.**

$= \boxed{}$ ← **Divide.**

Quick Check

1. Write 0.607 as a percent.

$\boxed{}$

2. Write each percent as a decimal.

a. 35% $\boxed{}$ **b.** 12.5% $\boxed{}$ **c.** 7.8% $\boxed{}$

Examples

❸ **Writing Percents as Fractions** Write each percent as a fraction in simplest form.

a. 12%

$$12\% = \dfrac{12}{\boxed{}}$$ ← Write as a fraction with a denominator of $\boxed{}$. →

$$= \dfrac{12 \div \boxed{}}{100 \div \boxed{}}$$ ← Divide the numerator and the denominator by the GCF. →

$$= \dfrac{\boxed{}}{\boxed{}}$$ ← Simplify the fraction. →

b. 45%

$$45\% = \dfrac{45}{\boxed{}}$$

$$= \dfrac{45 \div \boxed{}}{100 \div \boxed{}}$$

$$= \dfrac{\boxed{}}{\boxed{}}$$

❹ **Ordering Rational Numbers** Order $\frac{3}{5}, \frac{2}{10}$, 0.645, and 13% from least to greatest. Write all numbers as decimals. Then graph each number on a number line.

$\frac{3}{5} = \boxed{}$ ← Divide the $\boxed{}$ by the $\boxed{}$.

$\frac{2}{10} = \boxed{}$ ← Divide the $\boxed{}$ by the $\boxed{}$.

0.645 ← This number is already in decimal form.

13% = $\boxed{}$ ← Move the decimal point $\boxed{}$ places to the $\boxed{}$.

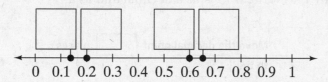

Quick Check

3. An elephant eats about 6% of its body weight in vegetation every day. Write this as a fraction in simplest form.

4. Order from least to greatest.

a. $\frac{3}{10}, 0.74, 29\%, \frac{11}{25}$

b. $15\%, \frac{7}{20}, 0.08, 50\%$

Lesson 6-3

Percents Greater Than 100% or Less Than 1%

Lesson Objective	NAEP 2005 Strand:
To convert between fractions, decimals, and percents greater than 100% or less than 1%	Topic:
	Local Standards: _____

Examples

❶ Rewriting Percents Greater Than 100% Write 140% as a decimal and as a fraction.

$140\% = \boxed{}$ ← Move the decimal point $\boxed{}$ places to the $\boxed{}$.

$140\% = \dfrac{140}{\boxed{}}$ ← Use the definition of percent.

$= \dfrac{\boxed{}}{\boxed{}}$ or $\boxed{}\dfrac{\boxed{}}{\boxed{}}$ ← Simplify the fraction.

140% equals $\boxed{}$ in decimal form and $\boxed{}$ in fraction form.

❷ Rewriting Percents Less Than 1% Write 0.75% as a decimal and as a fraction in simplest form.

$0.75\% = \boxed{}$ ← Move the decimal point $\boxed{}$ places to the $\boxed{}$.

$0.75\% = \dfrac{0.75}{\boxed{}}$ ← Use the definition of percent.

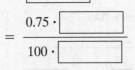

$= \dfrac{0.75 \cdot \boxed{}}{100 \cdot \boxed{}}$ ← Multiply numerator and denominator by $\boxed{}$ to get a whole number numerator.

$= \dfrac{\boxed{}}{10,000} = \dfrac{\boxed{}}{\boxed{}}$ ← Simplify.

0.75% equals $\boxed{}$ in decimal form and $\boxed{}$ in fraction form.

Quick Check

1. Write 125% as a decimal and as a fraction in simplest form.

2. Write 0.35% as a decimal and as a fraction in simplest form.

     Daily Notetaking Guide

Name _____ Class _____ Date _____

Examples

❸ **Writing Mixed Numbers as Percents** The sports stadium at a school has $4\frac{2}{3}$ as many seats as the auditorium. Write this mixed number as a percent. Round to the nearest hundredth.

$4\frac{2}{3} = $ ☐ ➕ ☐ ➗ ☐ 🟰 ☐ ← **Use a calculator.**

$\approx 4.66.67 = $ ☐ % ← **Move the decimal point** ☐ **places to the** ☐ **.**

The number of seats in the stadium is ☐ of the number of seats in the auditorium.

❹ **Multiple Choice** An animal shelter has 4 beagles available for adoption. There are 481 other dogs for adoption that are not beagles. About what percentage of the dogs are beagles?

A. 8%   **B.** 0.8%   **C.** 0.08%   **D.** 0.008%

☐ + ☐ = ☐ ← **Add.**

$\dfrac{☐}{☐} = \dfrac{☐}{☐}$ ← **Write the fraction.**

= ☐ ← **Use a calculator.**

= ☐ ← **Write as a percent and round.**

About ☐ of the dogs are beagles. The correct answer is choice ☐.

Quick Check

3. You plan to run $2\frac{4}{5}$ the distance you ran yesterday. Write this number as a percent.

☐

4. Idaho has 2 members in the U.S. House of Representatives. There are a total of 435 representatives. What percent of the representatives are from Idaho? Round to the nearest hundredth of a percent.

☐

Lesson 6-4

Finding a Percent of a Number

Lesson Objective	**NAEP 2005 Strand:** Number Properties and Operations
To find and estimate the percent of a number	**Topic:** Ratios and Proportional Reasoning
	Local Standards: _____

Examples

① **Finding a Percent of a Number** Find 80% of 460.

Method 1 Write the percent as a decimal.   **Method 2** Write the percent as a fraction.

$80\% = \boxed{}$ ← **Change 80% to an** → $80\% = \dfrac{\boxed{}}{\boxed{}}$
equivalent form.

$\boxed{} \cdot 460 = \boxed{}$ ← **Multiply.** → $\dfrac{\boxed{}}{\boxed{}} \cdot 460 = \boxed{}$

80% of 460 is $\boxed{}$.

② **Using Mental Math** Find 49% of 300.

What You Think

49% is 50% − $\boxed{}$%

50% of 300 is $\boxed{}$ · 300, or $\boxed{}$.

1% of 300 is $\boxed{}$ · 300, or $\boxed{}$.

$\boxed{}$ − $\boxed{}$ = $\boxed{}$, so 49% of 300 is $\boxed{}$.

Why It Works

49% of 300 = $\boxed{}$ · 300   ← **Write 49% as a decimal.**

= (0.50 − 0.01) · 300   ← **Substitute 0.50 − 0.01 for 0.49.**

= (0.50 · 300) − (0.01 · 300)   ← **Use the** $\boxed{}$ **Property.**

= $\boxed{}$ − $\boxed{}$ ← **Multiply.**

= $\boxed{}$ ← **Subtract.**

Quick Check

1. Find 75% of 140.

$$\boxed{}$$

2. Use mental math to find 40% of 2,400.

$$\boxed{}$$

Example

❸ **Estimating a Percent** Estimate each answer.

a. 76% of 405

76% ·   405   ← **Write an expression.**

  ↓   ↓

$\frac{3}{4}$ · [_____] = [_____]   ← **Use** [_____] **numbers such as** $\frac{3}{4}$ **and** [_____].

76% of 405 is about [_____].

b. 12% of 5,575

12% ·   5,575   ← **Write an expression.**

  ↓   ↓

$\frac{1}{10}$ · [_____] = [_____]   ← **Use** [_____] **numbers such as** $\frac{1}{10}$ **and** [_____].

12% of 5,575 is about [_____].

Quick Check

3. Estimate each answer.

a. 24% of 238

[_____]

b. 19% of 473

[_____]

c. 82% of 747

[_____]

Lesson 6-5

Solving Percent Problems Using Proportions

Lesson Objective	**NAEP 2005 Strand:** Number Properties and Operations
To use proportions to solve problems involving percent	**Topic:** Ratios and Proportional Reasoning
	Local Standards: _____

Key Concepts

Percents and Proportions

Finding a Percent
What percent of 25 is 5?

0   5   25

0% n%   100%

$$\frac{\boxed{}}{\boxed{}} = \frac{n}{100}$$

$$n = \boxed{}$$

Finding a Part
What is 20% of 25?

0   n   25

0% 20%   100%

$$\frac{n}{\boxed{}} = \frac{\boxed{}}{100}$$

$$n = \boxed{}$$

Finding a Whole
20% of what is 5?

0   5   n

0% 20%   100%

$$\frac{\boxed{}}{n} = \frac{\boxed{}}{100}$$

$$n = \boxed{}$$

Example

❶ Finding a Percent What percent of 150 is 45?

You can write a proportion to find the percent.

$$\frac{45}{\boxed{}} = \frac{n}{\boxed{}}$$ ← **Write a proportion.**

$$\boxed{}n = 45\left(\boxed{}\right)$$ ← **Write the cross products.**

$$\frac{150n}{\boxed{}} = \frac{45(100)}{\boxed{}}$$ ← **Divide each side by** $\boxed{}$.

$$n = \boxed{}$$ ← **Simplify.**

45 is $\boxed{}$% of 150.

Quick Check

1. What percent of 92 is 23?

_____

Examples

② **Finding a Part** 24% of 25 is what number?

$$\frac{n}{\boxed{}} = \frac{\boxed{}}{100}$$ ← **Write a proportion.**

$$\frac{n}{\boxed{}} = \frac{\boxed{}}{25}$$ ← **Simplify the fraction.**

$$n = \boxed{}$$ ← **Simplify.**

$\boxed{}$ is 24% of 25.

③ **Finding the Whole** Use a proportion to answer the question: 117 is 45% of what number?

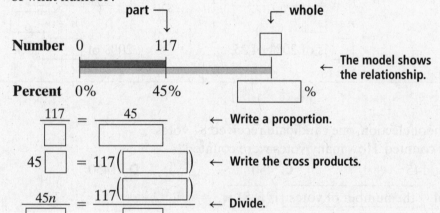

$$\frac{117}{\boxed{}} = \frac{45}{\boxed{}}$$ ← **Write a proportion.**

$$45 \boxed{} = 117 \left(\boxed{} \right)$$ ← **Write the cross products.**

$$\frac{45n}{\boxed{}} = \frac{117 \left(\boxed{} \right)}{\boxed{}}$$ ← **Divide.**

$$n = \boxed{}$$ ← **Simplify.**

Quick Check

2. 85% of 20 is what number?

$\boxed{}$

3. Your math teacher assigns 25 problems for homework. You have done 60% of them. How many problems have you done?

$\boxed{}$

Name _____ Class _____ Date _____

Lesson 6-6

Solving Percent Problems Using Equations

Lesson Objective	**NAEP 2005 Strand:** Algebra
To use equations to solve problems involving percent	**Topic:** Algebraic Representations
	Local Standards: _____

Key Concepts

Percents and Proportions

Finding a Percent

What percent of 25 is 5?

$n \cdot \boxed{} = \boxed{}$

$n = \boxed{}$

5 is $\boxed{}$ of 25.

Finding a Part

What is 20% of 25?

$n = \boxed{} \cdot \boxed{}$

$n = \boxed{}$

$\boxed{}$ is of 20% of 25.

Finding a Whole

20% of what is 5?

$\boxed{} \cdot n = \boxed{}$

$n = \boxed{}$

20% of $\boxed{}$ is 5.

Examples

❶ **Finding a Whole** In a school election, one candidate received 81 votes. This was 18% of the votes counted. How many votes were counted?

A. 45   **B.** 145   **C.** 450   **D.** 1450

Words $\boxed{18\%}$ of $\boxed{\text{the number of votes}}$ is $\boxed{81}$.

Let n = the number of votes counted.

Equation $\boxed{} \cdot \boxed{}$ $= \boxed{}$

$\boxed{} \cdot \boxed{} = \boxed{}$ ← **Write the equation.**

$\dfrac{0.18n}{\boxed{}} = \dfrac{81}{\boxed{}}$ ← **Divide each side by** $\boxed{}$.

$n = \boxed{}$ ← **Simplify.**

$\boxed{}$ votes were counted. The correct choice answer is $\boxed{}$.

❷ **Finding a Part** What number is 32% of 40?

Words $\boxed{\text{A number}}$ is $\boxed{32\%}$ of $\boxed{40}$.

Let $\boxed{}$ = the number.

Equation $\boxed{}$ $= \boxed{} \cdot \boxed{}$

$= \boxed{}$ ← **Simplify.**

❸ Finding a Percent Of the 257 sandwiches sold at a delicatessen one day, 45 were turkey sandwiches. What percent of the sandwiches were turkey?

Estimate About 50 of 250 sandwiches were turkey.

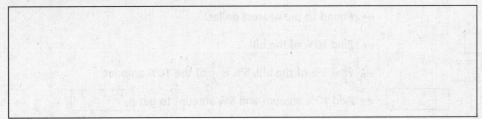

← Write an equation. Let *p* = the percent of sandwiches that are turkey.

$$\frac{257p}{\boxed{}} = \frac{45}{\boxed{}}$$

← Divide each side by $\boxed{}$.

$p \approx \boxed{}$ ← Use a calculator.

$p \approx \boxed{}$ %   ← Write the decimal as a percent.

Check for Reasonableness $\boxed{}$ % is close to the estimate $\boxed{}$ %.

Quick Check

1. A plane flies with 54% of its seats empty. If 81 seats are empty, what is the total number of seats on the plane?

2. 27% of 60 is what number?

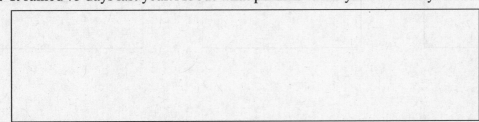

3. It rained 75 days last year. About what percent of the year was rainy?

Lesson 6-7

Applications of Percent

Lesson Objective	**NAEP 2005 Strand:** Number Properties and Operations
To find and estimate solutions to application problems involving percent	**Topic:** Ratios and Proportional Reasoning
	Local Standards: _____

Vocabulary

commission = [_____] · [_____]

Examples

1 **Finding Sales Tax** A video game costs $34.98. The sales tax rate is 5.5%. How much will you pay for the video game?

[_____] · 34.98 = [_____]   ← **Find the sales tax. Round to the nearest cent.**

34.98 + [_____] = [_____]   ← **Add the sales tax to the purchase price.**

You will pay [_____] for the video game.

2 **Estimating a Tip** Use estimation to calculate a 15% tip for $34.50.

34.50 ≈ [_____]   ← **Round to the nearest dollar.**

0.1 · [_____] = [_____]   ← **Find 10% of the bill.**

$\frac{1}{2}$ · [_____] = [_____]   ← **Find 5% of the bill. 5% is $\frac{1}{2}$ of the 10% amount.**

[_____] + [_____] = [_____]   ← **Add 10% amount and 5% amount to get** [_____].

A 15% tip for $34.50 is about [_____].

Quick Check

1. Find the total cost for a purchase of $185 if the sales tax rate is 5.5%.

[_____]

2. Estimate a 15% tip for each amount.
   a. $58.20   **b.** $61.80   **c.** $49.75

[_____]   [_____]   [_____]

Examples

❸ Finding a Commission Find the commission on a $300 sale, with a commission rate of 8.5%.

[　　　] · [　　　] = [　　　]   ← **Write 8.5% as** [　　　] **and multiply.**

The commission on the sale is [　　　] .

❹ Finding a Commission Find the total earnings for a salesperson with a salary of $550 plus 4% commission on sales of $1,485.

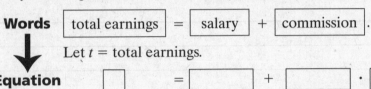

Words   [total earnings] = [salary] + [commission] .

Let t = total earnings.

Equation   [　] = [　　　] + [　　　] · [　　　]

t = [　　　] + [　　　] · [　　　]   ← **Write the equation.**

= 550 + [　　　]   ← **Multiply.**

= [　　　]   ← **Simplify.**

The salesperson earns [　　　] .

Quick Check

3. Find the commission on a $3,200 sale, with a commission rate of 6%.

[　　　　　　　　　　　　　　　　　　　]

4. Suppose you earn a weekly salary of $800 plus a commission of 3.5% on all sales. Find your earnings for a week with total sales of $1,400.

[　　　　　　　　　　　　　　　　　　　]

Lesson 6-8

Finding Percent of Change

Lesson Objective To find percents of increase and percents of decrease	**NAEP 2005 Strand:** Number Properties and Operations **Topic:** Ratios and Proportional Reasoning **Local Standards:** _____

Vocabulary

The percent of change is _____

_____

A markup is _____

_____

A discount is _____

_____

Example

① **Finding a Percent of Increase** Last year, a school had 632 students. This year the school has 670 students. Find the percent of increase in the number of students.

$670 - 632 = \boxed{}$ ← **Find the amount of change.**

$\dfrac{38}{\boxed{}} = \dfrac{n}{\boxed{}}$ ← **Write a proportion. Let n = percent of change.**

$100 \cdot \dfrac{38}{\boxed{}} = \dfrac{n}{\boxed{}} \cdot 100$ ← **Multiply each side by 100.**

$\dfrac{3800}{\boxed{}} = n$ ← **Simplify.**

$n \approx \boxed{}$ ← **Divide.**

The number of students increased by about $\boxed{}$.

Quick Check

1. In 2000, California went from 52 to 53 representatives. Find the percent of increase in representatives.

_____

Examples

❷ Finding a Percent of Markup Find the percent of markup for a car that a dealer buys for $10,590 and sells for $13,775.

$13,775 - 10,590 =$ [   ] ← **Find the amount of markup.**

$$\frac{3,185}{\boxed{}} = \frac{n}{\boxed{}}$$ ← **Write a proportion. Let n be the percent of markup.**

[   ]$n =$ [   ](100) ← **Write cross products.**

$$\frac{\boxed{}\,n}{\boxed{}} = \frac{\boxed{}(100)}{\boxed{}}$$ ← **Divide each side by** [   ].

$n \approx$ [   ] ← **Simplify.**

The percent of markup is about [   ].

❸ Finding a Percent of Discount Find the percent of discount for a $74.99 tent that is discounted to $48.75.

$74.99 - 48.75 =$ [   ] ← **Find the amount of the discount.**

$$\frac{26.24}{\boxed{}} = \frac{n}{\boxed{}}$$ ← **Write a proportion. Let n be the percent of discount.**

[   ]$n = 26.24\left(\boxed{}\right)$ ← **Write cross products.**

$$\frac{\boxed{}\,n}{\boxed{}} = \frac{26.24\left(\boxed{}\right)}{\boxed{}}$$ ← **Divide each side by** [   ].

$n \approx$ [   ] ← **Simplify.**

The percent of discount for the tent is about [   ].

Quick Check

2. Find the percent of markup for a $17.95 headset marked up to $35.79.

[   ]

3. Find the percent of discount of a $24.95 novel on sale for $14.97.

[   ]

Lesson 7-1

Lines and Planes

Lesson Objective To identify segments, rays, and lines	**NAEP 2005 Strand:** Geometry **Topic:** Relationships Among Geometric Figures **Local Standards:** _____

Vocabulary

A point _____

_____

A line is _____

A ray is _____

A segment is _____

A plane is _____

Intersecting lines are _____

_____

Parallel lines are _____

Skew lines are _____

_____

Example

① **Naming Segments, Rays, and Lines** Use the points in each diagram to name the figure.

a. _C _____ G_

[rectangle]

b. _J   K_

[rectangle]

c. _A   B_

[rectangle]

Quick Check

1. Use the points in each diagram to name the figure shown.

a. _P   D_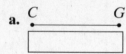

[rectangle]

b. _R _____ S_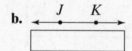

[rectangle]

c. _A   V_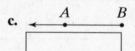

[rectangle]

Daily Notetaking Guide

Example

❷ **Intersecting, Parallel, and Skew** Name all the segments that have each characteristic.

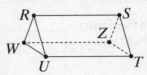

a. parallel to $\overline{UT}$

[ ] and [ ] are parallel to $\overline{UT}$.

b. intersecting $\overline{RU}$

[ ], [ ], [ ], and [ ] intersect $\overline{RU}$.

c. skew to $\overline{RS}$

[ ] and [ ] are skew to $\overline{RS}$.

Quick Check

2. Name the segments in the diagram that fit each description.

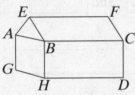

a. parallel to $\overline{BC}$

b. intersect $\overline{BH}$

c. skew to $\overline{AG}$

Lesson 7-2

Identifying and Classifying Angles

Lesson Objective To classify angles and to find angle measures using the relationship between pairs of angles	**NAEP 2005 Strand:** Measurement **Topic:** Measuring Physical Attributes **Local Standards:** _____

Vocabulary

An angle is _____

_____

A vertex is _____

_____

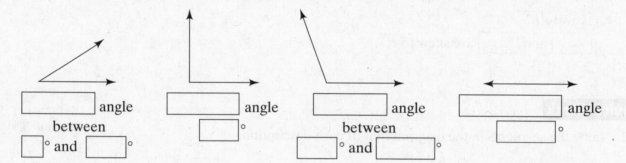

[____] angle	[____] angle	[____] angle	[____] angle
between [__]° and [____]°	[____]°	between [____]° and [____]°	[____]°

Adjacent angles are _____

_____

Vertical angles are _____

_____

Circle an angle adjacent to ∠1.

Circle the vertical angle to ∠1.

If the sum of the measure of two angles is 90°, the angles are [_____].
If the sum is 180°, the angles are [_____].

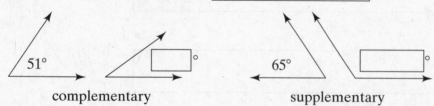

51°	[____]°	65°	[____]°
complementary		supplementary	

Congruent angles are _____

_____

Examples

❶ Identifying Angles Identify the acute angles, obtuse angles, and straight angle in the figure.

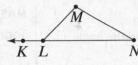

acute angles: [   ] and [   ]

obtuse angles: [   ] and [   ]

straight angle: [   ]

❷ Finding Angle Measures Find the measures of ∠1, ∠2, and ∠4, for $m\angle 3 = 32°$.

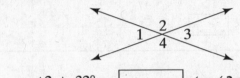

$m\angle 2 + 32° =$ [   ] ← ∠2 and ∠3 are [   ].

$m\angle 2 + 32° - 32° = 180° - 32°$ ← **Subtract 32° from each side.**

$m\angle 2 =$ [   ] ← **Simplify.**

$m\angle 1 =$ [   ] ← ∠1 and ∠3 are [   ] angles.

$m\angle 4 =$ [   ] ← ∠2 and ∠4 are [   ] angles.

Quick Check

1. Classify ∠AFE as *acute*, *right*, *obtuse*, or *straight*.

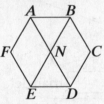

[   ]

2. Find the measure of the complement of ∠3 in Example 2.

[   ]

3. In the diagram at the right, $m\angle 8 = 72°$. Find the measures of ∠5, ∠6, and ∠7.

[   ]

Lesson 7-3

Triangles

Lesson Objective	**NAEP 2005 Strand:** Geometry
To classify triangles and to find the angle measures of triangles	**Topics:** Dimension and Shape; Relationships Among Geometric Figures
	Local Standards: _____

Vocabulary and Key Concepts

Angle Sum of a Triangle

The sum of the measures of the angles of a triangle is [ ].

Congruent sides are _____

_____

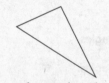

scalene triangle   isosceles triangle   equilateral triangle

congruent sides	congruent sides	congruent sides

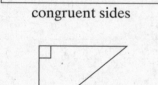
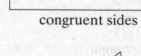
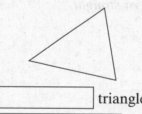
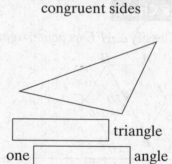

[ ] triangle	[ ] triangle	[ ] triangle
one [ ] angle	[ ] angles	one [ ] angle

Examples

① Classifying Triangles by Sides Classify each triangle by its sides.

a. There are two congruent sides, so the triangle is [   ].

b. There are no congruent sides, so the triangle is [   ].

❷ Classifying Triangles by Angles Classify each triangle by its angle measures.

a.

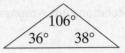

The triangle has ☐ obtuse angle,

so it is an ☐ triangle.

b.

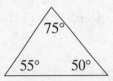

The triangle has ☐ acute angles,

so it is an ☐ triangle.

❸ Finding an Angle Measure Find the value of x in the triangle.

$$x + 78° + 56° = \boxed{}$$

$$x + \boxed{} = \boxed{}$$

$$x + \boxed{} - \boxed{} = \boxed{} - \boxed{}$$

$$x = \boxed{}$$

Quick Check

1. Classify $\triangle BCD$ by its sides.

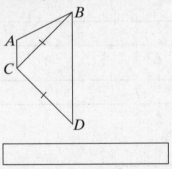

☐

2. Classify each triangle by its angle measures.

a.

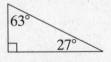

☐

b.

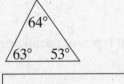

☐

3. Find the value of x in the triangle.

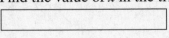

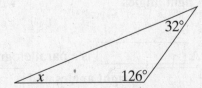

Lesson 7-4

Quadrilaterals and Other Polygons

Lesson Objective	NAEP 2005 Strand: Geometry
To classify polygons and special quadrilaterals	**Topics:** Dimension and Shape; Relationships Among Geometric Figures
	Local Standards: _____

Vocabulary

A polygon is _____

_____

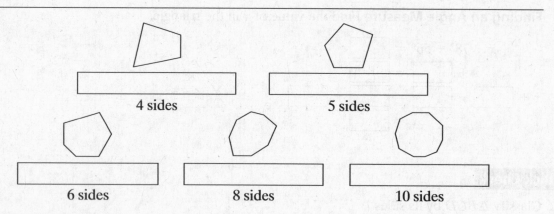

4 sides	5 sides

6 sides	8 sides	10 sides

A regular polygon is _____

_____

An irregular polygon is _____

_____

A [   ] is a quadrilateral with exactly [   ] pair of parallel sides.

A [   ] is a quadrilateral with [   ] pairs of opposite sides parallel.

There are three special types of parallelograms.

A [   ] is a parallelogram with [   ] right angles.

A [   ] is a parallelogram with [   ] congruent sides.

A [   ] is a parallelogram with [   ] right angles and [   ] congruent sides.

Daily Notetaking Guide

Examples

❶ Identifying Regular Polygons Identify the polygon and classify it as *regular* or *irregular*.

 The figure has ☐ sides. Not all sides are congruent.

The ☐☐☐☐ is ☐☐☐☐.

❷ Classifying Polygons Identify the polygons in the design.

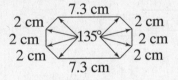 The outside polygon is a ☐☐☐☐. Inside the decagon are ☐☐☐☐,

☐☐☐☐, ☐☐☐☐, and a ☐☐☐☐.

❸ Using Dot Paper Draw a regular parallelogram.

 A ☐☐☐☐ is a regular parallelogram.

Quick Check

1. Identify each polygon and classify it as *regular* or *irregular*.

a.
2 cm 7.3 cm 2 cm
2 cm 135° 2 cm
2 cm   2 cm
    7.3 cm

b.
5 / 60° \ 5
60°   60°
    5

c. Reasoning How would you find the perimeter of a regular polygon? Explain.

2. Use the best names to identify the polygons in the pattern.

3. Use dot paper to draw a trapezoid with a pair of opposite sides that are congruent.

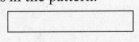

Lesson 7-5

Lesson Objective To identify congruent figures and to use them to find missing measures	**NAEP 2005 Strand:** Geometry **Topic:** Transformation of Shapes and Preservation of Properties **Local Standards:** _____

Vocabulary

Congruent polygons are _____

_____

Example

① **Identifying Congruent Figures** Are the figures *congruent* or *not congruent*? Explain.

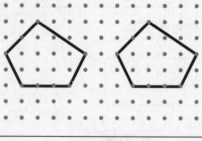

$\overline{AB} \cong$ [ ] , $\overline{BC} \cong$ [ ] , $\overline{CD} \cong$ [ ] , $\overline{DE} \cong$ [ ] , $\overline{EA} \cong$ [ ] ,

$\angle A \cong$ [ ] , $\angle B \cong$ [ ] , $\angle C \cong$ [ ] , $\angle D \cong$ [ ] , and $\angle E \cong$ [ ] .

The figures are [ ] .

Quick Check

1. Are the figures below *congruent* or *not congruent*? Explain.

[ ]

Examples

❷ Is the figure at the right congruent to the figure at the left?

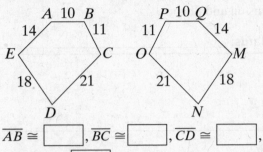

$\overline{AB} \cong$ [   ] , $\overline{BC} \cong$ [   ] , $\overline{CD} \cong$ [   ] , $\overline{DE} \cong$ [   ] ,

and $\overline{EA} \cong$ [   ] .

All corresponding sides and angles are congruent, so the figures are

[   ] .

❸ **Working With Congruent Figures** The triangles are congruent.
Write six congruences for the corresponding parts of the triangles.

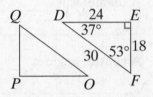

$\angle Q \cong$ [   ]   [   ] $\cong \angle E$ $\angle O \cong$ [   ]

$\overline{DF} \cong$ [   ] $\overline{EF} \cong$ [   ]   [   ] $\cong \overline{OP}$

Quick Check

2. Is the figure on the right congruent to the sample figure? Explain.

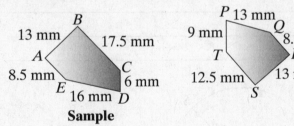

Sample

[   ]

3. The quadrilaterals are congruent.
   a. Write the congruences for the corresponding parts.

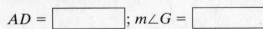

[   ] [   ] [   ] [   ]

[   ] [   ] [   ] [   ]

   b. Find AD and $m\angle G$.

$AD =$ [   ] ; $m\angle G =$ [   ]

Lesson 7-6

Circles

Lesson Objective	NAEP 2005 Strand: Geometry
To identify parts of a circle	Topic: Dimension and Shape
	Local Standards: _____

Vocabulary

A circle is _____

_____

A radius is _____

_____

A diameter is _____

_____

A central angle is _____

_____

A chord is _____

_____

An arc is _____

_____

A semicircle is _____

_____

$\overline{ST}$ is a [   ] .

$\overline{VW}$ is a [   ] .

$\overline{WX}$ is a [   ] .

$\angle STW$ is a [   ] .

$\overline{SV}$ is an [   ] .

$\overset{\frown}{WSV}$ is a [   ] .

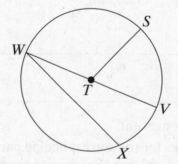

Examples

Use circle *F* for Examples 1–3.

❶ Naming Parts Inside a Circle Name all the radii, diameters, and chords shown for circle *F*.

radii: ☐ , ☐ , and ☐

diameter: ☐

chords: ☐ and ☐

❷ Naming Arcs Name three of the arcs in circle *F*.

☐

❸ Naming Arcs Name two different arcs between points *C* and *D*.

The shorter arc is ☐ .

The longer arc is ☐ .

Quick Check

1. Name all the central angles shown in circle *O*.

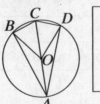

☐

2. Name three arcs in circle *F* not mentioned in Example 2.

☐

3. Name two different arcs between points *A* and *D* in circle *F*.

☐

Lesson 7-7

Circle Graphs

Lesson Objective To analyze and construct circle graphs	**NAEP 2005 Strand:** Data Analysis and Probability **Topic:** Data Representation **Local Standards:** _____

Vocabulary

A circle graph is _____

_____

Examples

1 Analyzing a Circle Graph Use the circle graph at the right to find how many of the days were cloudy.

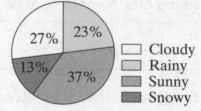

November Weather (30 days)

27% 23%
13% 37%

☐ Cloudy
☐ Rainy
☐ Sunny
☐ Snowy

☐ of 30 days = ☐ · 30 = ☐

☐ days were cloudy.

2 Constructing a Circle Graph Use the information in the table to make a circle graph.

Step 1 Add to find the total number of households.

$26{,}724 + 34{,}666 + 17{,}152 + 15{,}309 + 10{,}854 =$ ☐
(in thousands)

Size of U.S. Households (2000)

No. of People in Household	Number (in thousands)
1	26,724
2	34,666
3	17,152
4	15,309
5 or more	10,854

Step 2 For each central angle, set up a proportion to find the angle measure. Use a calculator to solve. Round to the nearest tenth.

$$\frac{\boxed{}}{104{,}705} = \frac{a}{360°} \qquad \frac{\boxed{}}{104{,}705} = \frac{b}{360°} \qquad \frac{\boxed{}}{104{,}705} = \frac{c}{360°}$$

$$a \approx \boxed{} \qquad b \approx \boxed{} \qquad c \approx \boxed{}$$

$$\frac{\boxed{}}{104{,}705} = \frac{d}{360°} \qquad \frac{\boxed{}}{104{,}705} = \frac{f}{360°}$$

$$d \approx \boxed{} \qquad f \approx \boxed{}$$

Step 3 Draw a circle. Draw the central angles using the measures found in Step 2. Label each section. Include a title and a key.

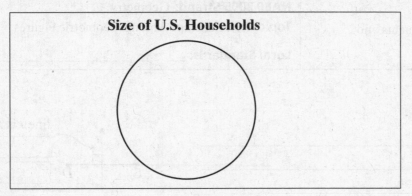

Size of U.S. Households

Quick Check

1. According to the circle graph in Example 1, how many days were sunny?

2. Human Blood Types

Blood Type	Percent
A	40%
B	11%
AB	4%
O	45%

Source: American Association of Blood Banks

a. Find the measure of the central angle that you would draw to represent blood type A.

b. Use the information in the table to make a circle graph.

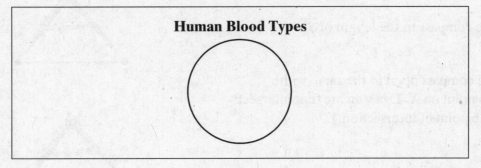

Human Blood Types

Lesson 7-8

Constructions

Lesson Objective	NAEP 2005 Strand: Geometry
To construct congruent segments and perpendicular bisectors	**Topic:** Relationships Among Geometric Figures
	Local Standards: _____

Vocabulary

A compass is _____

_____

A midpoint is _____

_____

A segment bisector is _____

_____

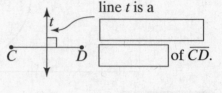

line t is a

of $\overline{CD}$.

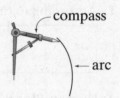

compass

arc

[ ] is congruent to $\overline{MB}$.

[ ] is the midpoint of $\overline{AB}$.

Line ℓ is a [   ] of $\overline{AB}$.

Perpendicular lines are _____

A perpendicular bisector is _____

_____

Examples

❶ Constructing a Congruent Segment Construct segment $\overline{XY}$ congruent to $\overline{ST}$.

Step 1 Draw a ray with endpoint X.

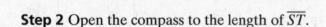

Step 2 Open the compass to the length of $\overline{ST}$.

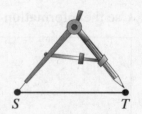

Step 3 Keep the compass open to the same width. Put the compass point on X. Draw an arc that intersects the ray. Label the point of intersection Y.

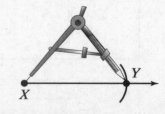

[ ] is congruent to $\overline{ST}$.

❷ Constructing a Perpendicular Bisector

Construct the perpendicular bisector of $\overline{PQ}$.

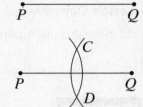

Step 1 Set the compass to more than half the length of $\overline{PQ}$. Put the tip of the compass at P and draw an arc intersecting $\overline{PQ}$. Keeping the compass set at the same width, put the tip at Q and draw another arc intersecting $\overline{PQ}$. Points C and D are where the arcs intersect.

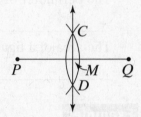

Step 2 Draw $\overleftrightarrow{CD}$. The intersection of $\overline{PQ}$ and $\overleftrightarrow{CD}$ is point $\boxed{}$. $\overleftrightarrow{CD}$ is the $\boxed{}$ of $\overline{PQ}$. Point M is the midpoint of $\boxed{}$.

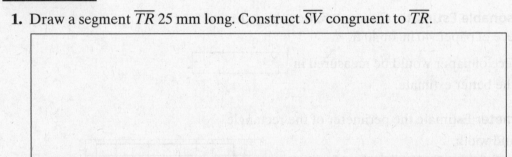

Quick Check

1. Draw a segment $\overline{TR}$ 25 mm long. Construct $\overline{SV}$ congruent to $\overline{TR}$.

2. Draw a segment 3 in. long. Label the segment $\overline{XY}$. Construct the perpendicular bisector of $\overline{XY}$.

Lesson 8-1

Estimating Perimeter and Area

Lesson Objective	NAEP 2005 Strand: Measurement
To estimate length, perimeter, and area	Topic: Measuring Physical Attributes
	Local Standards: _____

Vocabulary

The perimeter of a figure _____

_____

The area of a figure is _____

_____

Examples

1 Choosing a Reasonable Estimate Choose a reasonable estimate for the perimeter of a piece of paper: 40 in. or 40 ft.

The edges of a piece of paper would be measured in [   ].

So [   ] is the better estimate.

2 Estimating Perimeter Estimate the perimeter of the rectangle.

Estimate length and width.

The length is about 5 units. →
The width is about 8. →

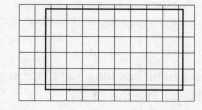

Use the formula for perimeter of a rectangle.

$2(\boxed{} + \boxed{}) = \boxed{}$

The perimeter is about [   ] units long.

Quick Check

1. Which is a reasonable estimate for the distance between Boston, Massachusetts, and Washington, D.C., 400 ft or 400 mi? Explain.

2. Estimate the perimeter of the rectangle.

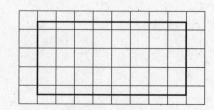

Example

③ Estimating Area Each square represents 50 yd². Estimate the area of the shaded figure.

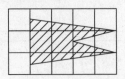

Count the number of squares filled or almost filled: ☐.

Then count the number of squares that are about half-filled: ☐.

Estimate the number of squares filled by ☐ the filled squares
and the half-filled squares, which is ☐ + ½(☐), or ☐.

Since each square represents 50 yd², multiply ☐ by ☐ yd². The area
is about ☐ yd².

Quick Check

3. Estimate the area of the shaded region. Each square represents 4 yd².

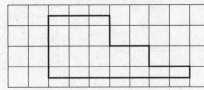

4. Each square represents 25 square feet. Estimate the area and perimeter of the figure.

Lesson 8-2

Lesson Objective To find the area and perimeter of a parallelogram	**NAEP 2005 Strand:** Measurement **Topic:** Measuring Physical Attributes **Local Standards:** _____

Vocabulary and Key Concepts

Area of a Parallelogram

The area of a parallelogram is equal to the product of any ⬚ *b* and the corresponding ⬚ *h*.

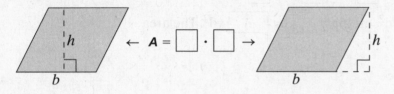

The height of a parallelogram is _____

_____

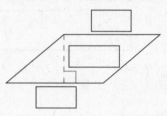

Examples

❶ Finding the Area of a Parallelogram Find the area of the parallelogram.

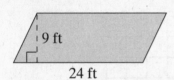

9 ft

24 ft

$A = \boxed{}\boxed{}$ ← **Use the area formula.**

$= (\boxed{})(\boxed{})$ ← **Substitute.**

$= \boxed{}$ ← **Simplify.**

The area is $\boxed{}$ ft².

❷ **Relating Perimeter and Area** Jacob wants to fence in a rectangular dog run in his back yard. He has 46 feet of fencing and wants the dog run to be as large as possible. Which dimensions should he use?

A. length of 9 ft and width of 14 ft   **B.** length of 10 ft and width of 14 ft

C. length of 11 ft and width of 12 ft   **D.** length of 12 ft and width of 12 ft

Since all answer choices give the length *l* and the width *w*, you can calculate both the perimeter $2l + 2w$, and the area [⬚].

Perimeter   **Area**

[⬚] (9) + [⬚] (14) = [⬚]   [⬚] [⬚] [⬚] = [⬚] ← Perimeter is correct; find the area.

[⬚] (10) + [⬚] (14) = [⬚]   ← Perimeter is greater than 46 ft.

[⬚] (11) + [⬚] (12) = [⬚]   [⬚] [⬚] [⬚] = [⬚] ← Perimeter is correct; the area in choice

                                                A is [⬚].

[⬚] (12) + [⬚] (12) = [⬚]   ← Perimeter is greater than 46 ft.

The rectangle with a length of [⬚] ft and a width of [⬚] ft will have the correct perimeter and the greatest area. The correct answer is choice [⬚].

Quick Check

1. Find the area of the parallelogram.

[⬚]

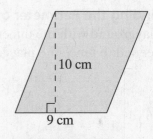

10 cm

9 cm

2. What is the perimeter of the rectangle?

[⬚]

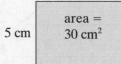

5 cm   area = 30 cm²

Name _____ Class _____ Date _____

Lesson 8-3   **Perimeter and Area of a Triangle**

Lesson Objective	**NAEP 2005 Strand:** Measurement
To find the perimeter and area of a triangle	**Topic:** Measuring Physical Attributes
	Local Standards: _____

Vocabulary and Key Concepts

Area of a Triangle

The area of a triangle is equal to half the product of any

[   ] and the corresponding [   ].

The height of a triangle _____
_____

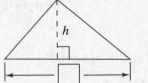 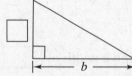 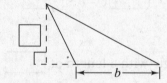

Example

1 **Finding the Perimeter of a Triangle** A school is creating a triangular playground with the dimensions shown. How many yards of fencing are needed to fence the playground?

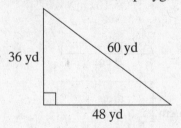

36 yd   60 yd
48 yd

$P =$ [   ] [   ] 48 [   ] 60   ← **Find the perimeter.**

= [   ]   ← **Simplify.**

The school needs [   ] yards of fencing to fence the playground.

Example

❷ Finding the Area of a Triangle Find the area of each triangle.

a.

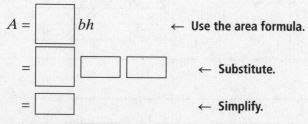

$A = \frac{1}{2}$ ☐ ☐ ← **Use the area formula.**

$= \frac{1}{2}$ (☐)(☐) ← **Substitute.**

$=$ ☐ ← **Simplify.**

The area is ☐ yd².

b. The triangle has side lengths of 16.2 cm, 15.4 cm, and 2.4 cm. Draw the height going to the base of length 2.4 cm. The height is 15 cm.

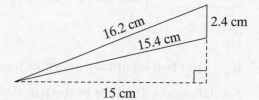

$A =$ ☐ bh ← **Use the area formula.**

$=$ ☐ ☐ ☐ ← **Substitute.**

$=$ ☐ ← **Simplify.**

The area is ☐ cm².

Quick Check

1. How much fabric do you need to border a triangular quilt piece whose sides are 6 cm, 8 cm, and 10 cm long?

☐

2. Find the area of each triangle.

a.

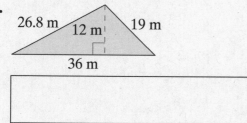

☐

b.

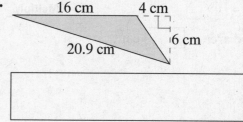

☐

Lesson 8-4

Areas of Other Figures

Lesson Objective	**NAEP 2005 Strand:** Measurement
To find the area of a trapezoid and the areas of irregular figures	**Topic:** Measuring Physical Attributes
	Local Standards: _____

Vocabulary and Key Concepts

Area of a Trapezoid

The area of a trapezoid is [　　　　] the product of the

[　　　　] and the sum of the lengths of the [　　　　].

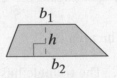

$A = \frac{1}{2}\,\boxed{}\,(\boxed{} + \boxed{})$

If you put two identical trapezoids together, you get a

paralellogram. The area of the parallelogram is [　　　　].

The area of one trapezoid is [　　　　].

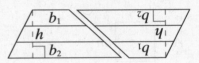

The bases of a trapezoid are _____

The height of a trapezoid is _____

_____

Examples

❶ **Finding the Area of a Trapezoid** Find the area of the trapezoid.

$A = \frac{1}{2}\,\boxed{}\,(\boxed{} + \boxed{})$ ← Use the area formula for a trapezoid.

$= \frac{1}{2}(\boxed{})(\boxed{} + \boxed{})$ ← Substitute for h, b_1, and b_2.

$= \frac{1}{2}(\boxed{})(16)$ ← Add.

$= \boxed{}$ ← Multiply.

The area is $\boxed{}$ cm^2.

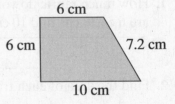

❷ Estimating Area Estimate the area of the figure by finding the area of the trapezoid.

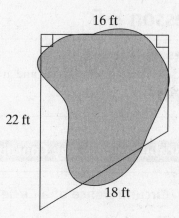

16 ft

22 ft

18 ft

$A = \frac{1}{2}\boxed{}(\boxed{} + b_2)$ ← **Use the area formula for a trapezoid.**

$= \frac{1}{2}(\boxed{})(\boxed{} + 22)$ ← **Substitute for h, b_1 and b_2.**

$= \frac{1}{2}(\boxed{})(\boxed{})$ ← **Add.**

$= \boxed{}$ ← **Multiply.**

The area of the figure is about $\boxed{}$ ft^2.

Quick Check

1. Find the area of each trapezoid.

a.

6 m

5 m   4.4 m   4.5 m

9.5 m

$\boxed{}$ m^2

b.

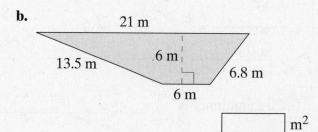

21 m

13.5 m   6 m   6.8 m

6 m

$\boxed{}$ m^2

2. Estimate the area of the figure by finding the area of the trapezoid.

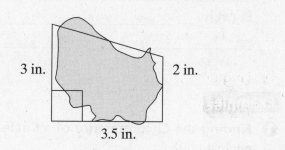

3 in.   2 in.

3.5 in.

Lesson 8-5

Circumference and Area of a Circle

Lesson Objective	NAEP 2005 Strand: Measurement
To find the circumference and area of a circle	**Topic:** Measuring Physical Attributes
	Local Standards: _____

Vocabulary and Key Concepts

Circumference of a Circle

The circumference of a circle is [ ] times the [_____].

$$C = \pi d = 2\pi r$$

Area of a Circle

The area of a circle is the product of [ ] and the square of the

[_____].

$$A = \pi r^2$$

Circumference is _____

_____

Pi (π) is _____

_____

Examples

1 **Finding the Circumference of a Circle** Find the circumference of each circle. Round to the nearest tenth.

a.

9 yd

b.

40 cm

$C =$ [_____]   ← **Use the formula for circumference.** → $C =$ [____]

$= 2\pi ($ [ ] $)$ ← **Substitute.** → $= \pi ($ [____] $)$

$=$ [_____]   ← **Use a calculator.** → $=$ [_____]

The circumference is approximately [_____] yd.

The circumference is approximately [_____] cm.

❷ Finding the Area of a Circle A pizza has a diameter of 28 cm. What is the area of the pizza? Round to the nearest tenth.

$r = \dfrac{\boxed{}}{2} = \boxed{}$ ← **The radius is half the diameter.**

$A = \boxed{}$ ← **Use the formula for the area of a circle.**

$ = \pi\left(\boxed{}\right)^2$ ← **Substitute** $\boxed{}$ **for the radius.**

$ \approx \boxed{}$ ← **Use a calculator.**

$ \approx \boxed{}$ ← **Round the solution to the nearest tenth.**

The area of the pizza is approximately $\boxed{}$ cm^2.

Quick Check

1. Find the circumference of the circle. Round to the nearest tenth.

$\boxed{}$ m

2. Find the area of the circle. Round to the nearest square unit.

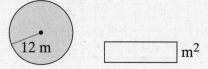

$\boxed{}$ m^2

Lesson 8-6

Square Roots and Irrational Numbers

Lesson Objective	**NAEP 2005 Strand:** Number Properties and Operations
To find and estimate square roots and to classify numbers as rational or irrational	**Topic:** Estimation
	Local Standards: _____

Vocabulary

A perfect square is _____
_____

Finding a square root is _____
_____

An irrational number is _____
_____

Examples

❶ Finding Square Roots of Perfect Squares Simplify $\sqrt{121}$.

Since $\boxed{}^2 = 121$, $\sqrt{121} = \boxed{}$.

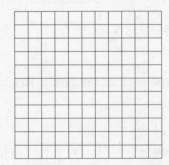

❷ Estimating Square Roots A square rug has an area of 68 ft². Use the formula for area of a square to estimate the dimensions of the rug.

$A = s^2$ ← Use the formula for the area of a square.

$\boxed{} = s^2$ ← Substitute $\boxed{}$ for the area.

$\boxed{} = \sqrt{s^2}$ ← Take the square root of each side.

$\boxed{} = s$ ← Simplify.

$\sqrt{64} < \boxed{} < \boxed{}$ ← Find the perfect squares close to $\boxed{}$.

$8 < \boxed{} < \boxed{}$ ← Simplify.

$\sqrt{68}$ is between 8 and $\boxed{}$. Since 68 is closer to $\boxed{}$ than to $\boxed{}$,

$\sqrt{68}$ is about $\boxed{}$. So the dimensions of the rug are about $\boxed{}$.

❸ Classifying Numbers Identify each number as rational or irrational.

a. $\sqrt{121}$ [   ]   ← **121** [   ] **a perfect square.**

b. $\sqrt{30}$ [   ]   ← **30** [   ] **a perfect square.**

c. 20.5167   [   ]   ← **It is a terminating decimal.**

d. 29.2992999...   [   ]   ← **The decimal neither terminates nor repeats.**

Quick Check

1. Simplify.

a. $\sqrt{64}$ b. $\sqrt{81}$ c. $\sqrt{225}$

[   ]   [   ]   [   ]

2. Suppose Juanita bought 80 tiles to tile a floor. They measured 1 ft^2 each. Use the formula for area of a square to estimate the dimensions of the floor.

[   ]

3. Identify each number as *rational* or *irrational*.

a. $\sqrt{2}$ b. $\sqrt{81}$ c. $0.\overline{6}$ d. $1\frac{2}{7}$

[   ]   [   ]   [   ]   [   ]

Lesson 8-7

Lesson Objective	**NAEP 2005 Strand:** Geometry
To use the Pythagorean Theorem to solve real-world problems	**Topic:** Relationships Among Geometric Figures
	Local Standards: _____

Vocabulary and Key Concepts

Pythagorean Theorem

The Pythagorean Theorem states that in any [____] triangle, the sum of the [_____] of the lengths of the [_____] equals the [_____] of the length of the [_____].

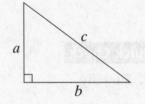

$$a^2 + b^2 = c^2$$

In a right triangle, the legs are _____

_____

The hypotenuse is _____

_____

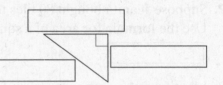

Examples

❶ Finding the Length of a Hypotenuse Find the length of the hypotenuse of the triangle.

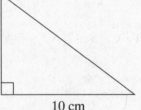

7.5 cm

10 cm

$c^2 = $ [____] $ + b^2$ ← **Pythagorean Theorem.**

$c^2 = $ [____] $ + 10^2$ ← **Substitute.**

$c^2 = $ [_____] $ + $ [_____] ← **Simplify.**

$c^2 = $ [_____]

$\sqrt{c^2} = $ [_____]

$c = $ [_____] ← **Take the square root of each side.**

The length of the hypotenuse is [_____] cm.

❷ Finding the Length of a Leg Find the length of the missing leg of the triangle.

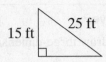

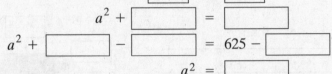

$a^2 + \boxed{}^2 = \boxed{}^2$ ← **Pythagorean Theorem.**

$a^2 + \boxed{}^2 = \boxed{}^2$ ← **Substitute.**

$a^2 + \boxed{} = \boxed{}$ ← **Simplify.**

$a^2 + \boxed{} - \boxed{} = 625 - \boxed{}$ ← **Subtract** $\boxed{}$ **from both sides.**

$a^2 = \boxed{}$ ← **Simplify.**

$\boxed{} = \boxed{}$ ← **Take the square root of each side.**

$a = \boxed{}$ ← **Simplify.**

The length of the leg is $\boxed{}$ ft.

❸ A ladder, placed 4 ft from a wall, touches the wall 11.3 ft above the ground. What is the approximate length of the ladder? A sketch shows that the length of the ladder is the length of the hypotenuse.

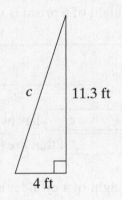

$\boxed{}^2 = \boxed{}^2 + \boxed{}^2$ ← **Use the Pythagorean Theorem.**

$c^2 = \boxed{}^2 + \boxed{}^2$ ← **Substitute.**

$c^2 = \boxed{}$ ← **Simplify.**

$\boxed{} = \boxed{}$ ← **Take the square root of each side.**

$c \approx \boxed{}$

The length of the ladder is about $\boxed{}$ ft.

Quick Check

1. Find the length of the hypotenuse in the triangle at the right.

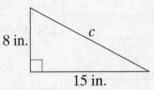

2. Find the missing length in the triangle at the right.

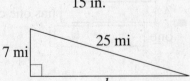

3. A support wire is attached to the top of a 60-m tower. It meets the ground 25 m from the base of the tower. How long is the wire?

Lesson 8-8

Three-Dimensional Figures

Lesson Objective	**NAEP 2005 Strand:** Geometry
To classify and draw three-dimensional figures	**Topic:** Dimension and Shape
	Local Standards: _____

Vocabulary

A three-dimensional figure, or solid, is _____

_____

A face is _____

_____

An edge is _____

_____

A prism is _____

_____

The bases of a prism are _____

The height of a prism is _____

_____

Prism

A cube is _____

A ⬚⬚⬚⬚⬚ has two congruent parallel

⬚⬚⬚⬚⬚ that are ⬚⬚⬚⬚ .

The height of a cylinder is _____

_____

A ⬚⬚⬚⬚ has ⬚⬚⬚⬚⬚ faces that meet at one point,

a ⬚⬚⬚⬚⬚ , and a base that is a ⬚⬚⬚⬚ .

A ⬚⬚⬚⬚ has one circular ⬚⬚⬚⬚ and

one ⬚⬚⬚⬚ .

A ⬚⬚⬚⬚ is the set of all points in space that are the same

distance from a ⬚⬚⬚⬚ point.

Examples

❶ Naming Figures Name the geometric figure.

The figure is a [   ].

❷ Drawing Three-Dimensional Figures Draw a pentagonal prism.

Step 1 Draw a
[   ].

Step 2 Draw a second
[   ]
congruent to the first.

Step 3 Connect the vertices.
Use [   ]
for hidden edges.

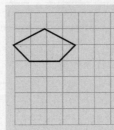

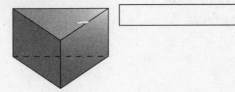

Quick Check

1. Name each figure.

a.
 [   ]

b. [   ]

2. Use the grid to draw a triangular prism.

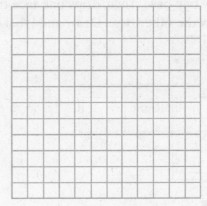

Lesson 8-9

Surface Areas of Prisms and Cylinders

Lesson Objective	**NAEP 2005 Strand:** Measurement
To find the surface areas of prisms and cylinders using nets	**Topic:** Measuring Physical Attributes
	Local Standards: _____

Vocabulary

A net is _____

The surface area of a prism is _____

Example

1 **Drawing a Net** Draw a net for the cube.

 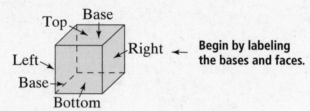

Begin by labeling the bases and faces.

First, draw one base. Then, draw one face that connects both bases.
Next, draw the other base. Draw and label the remaining faces.

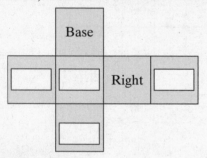

Quick Check

1. Draw a different net for the cube in Example 1.

Name _____ Class _____ Date _____

Examples

❷ **Finding the Surface Area of a Prism** Find the surface area of the prism.

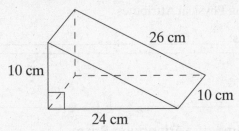

First, draw a net for the prism.

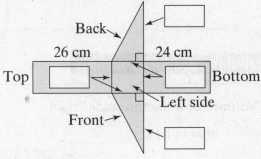

Then, find the total area of the five faces.

top   bottom   left side   front side   back side

$10(\boxed{}) + 10(\boxed{}) + 10(\boxed{}) + \frac{1}{2}(\boxed{})(\boxed{}) + \frac{1}{2}(\boxed{})(\boxed{}) = \boxed{}$

The surface area of the triangular prism is $\boxed{}$ cm^2.

❸ **Finding the Surface Area of a Cylinder** Find the surface area of the cylinder. Round to the nearest tenth.

Step 1 Draw a net.

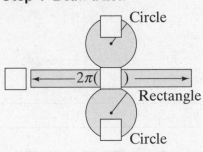

Step 2 Find the area of one circle.

$A = \pi r^2$

$\quad = \pi\left(\boxed{}\right)^2$

$\quad = \pi\left(\boxed{}\right)$

$\quad \approx \boxed{}$

Step 3 Find the area of the rectangle.

$(2\pi r)\boxed{} = 2\pi(3)(\boxed{}) = \boxed{}\pi \approx \boxed{}$ cm^2

Step 4 Add the areas of the two circles and the rectangle.

Surface Area $= \boxed{} + \boxed{} + \boxed{} = \boxed{}$

The surface area of the cylinder is about $\boxed{}$ cm^2.

Quick Check

2. Find the surface area of the prism.

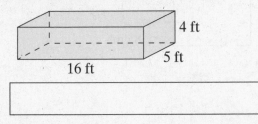

3. What is the surface area of the cylinder? Round to the nearest tenth.

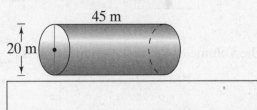

Name _____ Class _____ Date _____

Lesson 8-10

Volumes of Prisms and Cylinders

Lesson Objective	**NAEP 2005 Strand:** Measurement
To find the volume of prisms and cylinders	**Topic:** Measuring Physical Attributes
	Local Standards: _____

Vocabulary and Key Concepts

Volume of a Rectangular Prism

V = area of base · [   ]

    = Bh

    = [   ]

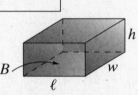

Volume of a Triangular Prism

V = area of base · height

    = Bh

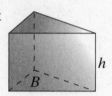

Volume of a Cylinder

V = area of base · [   ]

    = Bh

    = [   ]

The volume of a three-dimensional figure is _____

_____

A cubic unit is _____

Examples

❶ **Finding the Volume of a Rectangular Prism** Find the volume of the rectangular prism.

V = [   ]   ← **Use the formula.**

   = ([   ])([   ])([   ])   ← **Substitute.**

   = [   ]   ← **Multiply.**

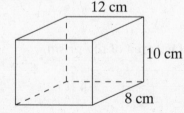

The volume of the rectangular prism is [   ] cm³.

❷ Finding the Volume of a Triangular Prism Find the volume of the triangular prism.

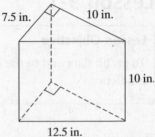

$V = Bh$ ← **Use the formula.**

= [＿＿＿](10)   ← **Substitute** $B = \frac{1}{2} \times 7.5 \times$ [＿＿＿] = [＿＿＿].

= [＿＿＿]   ← **Multiply.**

The volume of the triangular prism is [＿＿＿] cubic inches.

❸ Finding the Volume of a Cylinder A glass is 7.4 cm tall. The base of the glass has a diameter of 2.2 cm. Estimate the volume that the glass can hold if it is filled to the top. Then find the volume to the nearest cubic unit that the glass can hold if it is filled to the top.

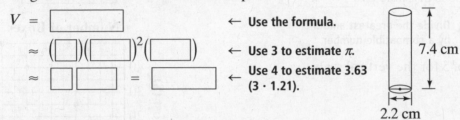

$V =$ [＿＿＿]   ← **Use the formula.**

$\approx$ ([＿＿])([＿＿])^2([＿＿])   ← **Use 3 to estimate** π.

$\approx$ [＿＿][＿＿] = [＿＿＿]   ← **Use 4 to estimate 3.63 (3 · 1.21).**

The estimated volume is [＿＿＿] cm^3.

Calculated volume: $V = \pi($[＿＿＿]$)^2($[＿＿＿]$) \approx$ [＿＿＿].   ← **Use a calculator.**

The calculated volume is about [＿＿＿] cm^3.   ← **Round to the nearest whole number.**

Quick Check

1. If the height of the prism in Example 1 is doubled, what is the volume?

[＿＿＿＿＿＿＿＿＿＿＿＿＿＿＿＿＿＿＿＿]

2. If the height of the prism in Example 2 is doubled, what is the volume?

[＿＿＿＿＿＿＿＿＿＿＿＿＿＿＿＿＿＿＿＿]

3. Estimate the volume of the cylinder. Then, find the volume to the nearest cubic centimeter.

Lesson 9-1

Patterns and Graphs

Lesson Objective	NAEP 2005 Strand: Algebra
To graph data and to use graphs to make predictions	Topic: Patterns, Relations, and Functions
	Local Standards: _____

Example

❶ Graphing Data Graph the data in the table.

The pattern in the first column of data suggests a horizontal interval of 20. Graphs that have from 6 to 10 intervals are easy to read. The greatest value in the second column is 50. Divide 50 by a factor from 6 to 10.

Choose [   ], since 50 is divisible by [   ].

$50 \div$ [   ] $=$ [   ] ← **Divide the greatest amount by a compatible number.**

Use [   ] intervals of 5 for the vertical scale.

No. of Boxes	Cost ($)
20	15
40	25
60	35
80	40
100	50

Number of Boxes

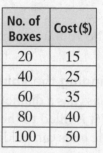

Quick Check

1. Graph the data in the table below.

Amount of Yogurt (c)	Price ($)
50	26
100	49
150	72
200	95

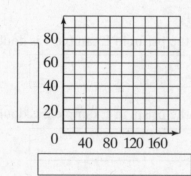

Examples

② **Estimating on a Graph** The graph shows the cost of renting a bowling lane for an hour. Which is the best estimate for the cost of the rental for 7 people?

A. about $15   **B.** about $20   **C.** about $25   **D.** about $30

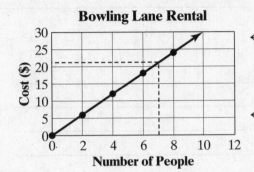

Bowling Lane Rental

← Draw lines to locate the value on the

[ ] axis that corresponds to 7

on the [ ] axis.

← The cost of the rental for 7 people is about [ ] .

The correct answer is choice [ ] .

③ **Making a Prediction** Estimate the cost of 600 gallons of water.

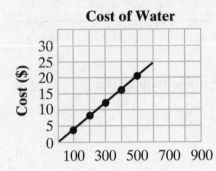

Cost of Water

← Extend the graph beyond 500 gallons.

← For 600 gallons, the cost is slightly less than $25. Estimate the answer.

The cost of 600 gallons is about [ ] .

Quick Check

2. Use the graph in Example 2 to estimate the cost of the rental for 5 people.

[ ]

3. Use the graph in Example 3 to estimate the cost of 800 gallons of water.

[ ]

Lesson 9-2

Number Sequences

Lesson Objective	NAEP 2005 Strand: Algebra
To describe the patterns in arithmetic and geometric sequences and use the patterns to find terms	**Topic:** Patterns, Relations, and Functions
	Local Standards: _____

Vocabulary

A sequence is _____

_____

An arithmetic sequence is _____

_____

A geometric sequence is _____

_____

A conjecture is _____

_____

Examples

❶ Describing an Arithmetic Sequence Describe the pattern in the sequence. Then find the next three terms in the sequence.

Position	1	2	3	4
Value of Term	100	93	86	79

+ (☐) + (☐) + (☐) ← **Find the common difference.**

Start with 100 and add ☐ *repeatedly.*

The next three terms are ☐ , ☐ , and ☐ .

❷ Describing Geometric Sequences Describe the pattern in 2, 6, 18, 54, ... Find the next three terms.

Position	1	2	3	4
Value of Term	2	6	18	54

· ☐ · ☐ · ☐ ← **Find the common ratio.**

Start with 2 and multiply by ☐ *repeatedly.*

54 · 3 = ☐ ; ☐ · 3 = ☐ ; ☐ · 3 = ☐ ← **Find the next three terms.**

The next three terms are ☐ , ☐ , and ☐ .

Name _____ Class _____ Date _____

❸ Geometry Describe the pattern to find the number of squares in each figure. Is the resulting sequence *arithmetic, geometric,* or *neither?*

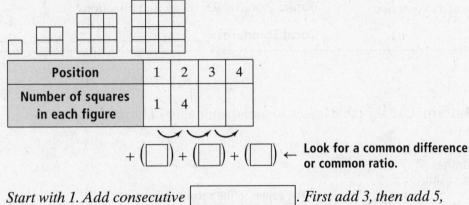

Position	1	2	3	4
Number of squares in each figure	1	4		

$+ (\Box) + (\Box) + (\Box)$ ← **Look for a common difference or common ratio.**

Start with 1. Add consecutive [_____] *. First add 3, then add 5, and so on.*

The sequence is [_____].

Quick Check

1. Describe the pattern in the sequence. Find the next 3 terms.

Position	1	2	3	4	5
Value of Term	44	35	26	17	8

[_____]

2. Describe the pattern in 1,000; 100; 10; …. Find the next 3 terms.

[_____]

3. Identify each sequence as *arithmetic, geometric, both,* or *neither.*

a. 1, 2, 6, 24, …   **b.** 2, 3, 6, 11, …   **c.** 10, 9, 8, 7, …

[_____]   [_____]   [_____]

Lesson 9-3

Patterns and Tables

Lesson Objective	NAEP 2005 Strand: Algebra
To use tables to represent and describe patterns	**Topic:** Patterns, Relations, and Functions
	Local Standards: _____

Examples

❶ **Representing a Pattern** Use the table below to find the number of horse shoes for 15 horses.

Number of Horses	Number of Horseshoes
1	4
3	12
5	
9	

$= 1 \times \boxed{}$
$= 3 \times \boxed{}$
$= 5 \times \boxed{}$
$= 9 \times \boxed{}$

← The values in the second column are $\boxed{}$ times the values in the first column.

To find the number of horseshoes for 15 horses, multiply 15 by $\boxed{}$.

The number of horseshoes for 15 horses is $\boxed{}$.

❷ **Finding the Value of a Term** Which sequence follows the rule $-4z + 12$, where z represents the position of a term in a sequence?

A. $16, 4, -8, -20, -32$

B. $-12, -8, -4, 0, 4$

C. $12, 8, 4, 0, -4$

D. $24, 12, 0, -12, -24$

Position	$-4z + 12$	Value of Term
0		12
	$-4(1) + 12$	
		-4

← Substitute 0, 1, 2, 3, and 4 for z.

The correct answer is choice $\boxed{}$.

❸ **Using a Table With a Sequence** Write an expression to describe the sequence 2, 4, 6, 8, 10, . . . Then, find the 10th term in the sequence.

2	4	6	8	10	...
↑	↑	↑	↑	↑	
Position 1	Position 2	Position 3	Position 4	Position 5	and so on.

Make a table that pairs the position of each term with its value.

Position	1	2	3	4	5	...	n
	↓☐	↓☐	↓☐	↓☐	↓☐	↓☐	↓☐
Value of Term	2	☐	6	☐	10	...	☐

The relationship is ⬚.

Let n = the term number. You can write the expression $n \cdot 2$, or ☐.

$n \cdot 2 = 10 \cdot 2 =$ ☐   ← **Substitute 10 for n to find the 10th term.**

Quick Check

1. The table shows the number of miles a car can travel using different amounts of gasoline. Complete the table. Find the distance the car can travel using 15 gallons of gasoline.

Gas (gal)	Miles Driven
1	18.1
2	36.2
3	54.3
4	☐
5	☐

2. Use the rule $2n + 3$, where n represents the position of a term in a sequence. Find the first four terms in the sequence.

3. Write an expression to describe the sequence $-8, -7, -6, -5, \ldots$. Find the 10th term in the sequence.

Lesson 9-4

Function Rules

Lesson Objective	NAEP 2005 Strand: Algebra
To write and evaluate functions	**Topics:** Algebraic Representations; Variables, Expressions, and Operations
	Local Standards: _____

Vocabulary

A function is _____

_____

Examples

1 **Writing a Function Rule** Suppose you can bicycle at an average speed of 10 mi/h. Write a function rule that describes the relationship between the time and distance you travel.

You can *make a table* to solve this problem.

Input: time (h)	1	2	3	4
Output: distance (mi)	10	20		

distance in miles = 10 · time in hours ← **Write the function rule in words.**

□ = 10□ ← **Use variables *d* for distance and *t* for time.**

2 **Using Tables to Analyze Functions** Write a rule for the function represented by each table.

x	y
0	−2
1	2
2	6
3	10
4	14

When *x* = 0, *y* = −2.
Each *y* equals □ times *x*, plus □.

The function rule is □.

Quick Check

1. Write a function rule for the relationship between the time and distance you travel at an average speed of 62 mi/h.

_____

Example

❸ **Evaluating Functions** Use the function $y = 2x - 3$. Find y when
$x = -1, 0, 2,$ and 3. Then make a table for the function.

$y = 2(-1) - 3 = \boxed{}$ ← **Substitute −1, 0, 2, and 3 for x.**

$y = 2(0) \ - 3 = \boxed{}$

$y = 2(2) \ - 3 = \boxed{}$ **List the values in a table. →**

$y = 2(3) \ - 3 = \boxed{}$

x	$y = 2x - 3$
−1	
0	
2	
3	

Quick Check

2. Write a rule for the function represented by the table below.

x	0	1	2	3
y	1	5	9	13

3. Use the function rule $y = 2x - 4$. Find y for $x = 0, 1, 2,$ and 3. Then make a table for the function.

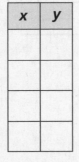

x	y

Lesson 9-5

Using Tables, Rules, and Graphs

Lesson Objective	NAEP 2005 Strand: Algebra
To find solutions to applications problems using tables, rules, and graphs	**Topic:** Algebraic Representations
	Local Standards: _____

Example

❶ **Graphing Using a Table** The table shows the relationship between gallons (input) and quarts (output). The rule $y = 4x$, where x represents the number of gallons, and y represents the number of quarts. Graph the relationship represented by the table. Graph gallons on the horizontal axis and quarts on the vertical axis. Draw a line through the points.

Gallons	Quarts
1	4
2	8
3	
4	

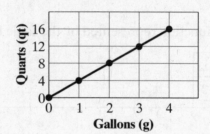

Quick Check

1. Graph the function represented by the table.

Input x	Output y
0	3
1	5
2	7
3	9

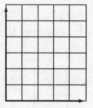

Example

❷ **Application: Plants** After one week, a 1-in. seedling grows to 3 inches. The second week, its height is 5 in., and the third week its height is 7 in. Write and graph a rule to find the height of the plant in week 4.

Step 1 Write a rule.

Words [   ] equals [ ] times [   ] plus 1

Let [ ] = plant height. Let [ ] = number of weeks.

Equation [ ] = [ ] · [ ] + 1

Step 2 Make a table of values. Graph the function.

Number of Weeks	Process	Plant Height (in.)
1	1 · [ ] + 1	3
2	2 · [ ] + 1	5
3	3 · [ ] + 1	7
4	4 · [ ] + 1	[ ]

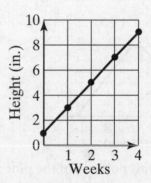

The height of the plant in week 4 is [   ]

Quick Check

2. A bus travels 60 miles per hours. Write and graph a rule to find the number of miles that can be traveled in 4.5 hours.

Number of Hours	Process	Distance (mi)

[   ]

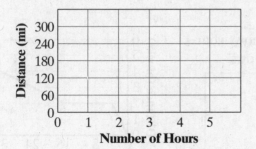

Lesson 9-6

Interpreting Graphs

Lesson Objective	NAEP 2005 Strand: Algebra
To describe and sketch graphs that represent real-world situations	**Topics:** Algebraic Representations; Variables, Expressions, and Operations
	Local Standards: _____

Example

① Describing a Graph Nancy took a roundtrip walk from home. The graph relates time and her distance from home. What can you tell about the trip from the graph?

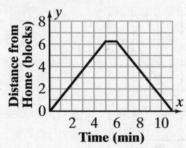

The first and third portions of the plot appear to have the same slope, disregarding the sign. This means that Nancy's speed would be

[   ] in both directions. The horizontal line

indicates that her distance from home did not change for one minute.

This means that she stopped walking for [   ].

Quick Check

1. You live 6 blocks from school. The graph at the right shows your walk home on a sunny day. Describe what the graph shows.

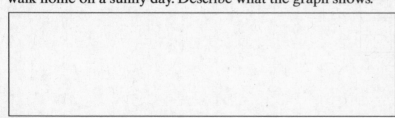

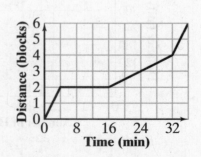

Daily Notetaking Guide

Example

❷ **Graphing Data** Souvenir mugs are on sale. You can buy one mug for $6, two for $10, three for $15, or four for $18. Graph the data.

Do not connect the points in the graph.

Mugs	Cost ($)
1	6

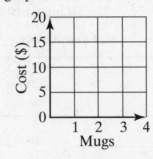

Check for Reasonableness Each cost is for a number of whole mugs. Since you cannot pay for part of a mug, connecting the points would not be meaningful.

Quick Check

2. Sketch a graph of the situation in Example 1 using *Total Distance Traveled (blocks)* instead of *Distance From Home* for the vertical axis.

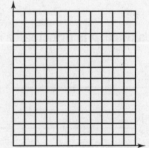

3. The table shows the number of cans in the cafeteria juice machine over time. Graph the data.

Time	Number of Cans
8 A.M.	30
9 A.M.	20
10 A.M.	19
11 A.M.	19

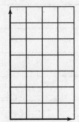

Lesson 9-7

Simple and Compound Interest

Lesson Objective To find simple interest and compound interest	**NAEP 2005 Strand:** Number Properties and Operations; Algebra **Topics:** Ratios and Proportional Reasoning; Algebraic Representations **Local Standards:** _____

Vocabulary and Key Concepts

Simple Interest Formula

$$I = \boxed{}$$

I is the interest earned, p is the principal, r is the interest rate per year, and t is the time in years.

Compound Interest Formula

$$B = \boxed{}$$

B is the balance, p is principal, r is annual interest rate, and t is the time in years.

Principal is _____

_____

Simple interest is _____

Compound interest is _____

_____

Balance is _____

_____

Examples

❶ Finding Simple Interest You invest $500 at a 3% annual interest rate for 4 years. What is the simple interest earned in dollars?

$I = prt$ ← Write the formula.

$I = (500)\left(\boxed{}\right)\left(\boxed{}\right)$ ← Substitute. Use $\boxed{}$ for 3%.

$= \boxed{}$ ← Simplify.

The interest is $\boxed{}$.

❷ Graphing Simple Interest You have $500 in an account that earns an annual rate of 3%. At the end of each year, you withdraw the interest you have earned. Graph the total interest you earn after 1, 2, 3, and 4 years.

Step 1 Make a table.

Time (yr)	Interest ($)
1	15
2	
3	
4	

Step 2 Draw a graph.

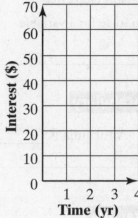

❸ Finding Compound Interest You deposit $500 in a bank account that pays 3% compound interest. What is your balance after 4 years?

$B = p(1 + r)^t$ ← **Write the formula.**

$= 500(1 + \boxed{})^4$ ← **Substitute. Use** $\boxed{}$ **for 3%.**

$= 500(\boxed{})$ ← **Use a calculator to simplify the power.**

$= \boxed{}$ ← **Round to the nearest cent.**

The balance after 4 years is $\boxed{}$.

Quick Check

1. Find the simple interest you pay on a $220 loan at a 5% annual interest rate for 4 years.

2. Graph the simple interest earned on $950 at an annual rate of 4.2%.

3. You deposit $3,000 in a bank account that pays 4.25% compound interest. What is your balance after 12 years?

Lesson 9-8

Transforming Formulas

Lesson Objective	NAEP 2005 Strand: Algebra
To solve for a variable	Topic: Equations and Inequalities
	Local Standards: _____

Vocabulary

A formula is _____

_____

Example

❶ **Transforming a Formula** Solve the formula $a = \frac{F}{m}$ for F.

 ← **Write the formula.**

 ← **Use the Multiplication Property of** ☐.

Quick Check

1. Solve each equation for x.

   a. $y = 2x - 4$

   ☐

   b. $y = x + 3$

   ☐

   c. $4y = 2x + 10$

   ☐

Example

❷ **Savings** You earn $60 interest for one year on a principal of $1,500. What is the interest rate?

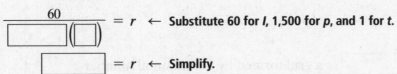

$$\frac{I}{\boxed{}\ \boxed{}} = r \quad \leftarrow \textbf{Use the simple interest formula } I = \textbf{\textit{prt}} \textbf{ and solve for } \textbf{\textit{r}}.$$

$$\frac{60}{\boxed{}\ |(\ \boxed{}\ )} = r \quad \leftarrow \textbf{Substitute 60 for } \textbf{\textit{I}}, \textbf{1,500 for } \textbf{\textit{p}}, \textbf{ and 1 for } \textbf{\textit{t}}.$$

$$\boxed{} = r \quad \leftarrow \textbf{Simplify.}$$

The interest rate is $\boxed{}$, or $\boxed{}$ %.

Quick Check

2. Find the interest rate that yields $120 interest each year on $2,000.

$$\boxed{}$$

Lesson 10-1

Graphing Points in Four Quadrants

Lesson Objective	**NAEP 2005 Strand:** Algebra
To name and graph points on a coordinate plane	**Topic:** Algebraic Representations
	Local Standards: _____

Vocabulary

A [box] is a grid formed by a horizontal number line called the [box] and a vertical number line called the [box].

O indicates the [box], where the axes intersect.

An ordered pair (x, y) gives _____

The x-coordinate is _____

The y-coordinate is _____

The x- and y-axes divide the coordinate plane into four [box].

Examples

❶ **Naming Coordinates** Name the coordinates of point D in the graph at the right.

A. $(2, 2)$ **B.** $(-2, 2)$ **C.** $(2, -2)$ **D.** $(-2, -2)$

Point D is 2 units to the left of the y-axis, so the x-coordinate is [box].

Point D is 2 units up from the x-axis, so the y-coordinate is [box].

The coordinates of point D is [box]. The correct answer is choice [box].

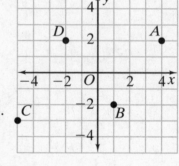

❷ **Graphing Points** Graph the point $D(4, -3)$ on a coordinate plane. In which quadrant does the point lie?

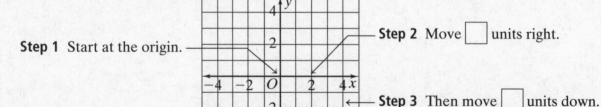

Step 1 Start at the origin.

Step 2 Move [box] units right.

Step 3 Then move [box] units down. Draw a dot. Label it D.

The point $D(4, -3)$ lies in quadrant IV.

❸ Graphing Polygons Draw a rectangle that measures 3 units by 5 units in a coordinate plane. Use $(0, 0)$ as one vertex and label all vertices.

Mark $(0, 0)$ as one vertex.

From the origin, count 3 units right and mark a vertex at [   ].

From the origin, count 5 units up and mark a vertex at [   ].

Mark the fourth vertex at [   ].

Draw the sides of the rectangle.

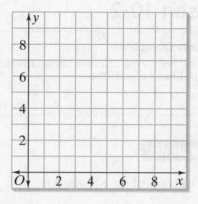

Quick Check

1. Name the coordinates of A, B, and C in the graph in Example 1.

[   ]

2. Graph point $R(-3, 5)$ on the grid at the right. In which quadrant does the point lie?

[   ]

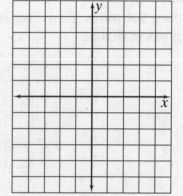

3. In a coordinate plane, draw a different rectangle for Example 3. Use $(0, 0)$ as one vertex and label all vertices.

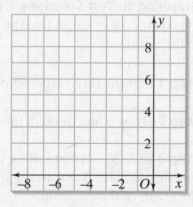

Lesson 10-2

Lesson Objective	NAEP 2005 Strand: Algebra
To find solutions of linear equations and to graph linear equations	**Topic:** Algebraic Representations; Equations and Inequalities
	Local Standards: _____

Vocabulary

A graph of an equation is _____

_____

An equation is a linear equation when _____

_____

Examples

1 **Finding Solutions** Find three solutions of $y = x - 5$. Organize your solutions in a table.

x	x − 5	y	Solution (x, y)
5	☐ − 5		
6	☐ − 5		
0	☐ − 5		

2 **Graphing to Test Solutions** Use the solutions from Example 1 to graph the equation $y = x - 5$. Use the graph to test whether $(3, -4)$ is a solution to the equation.

Step 1 Plot the three ordered-pair solutions.

Step 2 Draw a line through the points.

Step 3 Test $(3, -4)$ by plotting the point in the same coordinate plane. Look to see if the point lies on the line of the graph of the equation.

Since $(3, -4)$ ☐ on the line, $(3, -4)$ ☐ a solution of $y = x - 5$.

Example

❸ **Graphing a Linear Equation** Graph the linear equation $y = x - 1$.

Step 1 Make a table of solutions. Use zero as well as positive and negative values for x.

Step 2 Graph the points. Draw a line through the points.

x	$x - 1$	y	(x, y)
-4	☐ $- 1$		
-2	☐ $- 1$		
0	☐ $- 1$		
1	☐ $- 1$		
3	☐ $- 1$		

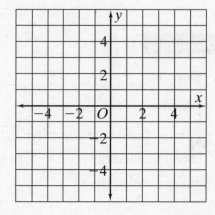

Quick Check

1. Find three solutions of each equation. Use $x = -2$, $x = 0$, and $x = 2$.

    a. $y = x + 8$ _____

    b. $y = x - 1$ _____

    c. $y = -2x$ _____

2. Tell whether $(7, 12)$ is a solution of $y = 3x - 1$.

    _____

3. Graph each linear equation.

    a. $y = x + 4$ **b.** $y = \frac{1}{2}x$ **c.** $y = -x$

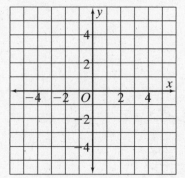
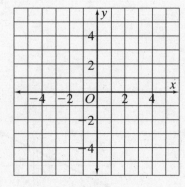
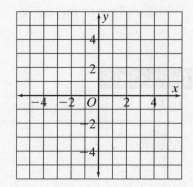

Lesson 10-3

Finding the Slope of a Line

Lesson Objective	**NAEP 2005 Strand:** Algebra
To find the slope of a line and use it to solve problems	**Topic:** Equations and Inequalities
	Local Standards: _____

Vocabulary

Slope is _____

_____

For any line, slope compares the vertical

change, called the [ ], to the horizontal

change, called the [ ].

slope = $\dfrac{\quad}{\quad}$

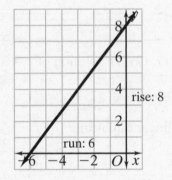

Example

① Finding Slope Find the slope of the line.

The rise of the line is [ ] and the run is [ ].

slope = $\dfrac{\text{rise}}{\boxed{}}$ ← **Use the definition of slope.**

= $\dfrac{\boxed{}}{\boxed{}}$ ← **Substitute rise and run.**

= $\dfrac{\boxed{}}{\boxed{}}$ ← **Simplify.**

The slope of the line is $\dfrac{\boxed{}}{\boxed{}}$.

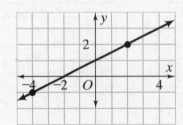

rise: 8

run: 6

Quick Check

1. Find the slope of the line.

Daily Notetaking Guide

Example

❷ **Drawing Lines on a Graph** Draw a line through the origin with a slope of $-\frac{5}{4}$.

Step 1 Graph a point at $(0, 0)$.

Step 2 Move 5 units [_____] and then 4 units to the [_____].

Graph a second point.

Step 3 Connect the points to form a line.

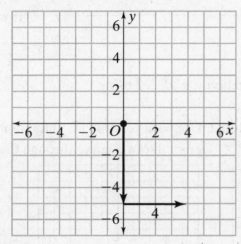

Quick Check

2. **a.** Slope is used to find the pitch, or steepness, of a roof. Roof *A* has a pitch of 3 to 12, which means it rises 3 in. for every 12 in. of run. What is the slope of Roof *A?*

[_____]

b. Draw a line through $P(2, 1)$ with a slope of $\frac{4}{3}$.

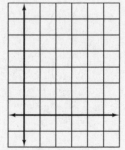

Lesson 10-4

Graphing Nonlinear Relationships

Lesson Objective	NAEP 2005 Strand: Algebra
To graph nonlinear relationships	**Topic:** Patterns, Relations, and Functions
	Local Standards: _____

Vocabulary

A nonlinear equation is _____

_____

Example

① **Graphing a Nonlinear Equation** Graph the equation $y = x^2 - 2$ using integer values of x from -3 to 3.

Step 1 Make a table of solutions.

Step 2 Use each solution (x, y) to graph a point. Draw a curve through the points.

x	$x^2 - 2$	y	(x, y)
−3	$(-3)^2 - 2$		
−2	$(-2)^2 - 2$		
−1	$(-1)^2 - 2$		
0	$(0)^2 - 2$		
1	$1^2 - 2$		
2	$2^2 - 2$		
3	$3^2 - 2$		

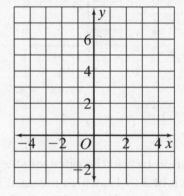

Quick Check

1. Graph $y = 2x^2$ using integer values of x from -3 to 3.

x	−3	−2	−1	0	1	2	3
y							

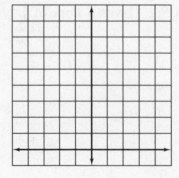

Example

❷ **Graphing Absolute Value Equations** Graph the equation $y = |x| + 2$ using integer values of x from -3 to 3.

x	$|x| + 2$	y	(x, y)
-3	$|-3| + 2$		
-2	$|-2| + 2$		
-1	$|-1| + 2$		
0	$|0| + 2$		
1	$|1| + 2$		
2	$|2| + 2$		
3	$|3| + 2$		

← Make a table of values.

Graph the ordered pairs. Then → connect the points.

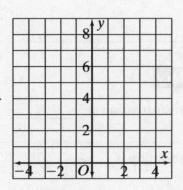

Quick Check

2. Graph $y = 2|x|$ using integer values of x from -3 to 3.

x	-3	-2	-1	0	1	2	3
y							

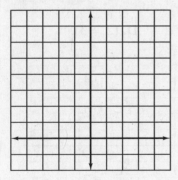

Lesson 10-5

Translations

Lesson Objective To graph and write rules for translations	**NAEP 2005 Strand:** Geometry **Topic:** Transformation of Shapes and Preservation of Properties **Local Standards:** _____

Vocabulary

A transformation is _____

_____

A translation is _____

_____

An image of a figure is _____

_____

Prime notation is _____

_____

Example

① **Translating a Point** Translate point $A(-3, -1)$ left 2 units and up 5 units.
What are the coordinates of image A'?

A. $(-5, 4)$ **B.** $(-1, 4)$ **C.** $(-1, -6)$ **D.** $(2, -3)$

Locate point A at $(-3, -1)$.
From point A, move 2 units left and 5 units up.
Graph the image point A'.

The coordinates of A' are (⬚ , ⬚).

The correct answer is choice ⬚ .

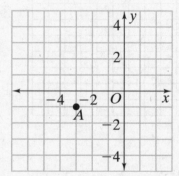

Quick Check

1. Translate point $G(-4, 1)$ right 1 unit and down 4 units. What are the
coordinates of the image G'? ⬚

Examples

❷ **Translating a Figure** The vertices of △ABC are A(−4, −3), B(−3, 1), and C(−1, −2). Translate △ABC right 5 units and down 2 units. Use arrow notation to describe the translation.

Graph and label vertices A, B, and C.
Draw △ABC.
From each vertex, move right 5 units and down 2 units, and then draw an image point.
Label A′, B′, and C′. Draw △A′B′C′.

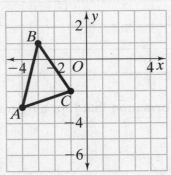

Use arrow notation: A(−4, −3), B(−3, 1), C(−1, −2) → A′ ⬚ , B′ ⬚ , C′ ⬚

❸ **Writing a Rule for a Translation** Write a rule for the translation shown in the graph.

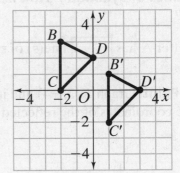

The horizontal change from B to B′ is ⬚ units right, so x → x + ⬚ .

The vertical change from B to B′ is ⬚ units down, so y → y + ⬚ .

The rule for the translation is
(x, y) → (x + ⬚ , y + ⬚).

Quick Check

2. Graph △ABC from Example 2. Translate it left 3 units and up 1 unit. Use arrow notation to describe the translation.

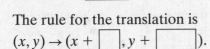

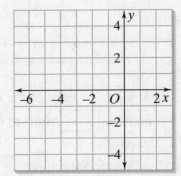

3. Write a rule for the translation of point D in Example 3 to (4, 3).

Lesson 10-6

Lesson Objective	**NAEP 2005 Strand:** Geometry
To identify lines of symmetry and to graph reflections	**Topics:** Transformation of Shapes and Preservation of Properties
	Local Standards: _____

Vocabulary

A figure has line symmetry if _____

_____

A line of symmetry is a line that _____

_____

A ⬚⬚⬚⬚⬚⬚⬚⬚⬚⬚ is a transformation that flips a figure

over a line called a ⬚⬚⬚⬚⬚⬚⬚⬚ .

Examples

❶ **Identifying Lines of Symmetry** How many lines of symmetry does the letter A have?

The capital letter A has ⬚⬚⬚ line(s) of symmetry.

❷ **Reflecting a Point** Graph $K(3, -4)$ and its reflection over the indicated axis. Write the coordinates of the reflected point.

   a. y-axis

                                            b. x-axis

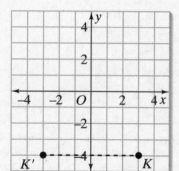 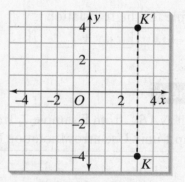

K is ⬚⬚⬚ units to the right of the y-axis,
so K' is ⬚⬚⬚ units to the ⬚⬚⬚ of the
y-axis.
K' has coordinates ⬚⬚⬚ .

K is ⬚⬚⬚ units below x-axis, so
K' is ⬚⬚⬚ units ⬚⬚⬚ the x-axis.
K' has coordinates ⬚⬚⬚ .

❸ Reflecting a Figure Draw the image of $\triangle ABC$ reflected over the x-axis. Use arrow notation to describe the original triangle and its image.

A is 1 unit above the x-axis, so A' is [ ] unit

[ ] the x-axis.

B is [ ] units above the x-axis, so B' is [ ] units

[ ] the x-axis.

C is [ ] unit above the x-axis, so C' is [ ] unit [ ]

the x-axis.

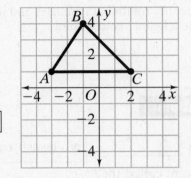

Draw $\triangle A'B'C'$ and use arrow notation:

$A(-3, 1), B(-1, 4), C(2, 1) \rightarrow A'$ [ ], B' [ ], C' [ ]

Quick Check

1. **Art** Draw the line(s) of symmetry on the mask. Does the mask have line symmetry?

[ ]

2. Graph the point $P(-4, 1)$ and its reflection over the indicated axis. Write the coordinates of the image.

   a. y-axis

   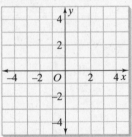

   [ ]

   b. x-axis

   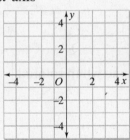

   [ ]

3. Graph $\triangle ABC$ from Example 3 above and its reflection over the y-axis. Use arrow notation to describe the original triangle and its image.

   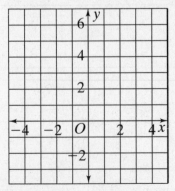

Lesson 10-7

Rotational Symmetry and Rotations

Lesson Objective To identify rotational symmetry and to rotate a figure about a point	**NAEP 2005 Strand:** Geometry **Topics:** Transformation of Shapes and Preservation of Properties **Local Standards:** _____

Vocabulary

A [_____] is a transformation that turns a figure about a fixed point called the [_____].

A figure has [_____] if it can be rotated 180° or less and match the original figure. When a figure has this property, the [_____] is the smallest angle measure the figure must rotate to match the original figure.

Example

❶ Identifying Rotational Symmetry As shown, do the letters H and N have rotational symmetry? Explain.

Both letters look the same when rotated [_____], so they have rotational symmetry.

Quick Check

1. Does the figure have rotational symmetry? Explain.

a.

b.

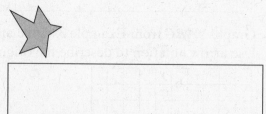

c.

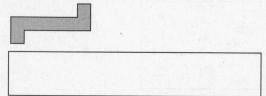

Examples

❷ Finding an Angle of Rotation The wheel below has rotational symmetry. Find the angle of rotation.

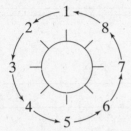

The wheel matches itself in ☐ positions. The angle of rotation is

$360° ÷$ ☐ , or ☐ .

❸ Rotating a Figure Graph $\triangle ABC$ with vertices $A(0,0)$, $B(3,1)$, and $C(2,5)$. Rotate the triangle 90° about A. Write the coordinates of A', B', and C'.

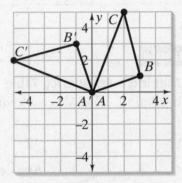

A' ☐ , B' ☐ , C' ☐

Quick Check

2. Find the angle of rotation of the flower.

☐

3. Graph $\triangle TRG$ with vertices $T(0,0)$, $R(3,3)$, and $G(5,1)$. Rotate $\triangle TRG$ 180° about T. Write the coordinates of T', R', and G'.

☐

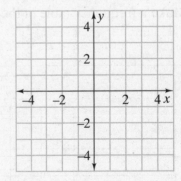

Lesson 11-1

Reporting Frequency

Lesson Objective To represent data using frequency tables, line plots, and histograms	**NAEP 2005 Strand:** Data Analysis and Probability **Topic:** Data Representation **Local Standards:** _____

Vocabulary

A frequency table is _____

_____

A line plot is _____

_____

A histogram is _____

_____

Example

1 Making a Frequency Table The data below show the ages of the students
in a karate class. Make a frequency table of the data.

| 11 | 5 | 9 | 13 | 8 | 9 | 11 | 10 | 8 | 6 | 7 |
| 12 | 11 | 13 | 12 | 7 | 6 | 11 | 12 | 10 | 8 | 9 |

Ages of Students in a Karate Class

Age	5	6	7	8	9	10	11	12	13
Tally	/	//	//	///	///				
Frequency	1	2							

Quick Check

1. The data below show the number of U.S. Representatives for 22 states.
Make a frequency table of the data.

| 4 | 3 | 1 | 2 | 1 | 5 | 4 | 1 | 7 | 2 | 8 |
| 1 | 3 | 8 | 5 | 9 | 3 | 5 | 7 | 3 | 1 | 9 |

Examples

➋ Making a Line Plot Make a line plot of the data in Example 1.

Step 1 Draw a number line from the least to the greatest value (from 5 to 13).

Step 2 Write an ✗ above each value for each time the value occurs in the data.

Step 3 Add a title.

Ages of Students in a Karate Class

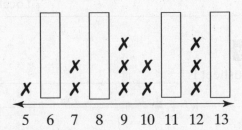

5 6 7 8 9 10 11 12 13

➌ Making a Histogram Make a histogram of the data in the frequency table below. Use the equal-sized intervals 1–4, 5–8, 9–12, 13–16, and 17–20.

Hours Spent on the Internet

Hours	Frequency
1–4	₩₩₩ ‖
5–8	₩₩₩₩₩ ‖
9–12	₩₩₩ ‖‖‖
13–16	₩₩₩
17–20	₩₩₩ ₩₩₩

← Add a title.

12
10
8
6
4
2
0
    1–4   9–12   17–20
        5–8   13–16

↑
Label each axis. →

Quick Check

2. Make a line plot of the number of students in math classes:

24 27 21 25 28 22 23 25 25 28 22 23 25
22 24 25 28 27 22

3. Make a histogram of the ages of employees at a retail store:

28 20 44 72 65 40 59 29 22 36 28 61 30
27 33 55 48 24 28 32

Lesson 11-2

Spreadsheets and Data Displays

Lesson Objective To interpret spreadsheets, double bar graphs, and double line graphs	**NAEP 2005 Strand:** Data Analysis and Probability **Topic:** Data Representation **Local Standards:** _____

Vocabulary

A spreadsheet is _____

_____

A cell is _____

_____

A double bar graph is _____

_____

A legend, or key, _____

_____

A double line graph is _____

_____

Example

① **Using a Spreadsheet** The spreadsheet shows the number of graduates in dentistry and medicine.

a. What value is in cell B5? What does the value represent?

Column B and row 5 meet at cell B5. The value is [____]. The value represents the number of graduates in [_____] in [_____].

b. In what year was the number of graduates from each school the same?

Cells B2 and C2 show that the number of graduates from each school was the same in [_____].

	A	B	C
1	Year	Dentistry	Medicine
2	1996	48	48
3	1997	36	51
4	1998	40	56
5	1999	43	42
6	2000	65	38
7	2001	61	46

Column →
← Cell B5
↑ Row

Quick Check

1. a. What value is in cell B4? What does the value represent?

[_____]

b. Which cell shows the number of graduates in Medicine in 2001?

[_____]

Examples

❷ Using a Double Bar Graph What was the first year in which more people obtained news from the radio than from the newspaper?

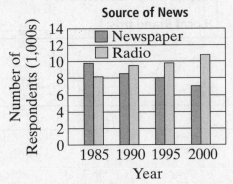

Source of News

The first year in which more people obtained news from the radio than the newspaper was [   ].

❸ Predicting With a Double Line Graph Use the graph to predict when low-fat milk consumption is 30,000 more pints than whole milk consumption.

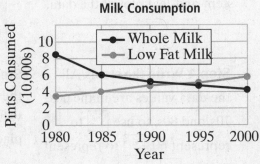

Milk Consumption

The line for whole milk consumption seems to be decreasing by about 5,000 pints every [   ] years. The line for low-fat milk consumption seems to be increasing by about 5,000 pints every [   ] years. You can estimate that low-fat consumption in

[   ] is 30,000 more pints than whole milk consumption.

Quick Check

2. In Example 2, in which year did the number of people who obtained news from the radio first exceed 10,000?

[   ]

3. Extend the graph of Example 3. Predict the number of pints of low-fat milk consumed in 2010.

[   ]

Lesson 11-3

Stem-and-Leaf Plots

Lesson Objective To represent and interpret data using stem-and-leaf plots	**NAEP 2005 Strand:** Data Analysis and Probability **Topic:** Data Representation **Local Standards:** _____

Vocabulary

A stem-and-leaf plot is _____

_____

Example

❶ **Making a Stem-and-Leaf Plot**
Use the table at the right. Make a stem-and-leaf plot of the data.

High Temperatures for Central City (°F) October 13–26

Week 1	81	73	67	81	77	79	73
Week 2	80	74	61	66	70	67	73

Step 1 Write the stems. All the data values are in the 60s, 70s, and 80s, so use ☐ to represent 60, ☐ to represent 70, and ☐ to represent 80. Draw a vertical line to the right of the stems.

$$6\,|$$
$$7\,| \leftarrow \textbf{Stems}$$
$$8\,|$$

Step 2 Write the leaves. For these data the leaves are the values in the ☐ place.

$$6\,|\,7\,1\,6\,7$$
$$7\,|\,3\,7\,9\,3\,4\,0\,3 \leftarrow \textbf{Leaves}$$
$$8\,|\,1\,1\,0$$

Step 3 Make the stem-and-leaf plot with the leaves in order from least to greatest. Add a key to explain the leaves. Add a title.

High Temperatures for Central City (°F) October 13–26

$$6\,|\,1\,6\,\square\,7$$
$$7\,|\,0\,3\,\square\,\square\,4\,7\,9$$
$$8\,|\,\square\,\square\,\square$$

Key → Key: 6 | 1 means 61.

Quick Check

1. Make a stem-and-leaf plot of the wind speeds (in miles per hour) recorded during a storm: 9, 14, 30, 16, 18, 25, 29, 25, 38, 34, 33.

Key: 0 | 9 means ☐ .

Daily Notetaking Guide

Examples

❷ Analyzing a Stem-and-Leaf Plot Compare the two sets of data in the stem-and-leaf plot.

a. Which day had the longest wait time?

[   ] had the longest wait time.

b. How long was the longest wait?

The longest wait was [   ].

Waiting for the Doctor

Monday		Friday
2 1	0	5 6
0	1	1 1 4
6 1	2	3 4 6 6
3	3	5 5
9	4	7 8 8	← Find the greatest value.

Key: 1 min ← 1 | 0 | 5 → 5 min

❸ Multiple Choice The stem-and-leaf plot shows the grades on a math test. Which statement is best supported by the stem-and-leaf plot?

A. The mean is 52.

B. The median is 82.5.

C. The mode is 72.

D. The range is 45.

The range is [   ] − [   ], or [   ].

The correct answer is choice [   ].

Grades on Math Test

5	2
6	8 8 9
7	1 2 2 5 9
8	0 0 0 4 5 6 9 9
9	1 1 3 6 7

Key: 9|1 means 91.

Quick Check

2. Which day had a higher median waiting time in Example 2? Explain.

[   ]

3. Find the correct values for mean, median, and mode in Example 3.

[   ]

Lesson 11-4

Lesson Objective To identify a random sample and to write a survey question	**NAEP 2005 Strand:** Data Analysis and Probability **Topic:** Experiments and Samples **Local Standards:** _____

Vocabulary

A population is _____

A sample is _____

A random sample is _____

_____

A biased question is _____

_____

Example

① **Identifying a Random Sample** You survey students in your school about their snacking habits. Would you get a random sample if you questioned different English classes? Explain.

Quick Check

1. You survey a store's customers. You ask why they chose the store. Which sample is more likely to be random? Explain.

  a. You survey 20 people at the entrance from 5:00 P.M. to 8:00 P.M.

  b. You survey 20 people outside the entrance throughout the day.

Example

❷ **Identifying Biased Questions** Is each question *biased* or *fair*? Explain.

a. "Which is a brighter color, pink, or green?"

This question is [   ]. The choices are presented equally.

b. "Is an electric pink shirt brighter than a green shirt?"

This question is [   ]. It implies that pink is brighter, thus influencing the responses.

Quick Check

2. Is each question *biased* or *fair*? Explain.

a. Do you prefer greasy meat or healthy vegetables on your pizza?

[   ]

b. Which pizza topping do you like best?

[   ]

Lesson 11-5

Estimating Population Size

Lesson Objective	**NAEP 2005 Strand:** Number Properties and Operations
To estimate population using size proportions	**Topic:** Ratios and Proportional Reasoning
	Local Standards: _____

Vocabulary

The capture/recapture method is used to _____

_____

Example

❶ Using the Capture/Recapture Method Researchers know that there are 63 marked gazelles in an area. On a flight over the area, they count 19 marked gazelles and a total of 412 gazelles. Write a proportion to estimate the gazelle population.

$$\frac{\text{number of marked gazelles counted}}{\text{total number of gazelles counted}} = \frac{\text{total number of marked gazelles}}{\text{estimate of gazelle population}}$$

$$\frac{\boxed{}}{\boxed{}} = \frac{63}{x} \qquad \leftarrow \textbf{Write a proportion.}$$

$$19x = 63 \cdot 412 \qquad \leftarrow \textbf{Write cross products.}$$

$$19x = \boxed{} \qquad \leftarrow \textbf{Multiply.}$$

$$\frac{19x}{\boxed{}} = \frac{25,956}{\boxed{}} \qquad \leftarrow \textbf{Divide each side by } \boxed{}.$$

$$x \approx \boxed{} \qquad \leftarrow \textbf{Round to the nearest integer.}$$

There are about $\boxed{}$ gazelles in the area.

Check: You can use an estimate to check your answer.

$$\frac{19}{412} \approx \frac{\boxed{}}{\boxed{}}, \text{ or } \frac{1}{20}$$

$$\frac{1}{20} = \frac{63}{x}$$

$$x = 63 \times 20 = 1,260$$

Since this is close to 1,366, the answer is reasonable.

Quick Check

1. Researchers know that there are 105 marked deer in an area. On a flight over the area, they count 35 marked deer and a total of 638 deer. Estimate the total deer population in the area.

Lesson 11-6

Using Data to Persuade

Lesson Objective	NAEP 2005 Strand: Data Analysis and Probability
To identify misleading graphs and statistics	Topic: Data Representation
	Local Standards: _____

Examples

1 **Redrawing Misleading Graphs** The graph shows the weekly earnings of four brothers.

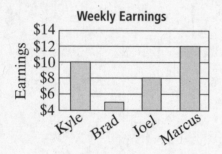

Redraw the graph so it is not misleading.

Method 1
Start the vertical scale at 0. Draw the bars to match the data.

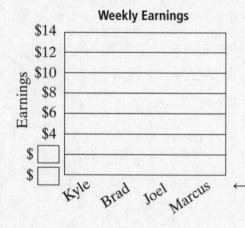

Method 2
Use a break in the vertical scale.

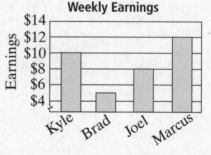

You can fix the graph by drawing it so that the vertical scale starts at [ ] .

2 **Misleading Intervals** A television station presented this graph to its advertisers to show how viewership has increased. Explain how the graph is misleading.

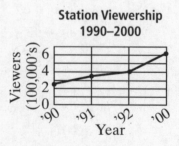

Station Viewership 1990–2000

The intervals on the horizontal axis are [   ] .

The number of viewers increases [   ] in the first 2 years and then another [   ] over the next 8 years.

Name _____ Class _____ Date _____

❸ **Misleading Use of Data Measures** The number of points scored by different players on a basketball team are listed below. Julio scored 7 points. Which measure of data makes Julio's performance seem the most impressive?

0   2   25   4   2   7   6

A. mean   **B.** median   **C.** mode   **D.** range

The range of [   ] is too large and only shows how much the

players' scores vary. The mean is about [   ] and makes 7 points

seem about average. The median score of [   ] makes 7 points

seem like a large number, but the mode of [   ] makes scoring 7

points seem even more impressive. The correct answer is choice [   ].

❹ **Advertising** The sign at the right is advertising for an auto dealership. Below it are the data for the cars at the dealership. Is the ad misleading?

Only [   ] of the 22 cars offered are under $10,000, and only by [   ]. There are many more over that amount, so the ad [   ] misleading.

Cars Under $10,000!

Model	Quantity	Price ($)
Pico	2	9,999
Toro	7	13,999
Enviro	9	15,999
Urban	4	22,999

Quick Check

1. When is a break in a vertical scale especially useful?

2. Redraw the graph in Example 2 using equal intervals on both axes.

3. Which value in the data in Example 3 would you consider an outlier?

4. How could you change the ad in Example 4 to better reflect the data?

Lesson 11-7

Exploring Scatter Plots

Lesson Objective	NAEP 2005 Strand: Data Analysis and Probability
To draw and interpret scatter plots	**Topic:** Data Representation
	Local Standards: _____

Vocabulary

A scatter plot is _____

_____

A positive trend exists when _____

_____

A negative trend exists when _____

_____

There is no trend when _____

_____

Examples

1 **Making Scatter Plots** Graph the data from the table in a scatter plot.

Each row in the table represents a point on the scatter plot.

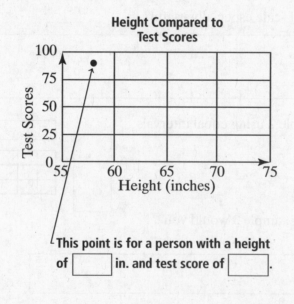

Height (in.)	Test Score
58	90
60	95
63	90
64	70
65	100
65	90
66	60
67	90
68	80
68	75
70	85
70	100
71	80
72	70

Height Compared to Test Scores

This point is for a person with a height of [ ] in. and test score of [ ].

❷ **Describing Trends in Scatter Plots** Describe the trend in the scatter plot for Example 1.

As the height increases, there is no upward or downward trend in the test scores. So the scatter plot shows [   ].

Quick Check

1. Graph the data in the table below in a scatter plot.

Height (in.)	58	64.5	67.5	65.5	63.5	64	71	62.5	69
Arm Span (in.)	57.5	64	68.5	66	62.5	66	72	63	70

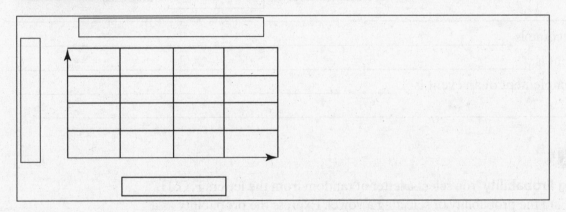

2. Suppose you draw a line that follows the trend shown in the scatter plot in Quick Check 1. Is the slope of the line positive or negative?

Lesson 12-1

Probability

Lesson Objective	NAEP 2005 Strand: Data Analysis and Probability
To find the probability and complement of an event	**Topic:** Probability
	Local Standards: _____

Vocabulary and Key Concepts

Theoretical Probability

theoretical probability = P(event) = $\dfrac{\text{number of } \boxed{} \text{ outcomes}}{\text{total number of } \boxed{} \text{ outcomes}}$

An outcome is _____

An event is _____

The complement of an event is _____

_____

Examples

❶ **Finding Probability** You select a letter at random from the letters F, G, H, and I. Find the probability of selecting a vowel. Express the probability as a fraction, a decimal, and a percent.

The event *vowel* has $\boxed{}$ outcome, $\boxed{}$, out of $\boxed{}$ possible outcomes.

P(vowel) = $\dfrac{\boxed{}}{\boxed{}}$ ← **number of favorable outcomes**

← **total number of possible outcomes**

= $\boxed{}$ = $\boxed{}$ % ← **Write as a decimal and percent.**

❷ Finding Probabilities from 0 to 1 A jar contains 1 blue marble, 3 green marbles, 3 yellow marbles, and 4 red marbles. You randomly select a marble from the jar. Find each probability.

a. $P(\text{red})$

There are ⬜ possible outcomes. Since there are ⬜ red marbles, there are ⬜ favorable outcomes.

$P(\text{red})$ ⬜/⬜   ← **number of favorable outcomes**
← **total number of possible outcomes**

b. $P(\text{orange})$

The event *orange* has ⬜ favorable outcomes.

$P(\text{orange})$ ⬜/⬜ , or ⬜   ← **number of favorable outcomes**
← **total number of possible outcomes**

c. $P(\text{not orange})$

$P(\text{not orange}) + P(\text{orange}) =$ ⬜   ← **The sum of the probabilities of an even and its complement is 1.**

⬜/⬜ + ⬜ = ⬜   ← **Substitute** ⬜ **for** $P(\text{orange})$**.**

$P(\text{not orange}) =$ ⬜   ← **Simplify.**

Quick Check

1. Find $P(\text{consonant})$ as a fraction for the letters in Example 1.

⬜

2. You roll a number cube once. Find each probability.

a. $P(\text{multiple of 3})$

⬜

b. $P(\text{not multiple of 2})$

⬜

c. $P(9)$

⬜

Lesson 12-2

Experimental Probability

Lesson Objective	**NAEP 2005 Strand:** Data Analysis and Probability
To find experimental probability and to use simulations	**Topic:** Probability
	Local Standards: _____

Vocabulary and Key Concepts

Experimental Probability

$$P(\text{event}) = \frac{\text{number of times an event occurs}}{\text{total number of trials}}$$

Experimental probability is _____

_____

Examples

1 **Finding Experimental Probability** A manufacturer of computer parts checks 100 parts each day. On Monday, two of the checked parts are defective.

a. What is the experimental probability that a part is defective?

$P(\text{defective part}) = \dfrac{\boxed{}}{\boxed{}}$ ← **number of defective parts**

← **total number of parts checked**

$= \dfrac{\boxed{}}{\boxed{}}$ ← **Simplify.**

The experimental probability is $\dfrac{\boxed{}}{\boxed{}}$.

b. Which is the best prediction of the number of defective parts in Monday's total production of 1,250 parts?

A. 13   **B.** 25   **C.** 125   **D.** 250

Let x represent the predicted number of defective parts.

defective → $\dfrac{1}{\boxed{}} = \dfrac{x}{\boxed{}}$ ← defective   ← **Write a proportion.**

total →   ← total

$\boxed{} = x$ ← **Solve the proportion.**

You can predict $\boxed{}$ parts out of 1,250 parts to be defective. The correct answer is choice $\boxed{}$.

❷ **Simulating an Event** A dog breeder knows that it is equally likely that a puppy will be male or female. Use a simulation to find the experimental probability that, in a litter of four puppies, all four will be male.

Simulate the problem by tossing four coins at the same time. Assume that male and female puppies are equally likely. Let "heads" represent a female and "tails" represent a male. A sample of 16 tosses is shown below.

Trial	Male	Female
1	✓✓	✓✓
2	✓	✓✓✓
3	✓✓✓✓	
4	✓✓	✓✓
5	✓✓✓	✓
6	✓✓	✓✓
7	✓	✓✓✓
8	✓✓	✓✓

Trial	Male	Female
9	✓✓	✓✓
10	✓✓✓	✓
11	✓✓	✓✓
12	✓	✓✓✓
13	✓✓	✓✓
14		✓✓✓✓
15	✓✓	✓✓
16	✓✓✓	✓

$P(\text{exactly four males}) = \dfrac{\boxed{}}{\boxed{}}$ ← **number of times four tails occurs**
   ← **total number of trials**

The experimental probability that, in a litter of four puppies,

all four will be male is $\boxed{}$.

Quick Check

1. In 60 coin tosses, 25 are tails. Find the experimental probability.

2. Use the data in Example 1. Predict the number of defective computer parts in a batch of 3,500.

3. Use the data in Example 2. What is the experimental probability that exactly three of the four puppies are male?

Lesson 12-3

Lesson Objective	**NAEP 2005 Strand:** Data Analysis and Probability
To make and use sample spaces and to use the counting principle	**Topic:** Probability
	Local Standards: _____

Vocabulary and Key Concepts

The Counting Principle

Suppose there are m ways of making one choice and n ways of making a second choice. There are $\boxed{} \times \boxed{}$ ways to make the first choice followed by the second choice.

Example If you can choose a shirt in 5 sizes and 7 colors, then you can choose $\boxed{} \times \boxed{}$, or $\boxed{}$, shirts.

A sample space is _____

_____

Example

1 Finding a Sample Space

a. A spinner is divided into five equal sections labeled A–E. Make a table to show the sample space for spinning the spinner twice. Write the outcomes as ordered pairs.

b. Find the probability of spinning at least one D.

There are $\boxed{}$ outcomes with at least one D. There are $\boxed{}$ possible outcomes. So, the probability of spinning at least one D is

$$\frac{\boxed{}}{\boxed{}}.$$

Quick Check

1. Give the sample space for tossing two coins. Find the probability of getting two heads.

Examples

❷ Using a Tree Diagram Suppose you can go west or northwest by train, bus, or car.

a. Draw a tree diagram to show the sample space for your journey.

Train ⟨ West ⟩ Train, [ ]

Northwest [ ], Northwest

Bus ⟨ West ⟩ Bus, [ ]

Northwest [ ], Northwest

← There are [ ] possible outcomes.

Car ⟨ West ⟩ Car, [ ]

Northwest [ ], Northwest

b. What is the probability of a random selection that results in a bus trip west?

There is [ ] favorable outcome (bus, [ ]) out

of [ ] possible outcomes. The probability is [ ].

❸ Using the Counting Principle How many kinds of coin purses are available if the purses come in small or large sizes and colors red, blue, yellow, and black?

Size	Colors
small	red
large	blue
	yellow
	black

Size   **Color**
number of choices × number of choices

[ ] × [ ] = [ ]

There are [ ] different kinds of coin purses available.

Quick Check

2. a. Suppose an airplane is added as another choice in Example 2.
Draw a tree diagram to show the sample space.

[ ]

b. Find the probability of selecting an airplane at random for your journey.

[ ]

3. A manager at Deli Counter decides to add chicken to the list of meat choices. How many different sandwiches are now available?

[ ]

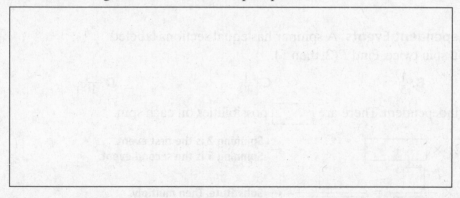

THE DELI COUNTER SANDWICHES

FRESH BREADS	DELI MEATS
Rye	Roast Beef
Wheat	Turkey
White	Ham
Pita	Pastrami
Wrap	Salami
	Liverwurst

Lesson 12-4

Compound Events

Lesson Objective	**NAEP 2005 Strand:** Data Analysis and Probability
To find the probability of independent and dependent events	**Topic:** Probability
	Local Standards: _____

Vocabulary and Key Concepts

Probability of Independent Events

If A and B are independent events,

then $P(A, \text{then } B) = $ [ ] $\times$ [ ].

Probability of Dependent Events

If event B depends on event A, then

$P(A, \text{then } B) = $ [ ] $\times$ [ ].

A compound event _____

Two events are independent if _____

_____

Two events are dependent if _____

_____

Examples

1 Probability of Independent Events A spinner has equal sections labeled 1 to 10. Suppose you spin twice. Find $P(2, \text{then } 5)$.

A. $\frac{1}{10}$ **B.** $\frac{1}{5}$ **C.** $\frac{1}{40}$ **D.** $\frac{1}{100}$

The two events are independent. There are [ ] possibilities on each spin.

$P(2, \text{then } 5) = P(2) \times$ [ ]   ← Spinning 2 is the first event.
                                         Spinning 5 is the second event.

$= \frac{1}{10} \times \dfrac{[\quad]}{[\quad]} = \dfrac{[\quad]}{[\quad]}$ ← Substitute. Then multiply.

The probability that you will spin a 2 and then a 5 is [ ]. The correct answer is choice [ ].

② **Probability of Dependent Events** You select two cards at random from those with the letters on them as shown below. The two cards do not show vowels. Without replacing the two cards, you select a third card. Find the probability that you select a card with a vowel after you select the two cards without vowels.

P R O B A B I L I T Y

There are ⬚ remaining after you select the first two cards.

$P(\text{vowel}) = \dfrac{\square}{\square}$ ← **number of remaining cards with vowels**
← **total number of remaining cards**

The probability of selecting a vowel for the third card is ⬚.

③ **Probability of Dependent Events** A bag contains 3 red marbles, 4 white marbles, and 1 blue marble. You draw one marble. Without replacing it, you draw a second marble. What is the probability that the two marbles you draw are red followed by white?

The two events are dependent. After the first selection, there are ⬚ marbles to choose from.

$P(\text{red, then white}) = P(\text{red}) \times \boxed{}$ ← **Use the formula for dependent events.**

$= \dfrac{3}{8} \times \dfrac{\square}{\square}$ ← **Substitute.**

$= \dfrac{\square}{\square} = \dfrac{\square}{\square}$ ← **Multiply. Then simplify.**

The probability that the two marbles are red and then white is ⬚.

Quick Check

1. You and a friend play a game twice. Assume the probability of winning is $\frac{1}{2}$. Find $P(\text{win, then lose})$.

2. Use the cards in Example 2. You select a B card at random. Without replacing the B card, you select a second card. Find $P(Y)$.

3. Suppose 26 cards lettered A–Z are put in a bucket. You select a card. Without replacing the first card, you select a second one. Find $P(J, \text{then } J)$.

Lesson 12-5

Permutations

Lesson Objective	NAEP 2005 Strand: Data Analysis and Probability
To find permutations	Topic: Probability
	Local Standards: _____

Vocabulary

A permutation is _____

_____

A factorial is _____

_____

Examples

① **Finding Permutations** Find the permutations of the letters T, I, G, E, and R.

The first letter can be any of the five letters. You have [   ] choices for the second, [   ] for the third, [   ] for the fourth, and [   ] for the fifth letter.

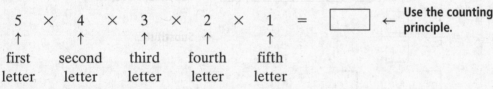

   5 × 4 × 3 × 2 × 1 = [   ] ← **Use the counting principle.**

   ↑   ↑   ↑   ↑   ↑

first second third fourth fifth
letter letter letter letter letter

There are [   ] different permutations.

② **Finding Permutations Using Factorials** How many different ways can you arrange a nickel, a dime, a penny, and a quarter in a row?

  4! = [   ] × [   ] × [   ] × [   ] = [   ]

   ↑   ↑   ↑   ↑   ↑

ways to first second third fourth
place coin coin coin coin
coins

You can make [   ] different arrangements of the coins.

❸ Horse Show Find the number of permutations for the blue, red, and green ribbons for 16 horses at a show.

There are [   ] possible horses that can win the blue ribbon. After that, there are [   ] horses that can win the red ribbon. Finally, there are [   ] horses that can win the green ribbon.

16 × [   ] × [   ] = [   ] ← **Use the counting principle.**

  ↑   ↑   ↑

blue   red   green
ribbon   ribbon   ribbon

There are [   ] different ways that horses could win blue, red, and green ribbons.

Quick Check

1. Find the number of permutations of the letters H, A, N, D, L, and E.

[   ]

2. Write the number of permutations for the letters G, R, A, V, I, E, and S in factorial form. Then multiply.

[   ]

3. a. Women's Olympic ice hockey tournaments have eight teams. Find the number of different ways that teams can win the gold, silver, and bronze medals.

[   ]

b. Reasoning In Example 3 above, the number is not found by finding 16!. Explain why.

[   ]

Lesson 12-6

Combinations

Lesson Objective To find combinations	**NAEP 2005 Strand:** Data Analysis and Probability **Topic:** Probability **Local Standards:** _____

Vocabulary

A combination is _____

_____

Examples

1 **Finding Combinations** You have one pen in each of these colors: red, green, blue, and purple. You lend three to a friend. How many different combinations of colors are possible in the pens you lend?

Color	Letter
Red	r
Green	g
Blue	b
Purple	p

Step 1 Let letters represent the four colors. Make a list of all possible permutations.

(r, g, b) (g, r, b) (b, r, g) (p, r, g)
(r, g, p) (g, r, p) (b, r, p) (p, r, b)
(r, b, g) (g, b, r) (b, g, r) (p, g, r)
(r, b, p) (g, b, p) (b, g, p) (p, g, b)
(r, p, g) (g, p, r) (b, p, r) (p, b, r)
(r, p, b) (g, p, b) (b, p, g) (p, b, g)

Step 2 Cross out any group containing the same letters as another group.

(r, g, b) (g, r, b) (b, r, g) (p, r, g)
(r, g, p) (g, r, p) (b, r, p) (p, r, b)
(r, b, g) (g, b, r) (b, g, r) (p, g, r)
(r, b, p) (g, b, p) (b, g, p) (p, g, b)
(r, p, g) (g, p, r) (b, p, r) (p, b, r)
(r, p, b) (g, p, b) (b, p, g) (b, p, g)

[____] different combinations of three colors are possible.

❷ Finding Combinations The county fair has 10 rides. You have time for three of them. How many different combinations of rides are available to you?

Step 1 Find the total number of permutations.

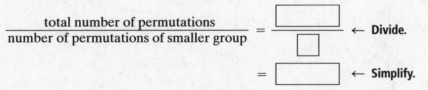

$$10 \ \times \ \boxed{} \ \times \ \boxed{} \ = \ \boxed{} \ \text{permutations} \quad \leftarrow \ \textbf{Use the counting principle.}$$

↑   ↑   ↑

first choice   second choice   third choice

Step 2 Find the number of permutations of the smaller group.

$$3 \ \times \ \boxed{} \ \times \ \boxed{} \ = \ \boxed{} \ \text{permutations} \quad \leftarrow \ \textbf{Use the counting principle.}$$

Step 3 Find the number of combinations.

$$\frac{\text{total number of permutations}}{\text{number of permutations of smaller group}} = \frac{\boxed{}}{\boxed{}} \quad \leftarrow \ \textbf{Divide.}$$

$$= \ \boxed{} \quad \leftarrow \ \textbf{Simplify.}$$

There are $\boxed{}$ combinations of rides available.

Quick Check

1. How many different combinations of two seashells can you make from three seashells?

2. On career day, an architect, an engineer, a carpenter, and a journalist speak at your school. If you go to two presentations, how many different combinations of presentations can you choose from?

Practice 1-1

Use rounding to estimate the nearest half-dollar.

1. $4.85
   + 1.47

   _____

2. $6.79
   − 3.95

   _____

3. $14.19
   + 5.59

   _____

4. $25.43
   − 21.20

   _____

Use front-end estimation to estimate each sum.

5. $4.76 + 6.15$

   _____

6. $1.409 + 3.512$

   _____

7. $2.479 + 6.518$

   _____

8. $3.17 + 2.72$

   _____

9. $9.87 + 2.16$

   _____

10. $5.89 + 7.21$

    _____

Use compatible numbers to estimate each quotient.

11. $76.32 \div 24.98$

    _____

12. $42.693 \div 4.7$

    _____

13. $54.36 \div 11.001$

    _____

Use any estimation strategy to calculate. Tell which strategy you used.

14. $66.93 + $72.18 + $69.18 + $71.94 + 65.75

    _____

15. $93.26 − 69.78$

    _____

16. 51.12×87.906

    _____

17. $457.03 + 592.8$

    _____

18. $702 \div 61$

    _____

19. $12.87 + 14.31 + 15.09$

    _____

20. $536 \div 41$

    _____

Find each estimate.

21. A rare truffle once sold for $13.20 for a 0.44 oz can.
    Approximately how much would 1 lb of this truffle cost?

    _____

22. The length of the longest loaf of bread measured 1,405 ft $1\frac{3}{4}$ in. It
    was cut into slices $\frac{1}{2}$ in. thick. How many slices were there?

    _____

1-1 • Guided Problem Solving

GPS Student Page 7, Exercise 32:

Travel On vacation, you wish to send eight postcards to friends at home. You find cards costing $.59 each. Eight postcard stamps cost about $2 total. About how much will it cost to buy and mail the cards?

Understand

1. Circle the information you will need to solve the problem.

2. What are you being asked to do?

_____

_____

3. Before you estimate the total cost, what do you have to estimate

first? _____

_____

Plan and Carry Out

4. Round $.59 to the nearest tenth. _____

5. Use the answer to Step 4 to estimate the product 8 × 0.59.

_____

6. About how much are eight postcard stamps?

_____

7. About how much will it cost to buy and mail the cards?

_____

Check

8. Is your estimate reasonable? Multiply 8 by 0.59 and then add 2.

_____

_____

Solve Another Problem

9. Paul stops by the market to buy his lunch. The market is selling bananas for $.22 each and sandwiches for $3.95. About how much does Paul spend if he buys a sandwich and 4 bananas?

_____

_____

Practice 1-2

Adding and Subtracting Decimals

Identify each property shown.

1. $(8.7 + 6.3) + 3.7 = 8.7 + (6.3 + 3.7)$

_____

2. $9.06 + 0 = 9.06$

_____

3. $4.06 + 8.92 = 8.92 + 4.06$

_____

4. $0 + 7.13 = 7.13 + 0$

_____

Find each sum.

5. $4.6 + 8.79$

6. $14.8 + 29.07$

7. $20.16 + 15.703$

8. $36.12 + 5.793$

9. $8.9 + 2.14 + 7.1$

10. $3.6 + 5.27 + 8.93$

11. $107.5 + 6$

12. $15.26 + 13.29 + 38.96$

13. $46.21 + 53.942$

Find each difference.

14. $8.7 - 2.03$

15. $53.86 - 4.02$

16. $14.59 - 8.3$

17. $42.75 - 26.36$

18. $53.86 - 16.47$

19. $56.89 - 48.91$

20. $5.06 - 3.297$

21. $3.4 - 2.768$

22. $5.002 - 4.3$

Use the advertisement at the right. Find each cost.

23. 1 egg _____

24. toast _____

25. bacon _____

26. milk _____

27. 1 egg and milk _____

28. 1 egg and bacon _____

2 eggs, toast, bacon, milk	$2.75
1 egg, toast, bacon, milk	$2.20
toast, milk	$0.90
toast, bacon, milk	$1.65
1 egg, toast	$0.95

1-2 • Guided Problem Solving

GPS **Student Page 11, Exercise 39:**

Weather During a 3-day storm, 8.91 in. of rain fell in Tallahassee and 4.24 in. fell in St. Augustine. How much more rain fell in Tallahassee than in St. Augustine?

Understand

1. Circle the information you will need to solve the problem.

2. What are you being asked to do?

   _____

   _____

3. Which word group tells you what operation to perform?

   _____

   _____

Plan and Carry Out

4. How do you align the addends in 8.91 and 4.24? Show your work.

   _____

5. What do you need to do in order to subtract these two numbers?

   _____

6. How much more rain was there in Tallahassee than in St. Augustine?

   _____

Check

7. How would you check the result in Step 6?

   _____

Solve Another Problem

8. Laurie has $10.59 left after buying a refreshment. If the refreshment cost $3.91 after tax, how much did Laurie have before she bought it?

   _____

Practice 1-3

Find each product.

1. 28×6

2. $7.3 \cdot 0.9$

3. $58 \cdot 2.1$

4. $15(187)$

5. 6.6×25

6. $(1.8)(0.7)$

7. $0.91 \cdot 2.7$

8. $4.6(3.9)$

9. 17.3×15.23

10. $2.33(3.56)$

11. 12.15×19

12. 481.51×623.42

Rewrite each equation with the decimal point in the correct place in the product.

13. $5.6 \times 1.2 = 672$

14. $3.7 \times 2.4 = 888$

15. $6.5 \times 2.5 = 1625$

16. $1.02 \times 6.9 = 7038$

17. $4.4 \times 6.51 = 28644$

18. $0.6 \times 9.312 = 55872$

Name the property of multiplication shown.

19. $3 \times 4 = 4 \times 3$

20. $9 \times (6 \times 3) = (9 \times 6) \times 3$

21. $2 \times 0 = 0$

22. $10 \times 1 = 10$

Solve.

23. Each trip on a ride at the carnival costs $1.25. If Tara goes on 4 rides, how much will it cost her?

24. Postage stamps cost $0.37 each. How much does a book of 50 stamps cost?

1-3 • Guided Problem Solving

GPS **Student Page 17, Exercise 39:**

One year, Texas had about 2.6 times as many head of cattle as Oklahoma. Oklahoma had 5.2 million. How many head of cattle did Texas have?

Understand

1. Circle the information you will need to solve the problem.

2. What are you being asked to do? _____

   _____

Plan and Carry Out

3. How many million head of cattle were in Oklahoma?

   _____

4. How many times more cattle did Texas have than Oklahoma?

   _____

5. Write an expression for the number of cattle in Texas (in millions).

   _____

6. How many decimal places are in both factors?

   _____

7. Multiply as if the numbers are whole numbers.

   _____

8. Place the decimal in the product using the total number of decimal places from Step 6.

   _____

Check

9. Estimate the product of 2.6 × 5.2, and compare it to your answer. Is your answer reasonable?

   _____

Solve Another Problem

10. You buy 6.5 yards of fabric that costs $7.95 per yard. How much money does it cost?

    _____

Guided Problem Solving

Practice 1-4

Find each quotient.

1. $0.7 \div 100$ _____

2. $4.85 \div 0.1$ _____

3. $7.08 \div 10$ _____

4. $3.5 \div 0.1$ _____

5. $847 \div 0.01$ _____

6. $0.3 \div 0.1$ _____

7. $32.6 \div 0.01$ _____

8. $5.02 \div 0.1$ _____

9. $2.1\overline{)12.6}$ _____

10. $29.75 \div 0.7$ _____

11. $37 \div 0.2$ _____

12. $4.74 \div 0.06$ _____

13. $1.414 \div 1.4$ _____

14. $0.78\overline{)0.16614}$ _____

15. $0.154 \div 5.5$ _____

16. $0.85\overline{)0.0527}$ _____

Annex zeros to find each quotient.

17. $1.3 \div 0.8$ _____

18. $2.4\overline{)5.4}$ _____

19. $79.04 \div 9.5$ _____

20. $36.78 \div 2.4$ _____

21. $\dfrac{58.5}{10.4}$ _____

22. $1.2\overline{)38.7}$ _____

Solve.

23. Alicia paid $1.32 for a bag of pinto beans. The beans cost $.55 per lb. How much did the bag of pinto beans weigh?

_____

24. Nina and 3 friends ate lunch at a cafe. They decided to split the bill evenly. The total bill was $17.84. How much was each person's share?

_____

1-4 • Guided Problem Solving

GPS **Student Page 23, Exercise 33:**

Landscaping After digging up lilac bushes in the garden, a landscape architect uses sod to cover the dirt. The sod costs $2.25/yd. He pays $31.50. How much sod does he buy?

Understand

1. Circle the information you will need to solve the problem.

2. What are you being asked to do?

   _____

   _____

3. Which operation must you perform to determine the answer?

   _____

Plan and Carry Out

4. How much money does the landscape architect spend?

   _____

5. How much is each yard of sod?

   _____

6. What is $31.50 ÷ $2.25/yd?

   _____

Check

7. Calculate $2.25/yd × 14 yd. Does your answer equal the total amount of money spent?

   _____

Solve Another Problem

8. Marissa created a platform for the set of the school play. She used boards that are each 3.15 in. wide. If the platform is 37.8 inches wide, how many boards did Marissa use?

   _____

Practice 1-5

Choose a reasonable estimate.

1. Length of a calculator   18 m   18 cm   18 mm

2. Length of a football field   100 km   100 m   100 cm

3. Thickness of a paperback book   25 km   25 m   25 mm

4. Capacity of a bottle of shampoo   250 mL   250 L   250 kL

Complete each statement. If necessary, use a number line.

5. 0.7 km = _____ m   6. _____ L = 40 mL   7. 83 m = _____ mm

8. 9,500 m = _____ km   9. 8 g = _____ kg   10. _____ m = 800 km

Change each measurement to the given unit.

11. 43 km 14 m to kilometers _____

12. 84 m 15 cm to centimeters _____

13. 9 kg 421 g to kilograms _____

14. 14 L 7 mL to liters _____

Write the metric unit that makes each statement true.

15. 9.85 kg = 9,850 _____   16. 87.43 m = 8,743 _____

17. 10,542 mL = 10.542 _____   18. 8.42 mm = 0.842 _____

19. 2,347 m = 2.347 _____   20. 0.356 m = 356 _____

Solve.

21. The capacity of a beaker is 150 mL. How many beakers can be filled from a 4 L container?

_____

22. Vitamin C comes in pills with a strength of 500 mg. How many pills would you need to take if you want a dosage of one gram?

_____

23. Your science teacher mixes the contents of two beakers containing 2.5 L and 800 mL of a liquid. What is the combined amount?

_____

24. A teaspoon of common table salt contains about 2,000 mg of sodium. How many grams of sodium is this?

_____

1-5 • Guided Problem Solving

GPS **Student Page 30, Exercise 35:**

Food The capacity of a coffee mug is 350 mL. How many coffee mugs can you fill from a 2 L container?

Understand

1. Circle the information you will need to solve the problem.

2. What are you being asked to do?

    _____

    _____

3. How many milliliters are there in one liter?

    _____

Plan and Carry Out

4. How many liters does the container hold?

    _____

5. Do you multiply or divide to change liters into milliliters?

    _____

6. How many milliliters are there in 2 L?

    _____

7. Do you multiply or divide to find how many coffee mugs can be filled?

    _____

8. How many coffee mugs can be filled from a 2 L container?

    _____

Check

9. Is the total capacity of the coffee mugs filled less than or equal to 2,000 mL? Does your answer make sense?

    _____

Solve Another Problem

10. Lily drinks 0.5 L of water during her exercise routine. If her aerobics instructor tells her that she should be drinking at least 300 mL of water, is Lily drinking enough? Explain.

    _____

Name _____ Class _____ Date _____

Practice 1-6

Comparing and Ordering Integers

Name the integer represented by each point on the number line.

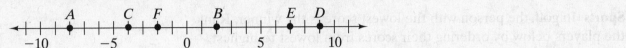

1. A _____ 2. B _____ 3. C _____ 4. D _____ 5. E _____ 6. F _____

Compare. Use <, >, or =.

7. -8 ☐ 8 8. 4 ☐ -4 9. $|5|$ ☐ $|-5|$ 10. -8 ☐ 0

11. -6 ☐ -2 12. -1 ☐ -3 13. $|-4|$ ☐ 0 14. $|-3|$ ☐ 2

Graph each integer and its opposite on the number line.

15. -9

    −8 −6 −4 −2 0 2 4 6 8

16. 5

    −8 −6 −4 −2 0 2 4 6 8

17. 8

    −8 −6 −4 −2 0 2 4 6 8

18. -2

    −8 −6 −4 −2 0 2 4 6 8

Find each absolute value.

19. $|2|$ 20. $|-3|$ 21. $|-38|$ 22. $|-2 + 5|$

_____ _____ _____ _____

23. $|-44|$ 24. $|5 + 2|$ 25. $|-16|$ 26. $|3 - 7|$

_____ _____ _____ _____

Write an integer to represent each situation.

27. a gain of 5 yards 28. a debt of $5

_____ _____

29. a temperature of 100°F 30. 135 feet below sea level

_____ _____

1-6 • Guided Problem Solving

GPS **Student Page 34, Exercise 48:**

Sports In golf, the person with the lowest score is the winner. Rank the players below by ordering their scores from lowest to highest.

Player	Score
T. Woods	−12
V. Singh	−4
E. Els	+10
P. Mickelson	−3
R. Goosen	−5

Understand

1. Who wins in a golf game?

   _____

2. How will you determine the lowest number?

   _____

Plan and Carry Out

3. Draw a number line. Plot each score. Which number is the farthest to the left of zero on the number line?

   _____

4. What is the order of all five numbers? _____

5. Rank the players from lowest score to highest score.

   _____

   _____

Check

6. Is the person with the highest score last? Is the person with the lowest score first?

   _____

   _____

Solve Another Problem

7. Anne had the following golf scores this week: −6, +5, −4, +13, −2, +4, +6, −11. Which was her best score? Which was her worst score?

   _____

Practice 1-7

Find each sum.

1. $-2 + (-3)$ 　　　　**2.** $8 - 7 + 4$ 　　　　**3.** $8 + (-5)$ 　　　　**4.** $15 + (-3)$

_____　_____　_____　_____

5. $-16 + 8$ 　　　　**6.** $7 + (-10)$ 　　　　**7.** $-9 + (-5)$ 　　　　**8.** $-12 + 14$

_____　_____　_____　_____

Find each difference.

9. $9 - 26$ 　　　　**10.** $-4 - 15$ 　　　　**11.** $21 - (-7)$ 　　　　**12.** $27 - (-16)$

_____　_____　_____　_____

13. $-16 - (-43)$ 　　**14.** $47 - 19$ 　　　　**15.** $-156 - 98$ 　　　　**16.** $-192 - 47$

_____　_____　_____　_____

17. $0 - (-51)$ 　　　**18.** $-63 - 89$ 　　　　**19.** $-12 - (-21)$ 　　　**20.** $92 - (-16)$

_____　_____　_____　_____

Find the value of each expression.

21. $3 + 8 + (-4)$ 　　　**22.** $2 + |-3| + (-3)$ 　　　**23.** $9 + 7 - 6$

_____　　_____　　_____

24. $56 + (-4) + (-58)$ 　**25.** $-4 - 3 + (-2)$ 　　**26.** $|-8| - 15 + (-8)$

_____　　_____　　_____

Use >, <, or = to complete each statement.

27. $-9 - (-11)$ ☐ 0 　　**28.** $-17 + 20$ ☐ 0 　　**29.** $11 - (-4)$ ☐ 0

30. $28 - 19$ ☐ 0 　　　**31.** $52 + (-65)$ ☐ 0 　　**32.** $-28 - (-28)$ ☐ 0

Solve.

33. The highest and lowest temperatures ever recorded in Africa are 136°F and −11°F. The highest temperature was recorded in Libya, and the lowest temperature was recorded in Morocco. What is the difference in these temperature extremes?

_____

34. The highest and lowest temperatures ever recorded in South America are 120°F and −27°F. Both the highest and lowest temperatures were recorded in Argentina. What is the difference in these temperature extremes?

_____

1-7 • Guided Problem Solving

GPS Student Page 41, Exercise 27:

Temperature The highest temperature ever recorded in the United States was 134°F, measured at Death Valley, California. The coldest temperature, −80°F, was recorded at Prospect Creek, Alaska. What is the difference between these temperatures?

Understand

1. Circle the information you will need to solve the problem.

2. What are you being asked to do?

   _____

3. Which word tells you what operation to perform?

   _____

Plan and Carry Out

4. Write a subtraction expression for the problem.

   _____

5. Subtracting a negative number is the same as adding what type of number?

   _____

6. Write an addition expression that is the same as the expression you wrote in Step 4.

   _____

7. What is the difference between these temperatures?

   _____

Check

8. What is 134°F − 214°F?

   _____

Solve Another Problem

9. At 6:00 A.M. the temperature was 25°F. At 9:00 P.M. the temperature was −13°F. What was the difference in the temperature?

   _____

Guided Problem Solving

Practice 1-8

Multiplying and Dividing Integers

Complete each statement. Then write two examples to illustrate each relationship.

1. positive ÷ positive = ?

_____

2. negative · positive = ?

_____

3. positive · positive = ?

_____

4. negative ÷ negative = ?

_____

5. negative ÷ positive = ?

_____

6. positive · positive = ?

_____

7. positive ÷ negative = ?

_____

8. negative · negative = ?

_____

Estimate each product or quotient.

9. $-72 \cdot 57$

_____

10. $-92 \cdot (-41)$

_____

11. $-476 \div 90$

_____

12. $-83 \cdot 52$

_____

13. $538 \div (-63)$

_____

14. $-803 \cdot (-106)$

_____

15. $49 \cdot 61$

_____

16. $479 \div (-61)$

_____

Find each product or quotient.

17. $\dfrac{-36}{9}$

_____

18. $\dfrac{-52}{-4}$

_____

19. $(-5) \cdot (-20)$

_____

20. $\dfrac{-63}{-9}$

_____

21. $(-15) \cdot (2)$

_____

22. $\dfrac{22}{-2}$

_____

23. $(13) \cdot (-6)$

_____

24. $\dfrac{-100}{-5}$

_____

25. $(-60) \cdot (-3)$

_____

26. $\dfrac{-240}{30}$

_____

27. $(43) \cdot (-8)$

_____

28. $\dfrac{-169}{-13}$

_____

1-8 • Guided Problem Solving

GPS Student Page 47, Exercise 35:

Hobbies A scuba diver is 180 ft below sea level and rises to the surface at a rate of 30 ft/min. How long will the diver take to reach the surface?

Understand

1. Circle the information you will need to solve the problem.

2. What are you being asked to do?

   _____

   _____

Plan and Carry Out

3. Will you multiply or divide to solve this problem?

   _____

4. How far below sea level is the diver?

   _____

5. How fast is the diver rising?

   _____

6. How long will the diver take to reach the surface?

   _____

Check

7. What is 30 ft/min × 6 min? Does your answer equal the original distance below sea level?

   _____

Solve Another Problem

8. A rock climber climbs down into the Grand Canyon at a rate of 2 ft/min. How long will it take him to climb down 50 ft?

   _____

Practice 1-9

Order of Operations and the Distributive Property

Find the value of each expression.

1. $(8 + 2) \times 9$

2. $5 - 1 \div 4$

3. $(6 + 3) \div 18$

4. $80 - 6 \times 7$

_____   _____   _____   _____

5. $4 \times 6 + 3$

6. $4 \times (6 + 3)$

7. $35 - 6 \times 5$

8. $9 \div 3 + 6$

_____   _____   _____   _____

Find the missing numbers. Then simplify.

9. $5(9 + 6) = 5\,(\underline{\ ?\ }) + 5\,(\underline{\ ?\ })$

10. $4(9.7 - 8.1) = \underline{\ ?\ }(9.7) - \underline{\ ?\ }(8.1)$

_____   _____

11. $\underline{\ ?\ }(3.8) = 9(4) - 9(\underline{\ ?\ })$

12. $\underline{\ ?\ }(17.1 + 12.6) = 6(17.1) + 6(12.6)$

_____   _____

Use the Distributive Property and mental math to find each product.

13. $3(6.4)$

14. $5(7.1)$

15. $5(8.9)$

_____   _____   _____

16. $4(9.2)$

17. $9(11.1)$

18. $7(8.9)$

_____   _____   _____

Copy each statement and add parentheses to make it true.

19. $6 + 6 \div 6 \times 6 + 6 = 24$

20. $6 \times 6 + 6 \times 6 - 6 = 426$

_____   _____

21. $6 + 6 \div 6 \times 6 - 6 = 0$

22. $6 - 6 \times 6 + 6 \div 6 = 1$

_____   _____

23. A backyard measures 80 ft $\times$ 125 ft. A garden is planted in one corner of it. The garden measures 15 ft $\times$ 22 ft. How much of the backyard is *not* part of the garden?

_____

1-9 • Guided Problem Solving

GPS **Student Page 51, Exercise 30:**

Business A florist is buying flowers to use in centerpieces. Each centerpiece has 3 lilies. There are a total of 10 tables. Each lily costs $.98. Use mental math to find the cost of the lilies.

Understand

1. What are you being asked to do?

   _____

2. Which method are you to use to determine the cost?

   _____

Plan and Carry Out

3. How many lilies do you need in all?

   _____

4. Write an expression to find the total cost of the lilies.

   _____

5. The amount $.98 can also be written as $1.00 – $.02. Rewrite your expression from Step 4 using $1.00 – $.02.

   _____

6. Simplify the expression using mental math.

   _____

7. How much do the lilies cost?

   _____

Check

8. Use a calculator to determine the cost of the lilies. Is your answer from step 7 correct?

   _____

Solve Another Problem

9. Your horticulture club is planting a garden at school as a beautification project. The principal is allowing you to use an area that is 5 yd². If it costs $8.93 to buy enough rose bulbs to plant 1 yd², how much will it cost to buy bulbs to fill 5 yd²?

   _____

Name _____ Class _____ Date _____

Practice 1-10

Mean, Median, Mode, and Range

The sum of the heights of all the students in a class is 1,472 in.

1. The mean height is 5 ft 4 in. How many students are in the class?
   (1 ft = 12 in.)

   _____

2. **a.** The median height is 5 ft 2 in. How many students are 5 ft 2 in.
   or taller?

   _____

   b. How many students are shorter than 5 ft 2 in.?

   _____

The number of pages read (to the nearest multiple of 50) by the students in history class last week are shown in the tally table at the right.

Pages	Tally
50	I
100	
150	II
200	IIII I
250	I
300	IIII
350	III
400	IIII
450	I
500	I

3. Find the mean, median, mode, and range of the data.

   _____

4. What is the outlier in this set of data? _____

5. Does the outlier raise or lower the mean? _____

A student hopes to have a 9-point average on his math quizzes. His quiz scores are 7, 6, 10, 8, and 9. Each quiz is worth 12 points.

6. What is his average quiz score?

   _____

7. There are two more quizzes. How many more points will be
   needed to give a 9-point quiz average?

   _____

Find the mean, median, mode, and range for each situation.

8. number of miles biked in one week

   21, 17, 15, 18, 22, 16, 20 _____

9. number of strikeouts per inning

   3, 2, 0, 0, 1, 2, 3, 0, 2 _____

1-10 • Guided Problem Solving

GPS Student Page 56, Exercise 26:

Find the mean, median, and mode for the hours of practice before a concert:

2 1 0 1 5 3 4 2 0 3 1 2

Understand

1. What does this data set refer to?

   _____

2. What are you being asked to do?

   _____

3. How many numbers are in the data set?

Plan and Carry Out

4. Find the sum of the numbers in the data set. _____

5. Find the mean by dividing the sum of the numbers by the total number of numbers. _____

6. Order the numbers in the data set in increasing order.

   _____

7. What are the two middle numbers? _____

8. Find the median of the data by finding the mean of the two middle numbers. _____

9. Find the mode by finding which number is listed most often. _____

10. How many modes are there? _____

Check

11. What do you notice about the mean, median, and mode of this data?

    _____

Solve Another Problem

12. Millie has 3 siblings, Peggy has one sister, Larry has 5 brothers, Joey is an only child, and Marie has 6 siblings. What is the mean number of siblings for this group of people? _____

1A: Graphic Organizer

For use before Lesson 1-1

Study Skill As you begin a new textbook, look through the table of contents to see what kind of information you will be learning during the year. Notice that some of the topics were introduced last year. Get a head start by reviewing your old notes and problems.

Write your answers.

1. What is the chapter title? _____

2. How many lessons are there in this chapter? _____

3. What is the topic of the Test-Taking Strategies page? _____

4. Complete the graphic organizer below as you work through the chapter.
   - In the center, write the title of the chapter.
   - When you begin a lesson, write the lesson name in a rectangle.
   - When you complete a lesson, write a skill or key concept in a circle linked to that lesson block.
   - When you complete the chapter, use this graphic organizer to help you review.

1B: Reading Comprehension

For use after Lesson 1-5

Study Skill Practice reading charts and tables in books, magazines, or newspapers since information is often organized this way.

The table below contains information about four of the highest-ranked centers in the history of the National Basketball Association (NBA).

Use the table below to answer the questions.

Player	Height, Weight	Number of Seasons to Playoffs	Points Per Game (PPG) During Regular Season	PPG During Playoffs	NBA Titles	Age at Retirement
Kareem Abdul-Jabbar	7 ft 2 in. 267 lb	20 to 18	24.6	24.3	6	42
Wilt Chamberlain	7 ft 1 in. 275 lb	14 to 13	30.1	22.5	2	37
Shaquille O'Neal	7 ft 1 in. 325 lb	13 to 12	27.6	26.7	2	*
Bill Russell	6 ft 10 in. 220 lb	13 to 13	15.1	16.2	11	35

* still playing

1. Which of these centers is the tallest? _____

2. Which center is the shortest? _____

3. Which center won the most NBA titles? _____

4. Which center weighed the greatest amount? _____

5. Which center played the most regular seasons? _____

6. Which center(s) played in the playoffs 13 times?

   _____

7. What does PPG stand for? _____

8. Which center had the highest PPG during the regular season?

   _____

9. **High-Use Academic Words** In the directions, you are told that the NBA centers in the table are *ranked* the highest. What does it mean to *rank*?

   a. to show clearly   b. to determine the relative position of

1C: Reading/Writing Math Symbols

For use after Lesson 1-6

Study Skill Finish one homework assignment before beginning another. Sometimes it helps to start with the most difficult assignment first.

Match the symbol in Column A with its meaning in Column B.

Column A	Column B
1. ·	**A.** division
2. ≈	**B.** degrees
3. ÷	**C.** is approximately equal to
4. ||	**D.** the opposite of
5. °	**E.** multiplication
6. ≤	**F.** is less than or equal to
7. −	**G.** absolute value

Match the metric abbreviation in Column A with the appropriate word in Column B.

Column A	Column B
8. mL	**A.** kilometers
9. L	**B.** decimeters
10. dm	**C.** milliliters
11. cL	**D.** centiliters
12. mg	**E.** grams
13. km	**F.** liters
14. g	**G.** milligrams

1D: Visual Vocabulary Practice

For use after Lesson 1-10

Study Skill If a word is not in the glossary, use a dictionary to find its meaning.

Concept List

Associative Property of Addition	Associative Property of Multiplication
Commutative Property of Addition	Distributive Property
mean	order of operations
median	range
mode	

Write the concept that best describes each exercise. Choose from the concept list above.

1.	2.	3.
$(3 - (-2)^2) \times 5 + 3 =$ $(3 - 4) \times 5 + 3 =$ $-1 \times 5 + 3 = -5 + 3 = -2$	$(8 + x) + 2x = 8 + (x + 2x)$	The number 14 represents this in the data set $\{14, 30, 14, 31, 30, 18, 14, 12\}$.
4. The average temperatures in a city over seven days included 54°F, 51°F, 42°F, 47°F, 58°F, 54°F, and 53°F. What does the number $58 - 42 = 16$ represent for this set of temperatures?	5. Blanes's grades in history class are 82, 82, 92, 90, and 84. What does the number $\dfrac{82 + 82 + 92 + 90 + 84}{5} = 86$ represent for this set of grades?	6. $8(2^3 + 16) = 8(2^3) + 8(16)$
7. $b + c = c + b$	8. $14 \times (50 \times 21) =$ $(14 \times 50) \times 21$	9. The set $\{1, 1, 3, 5, 10\}$ represents the number of hours that five students watched TV last week. What does the number 3 represent for this set of hours?

Vocabulary and Study Skills

1E: Vocabulary Check

Study Skill Strengthen your vocabulary. Use these pages and add cues and summaries by applying the Cornell Notetaking style.

Write the definition for each word or term at the right. To check your work, fold the paper back along the dotted line to see the correct answers.

_____   absolute value

_____

_____

_____   integers

_____

_____

_____   compatible numbers

_____

_____

_____   Zero Property

_____

_____

_____   additive inverses

_____

_____

1E: Vocabulary Check (continued)

Write the vocabulary word or term for each definition. To check your work, fold the paper forward along the dotted line to see the correct answers.

the distance of a number from 0 on the number line

_____

the set of positive whole numbers, their opposites, and 0

_____

numbers that are easy to compute mentally

_____

The product of 0 and any number is 0.

_____

any two numbers whose sum is 0

_____

1F: Vocabulary Review Puzzle

For use with the Chapter Review

Study Skill Vocabulary is an important part of every subject you learn. Review new words and their definitions using flashcards.

Find each of the following words in the word search. Circle the word and then cross it off the word list. Words can be displayed forwards, backwards, up, down, or diagonally.

absolute value	integers	order
median	mode	mean
opposites	outlier	range
compatible	distributive	multiplication

```
C Q E D E T A J P K A Z L H N
F K E E R E D R O N D A H U N
M Z D W I T E P I E B B I P O
R N O U R O L C C V E S E F I
A O M B A P B M E I T O V X T
N P R J N P I E P T I L A S A
G F I R L O T T E U F U T E C
E I N P M S A R T B E T K T I
Y O T H G I P A A I I E O R L
I D E O O T M N R R N V U O P
W A G R F E O V O T K A T I I
P D E F N S C O O S E L L J T
G K R N N A W S O I G U I R L
N M S D K A E V N D S E E U U
M E D I A N F M A R O M R L M
```

Practice 2-1

Exponents and Order of Operations

Write using exponents.

1. $3 \times 3 \times 3 \times 3 \times 3$ _____

2. $2.7 \times 2.7 \times 2.7$ _____

3. $11.6 \times 11.6 \times 11.6 \times 11.6$ _____

4. $2 \times 2 \times 2 \times 2 \times 2 \times 2$ _____

5. $8.3 \times 8.3 \times 8.3 \times 8.3 \times 8.3$ _____

6. $4 \times 4 \times 4 \times 4 \times 4 \times 4 \times 4 \times 4$ _____

Write as the product of repeated factors. Then simplify.

7. $(0.5)^3$ _____

8. $(-4)^5$ _____

9. $(2.7)^2$ _____

10. 2^3 _____

11. $(-5)^6$ _____

12. $(8.1)^3$ _____

Simplify. Use a calculator, paper and pencil, or mental math.

13. -4^3

14. $11 + (-6^3)$

15. $14 + 16^2$

16. $8 + 6^4$

17 $3^2 \cdot 5^4$

18. $6^2 - 2^4$

19. $4(0.9 + 1.3)^3$

20. $35 - (4^2 + 5)$

21. $(3^3 + 6) - 7$

22. $5(0.3 \cdot 1.2)^2$

23. $5(4 + 2)^2$

24. $(8 - 6.7)^3$

25. A cubic aquarium has edges measuring 4.3 ft each. Find the volume of the aquarium in cubic feet.

_____

26. Lana is 2^3 in. taller than her little sister. How many inches taller is Lana than her sister?

_____

2-1 • Guided Problem Solving

GPS Student Page 71, Exercise 36:

A Scanning Electron Microscope (SEM) can magnify an image to as much as 10^5 times the actual size. How many times is this?

Understand

1. What are you being asked to do?

   _____

   _____

2. What do you call the 5 in 10^5?

   _____

3. What do you call the 10 in 10^5?

   _____

Plan and Carry Out

4. The number 10^5 is what number? _____

5. How many zeros are in the number 10^5? _____

6. How many times does the SEM magnify? _____

Check

7. Does your answer follow the pattern of powers of 10? Explain.

   _____

   _____

   _____

Solve Another Problem

8. Lucy has a microscope that magnifies an image to as much as 10^3 times the actual size. Aaron has a microscope that magnifies an image to as much as 10^4 times the actual size. What is the difference in these two numbers?

   _____

   _____

Name _____ Class _____ Date _____

Practice 2-2

• •

Find the LCM of each pair of numbers.

1. 11, 5 _____   **2.** 5, 12 _____   **3.** 12, 7 _____

4. 5, 9 _____   **5.** 5, 18 _____   **6.** 5, 20 _____

7. 7, 10 _____   **8.** 17, 13 _____   **9.** 14, 8 _____

10. 11, 23 _____   **11.** 14, 5 _____   **12.** 16, 9 _____

13. Cameron is making bead necklaces. He has 90 green beads and 108 blue beads. What is the greatest number of identical necklaces he can make if he wants to use all of the beads?

_____

14. One radio station broadcasts a weather forecast every 18 minutes and another station broadcasts a commercial every 15 minutes. If the stations broadcast both a weather forecast and a commercial at noon, when is the next time that both will be broadcast at the same time?

_____

Determine whether each number is prime or composite.

15. 97 _____   **16.** 63 _____   **17.** 29 _____   **18.** 120 _____

Write the prime factorization. Use exponents where possible.

19. 42 _____   **20.** 130 _____

21. 78 _____   **22.** 126 _____

23. 125 _____   **24.** 90 _____

25. 92 _____   **26.** 180 _____

Find the GCF of each pair of numbers.

27. 45, 60 _____   **28.** 18, 42 _____   **29.** 32, 80 _____

30. 20, 65 _____   **31.** 24, 90 _____   **32.** 17, 34 _____

33. 14, 35 _____   **34.** 51, 27 _____   **35.** 42, 63 _____

• •

2-2 • Guided Problem Solving

GPS **Student Page 78, Exercise 48:**

A movie theatre just added two rooms. One room is large enough for 125 people, and the other can seat up to 350 people. In each room, the seating is arranged in horizontal rows with the same number of seats in each row. What is the greatest number of seats that can make up each row?

Understand

1. Circle the information you will need to solve.

2. What do you need to do to answer the question?

   _____

   _____

Plan and Carry Out

3. List the prime factors of 350.   _____

4. List the prime factors of 125.   _____

5. List the factors that 350 and
   125 have in common.   _____

6. What is the greatest common
   factor of 350 and 125?   _____

7. What is the largest number of seats
   that can make up each row?   _____

Check

8. What is 350 ÷ 25? What is 125 ÷ 25? Do these quotients have any common factors besides 1?

   _____

   _____

Solve Another Problem

9. For graduation, the left side of the gymnasium can seat 228 people and the right side can seat 144 people. The principal wants the same number of chairs in each row on both sides. How many chairs does the setup committee need to put in each row?

   _____

Practice 2-3

Simplifying Fractions

Write each fraction in simplest form.

1. $\frac{8}{12}$ _____

2. $\frac{9}{15}$ _____

3. $\frac{16}{20}$ _____

4. $\frac{20}{25}$ _____

5. $\frac{15}{18}$ _____

6. $\frac{14}{30}$ _____

7. $\frac{11}{44}$ _____

8. $\frac{24}{36}$ _____

Write each fraction in simplest form. Give the GCF of the numerator and denominator.

9. $\frac{125}{200}$ ____ GCF = ____

10. $\frac{36}{64}$ ____ GCF = ____

11. $\frac{65}{90}$ ____ GCF = ____

12. $\frac{45}{72}$ ____ GCF = ____

13. $\frac{35}{85}$ ____ GCF = ____

14. $\frac{30}{42}$ ____ GCF = ____

Solve.

15. Emily exercised from 4:05 P.M. to 4:32 P.M. For what part of an hour did Emily exercise? Write the fraction in simplest form.

_____

16. Luis rode his bike after school for 48 min. For what part of an hour did he ride his bike? Write the fraction in simplest form.

_____

17. Philip played video games for 55 min before dinner. For what part of an hour did he play?

_____

18. What part of an hour is your school lunch time?

_____

19. Survey 12 people to find their favorite kind of pizza from the following choices. Write the results in fraction form. Then shade the pizza shapes using different colors to indicate their choices.

Pizza Favorites

Cheese _____

Green Pepper _____

Olive _____

Mushroom _____

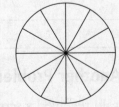

2-3 • Guided Problem Solving

GPS Student Page 84, Exercise 28:

Weather The city of Houston, Texas, typically has 90 clear days out of the 365 days in a year. Houston's clear days represent what fraction of a year? Write your answer in simplest form.

Understand

1. Circle the information you will need to solve.

2. What are you being asked to do?

   _____

   _____

Plan and Carry Out

3. Write the fraction for the expression 90 out of 365.

   _____

4. List the prime factors of 90.

   _____

5. List the prime factors of 365.

   _____

6. List the factors that 90 and 365 have in common.

   _____

7. Divide both 90 and 365 by the common factors.

   _____

8. Write the fraction in simplest form. _____

Check

9. Is 365 ÷ 90 the same as 73 ÷ 18? Explain.

   _____

   _____

Solve Another Problem

10. Gerald received a score of 66 out of 72 on his vocabulary test. Write his score as a fraction in simplest form.

    _____

Practice 2-4

Comparing and Ordering Fractions

Write the two fractions for these models and compare them with <, >, or =.

1.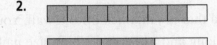

2.

3.

_____   _____   _____

Find the LCD of each pair of fractions.

4. $\frac{5}{8}, \frac{5}{6}$ _____

5. $\frac{5}{12}, \frac{7}{8}$ _____

6. $\frac{9}{10}, \frac{1}{2}$ _____

7. $\frac{1}{6}, \frac{3}{10}$ _____

8. $\frac{1}{4}, \frac{2}{15}$ _____

9. $\frac{5}{6}, \frac{8}{15}$ _____

Compare each pair of fractions. Use <, >, or =.

10. $\frac{7}{8}$ ☐ $\frac{3}{10}$

11. $\frac{6}{12}$ ☐ $\frac{4}{8}$

12. $\frac{7}{15}$ ☐ $\frac{11}{15}$

13. $\frac{4}{5}$ ☐ $\frac{6}{10}$

14. $\frac{8}{15}$ ☐ $\frac{1}{2}$

15. $\frac{10}{15}$ ☐ $\frac{8}{12}$

16. $\frac{4}{9}$ ☐ $\frac{7}{9}$

17. $\frac{1}{2}$ ☐ $\frac{11}{20}$

18. $\frac{7}{16}$ ☐ $\frac{1}{2}$

Order from least to greatest.

19. $\frac{1}{4}, \frac{1}{3}, \frac{1}{6}$ _____

20. $\frac{1}{2}, \frac{5}{6}, \frac{7}{8}$ _____

21. $\frac{1}{4}, \frac{2}{5}, \frac{3}{8}$ _____

22. $\frac{7}{8}, \frac{5}{9}, \frac{2}{3}$ _____

23. $\frac{3}{8}, \frac{5}{6}, \frac{1}{2}$ _____

24. $\frac{9}{10}, \frac{11}{12}, \frac{15}{16}$ _____

25. $\frac{3}{4}, \frac{1}{2}, \frac{7}{8}$ _____

26. $\frac{5}{9}, \frac{2}{3}, \frac{7}{12}$ _____

27. $\frac{15}{16}, \frac{7}{8}, \frac{1}{2}$ _____

Solve.

28. A pattern requires a seam of at least $\frac{5}{8}$ in. Rachel sewed a seam $\frac{1}{2}$ in. wide. Did she sew the seam wide enough? Explain.

_____

29. Marc needs $\frac{3}{4}$ cup of milk for a recipe. He has $\frac{2}{3}$ cup. Does he have enough? Explain.

_____

30. Monica is growing three bean plants as part of a science experiment. Plant A is $\frac{1}{2}$ in. tall. Plant B is $\frac{3}{4}$ in tall. Plant C is $\frac{3}{8}$ in. tall. Order the plants from shortest to tallest.

_____

31. During a rainstorm Willow received $\frac{7}{16}$ in. of rain and Riverton received $\frac{5}{8}$ in. of rain. Which community received more rain?

_____

2-4 • Guided Problem Solving

GPS Student Page 89, Exercise 29:

Carpentry You want to nail a board that is $\frac{1}{2}$ in. thick onto a wall. You can choose from nails that are $\frac{3}{8}$ in. long and $\frac{3}{4}$ in. long. Which size nail is the better choice? Explain.

Understand

1. Circle the information you will need to solve.

2. What are you being asked to do?

   _____

   _____

3. In order to compare fractions what must you do?

   _____

Plan and Carry Out

4. What is the common denominator for $\frac{1}{2}, \frac{3}{8}, \frac{3}{4}$? _____

5. Write an equivalent fraction for $\frac{1}{2}$ and $\frac{3}{4}$
   with the denominator found in Step 4.   _____

6. Which nail is longer than $\frac{4}{8}$ in.?   _____

7. Which size nail is the better
   choice, the $\frac{3}{8}$ in. nail or the $\frac{3}{4}$ in. nail?   _____

8. Explain why you chose the nail you did in Step 8.

   _____

   _____

   _____

Check

9. What is $\frac{3}{4} - \frac{1}{2}$? What is $\frac{3}{8} - \frac{1}{2}$?

   _____

Solve Another Problem

10. Louise used the $\frac{1}{2}$ in., the $\frac{11}{16}$ in., and the $\frac{5}{8}$ in. wrench from her
    dad's toolbox. Now he wants her to put them back in his toolbox
    from smallest to largest. What order should the wrenches be in?

    _____

Practice 2-5

Mixed Numbers and Improper Fractions

1. Write a mixed number and an improper fraction for the model below.

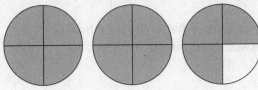

_____

Write each mixed number as an improper fraction.

2. $2\frac{3}{8}$ _____

3. $5\frac{1}{3}$ _____

4. $1\frac{7}{10}$ _____

5. $4\frac{5}{8}$ _____

6. $3\frac{5}{12}$ _____

7. $1\frac{15}{16}$ _____

Write each improper fraction as a mixed number in simplest form.

8. $\frac{25}{3}$ _____

9. $\frac{42}{7}$ _____

10. $\frac{18}{4}$ _____

11. $\frac{27}{12}$ _____

12. $\frac{11}{6}$ _____

13. $\frac{20}{3}$ _____

14. $\frac{125}{5}$ _____

15. $\frac{34}{7}$ _____

16. $\frac{40}{6}$ _____

The distance around the inside of a shopping mall is $\frac{12}{16}$ mi.

17. Juan jogged around the mall 4 times. How far did he jog?

_____

18. Aaron walked around the mall 3 times. How far did he walk?

_____

The distance around an indoor running track is $\frac{1}{6}$ mile.

19. Aruna jogged around the track 16 times. How far did she jog?

_____

20. Theresa walked around the track 22 times. How far did she walk?

_____

21. Shade the figures below to represent $3\frac{5}{8}$. How many eighths are shaded?

_____

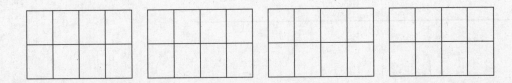

2-5 • Guided Problem Solving

GPS **Student Page 94, Exercise 38:**

A tailor designs a skirt that is $25\frac{1}{4}$ in. long. What is the length in eighths of an inch? Write your answer as an improper fraction.

Understand

1. What are you being asked to do?

_____

_____

2. What is an improper fraction?

_____

_____

3. How many eighths of an inch are in one inch? _____

Plan and Carry Out

4. Write an expression that will be used to solve the problem.

_____

5. In order to combine these two numbers, what must you do first?

_____

6. How many eighths of an inch are in $25\frac{1}{4}$ in. ? _____

7. What is the length in eighths of an inch?

_____

Check

8. Rewrite the answer to Step 7 as a mixed number.

_____

Solve Another Problem

9. There are $8\frac{3}{4}$ cups of flour in a batch of cookies. If there are 6 servings in a batch of cookies, how many cups of flour are in each serving? Write your answer as an improper fraction.

_____

Practice 2-6

Write each fraction as a decimal.

1. $\frac{3}{5}$ _____

2. $\frac{7}{8}$ _____

3. $\frac{7}{9}$ _____

4. $\frac{5}{16}$ _____

5. $\frac{1}{6}$ _____

6. $\frac{5}{8}$ _____

7. $\frac{1}{3}$ _____

8. $\frac{2}{3}$ _____

9. $\frac{9}{10}$ _____

10. $\frac{7}{11}$ _____

11. $\frac{9}{20}$ _____

12. $\frac{3}{4}$ _____

13. $\frac{4}{9}$ _____

14. $\frac{9}{11}$ _____

15. $\frac{11}{20}$ _____

Write each decimal as a mixed number or fraction in simplest form.

16. 0.6 _____

17. 0.45 _____

18. 0.62 _____

19. 0.8 _____

20. 0.325 _____

21. 0.725 _____

22. 4.75 _____

23. 0.33 _____

24. 0.925 _____

25. 3.8 _____

26. 4.7 _____

27. 0.05 _____

28. 0.65 _____

29. 0.855 _____

30. 0.104 _____

31. 0.47 _____

32. 0.894 _____

33. 0.276 _____

Order from least to greatest.

34. $0.\overline{2}, \frac{1}{5}, 0.02$

35. $1.\overline{1}, 1\frac{1}{10}, 1.101$

_____

_____

36. $\frac{6}{5}, 1\frac{5}{6}, 1.\overline{3}$

37. $4.\overline{3}, \frac{9}{2}, 4\frac{3}{7}$

_____

_____

38. A group of gymnasts were asked to name their favorite piece of equipment. 0.33 of the gymnasts chose the vault, $\frac{4}{9}$ chose the beam, and $\frac{1}{7}$ chose the uneven parallel bars. List their choices in order of preference from greatest to least.

_____

2-6 • Guided Problem Solving

GPS Student Page 99, Exercise 28:

Biology DNA content in a cell is measured in picograms (pg). A sea star cell has $\frac{17}{20}$ pg of DNA, a scallop cell has $\frac{19}{25}$ pg, a red water mite cell has 0.19 pg, and a mosquito cell has 0.024 pg. Order the DNA contents from greatest to least.

Understand

1. What are you being asked to do?

_____

2. To order fractions and decimals, what must you do first?

_____

_____

Plan and Carry Out

3. Write the fraction $\frac{17}{20}$ as a decimal. _____

4. Write the fraction $\frac{19}{25}$ as a decimal. _____

5. Which organism has the smallest DNA content? _____

6. Which organism has the largest DNA content? _____

7. Order the DNA contents from greatest to least.

_____

Check

8. Write 0.19 and 0.024 as fractions in simplest form. Order the DNA contents from greatest to least. Does your order check with that of Step 7?

_____

_____

Solve Another Problem

9. A solution calls for 0.25 oz of water, $\frac{2}{3}$ oz of vinegar, 0.6 oz of carbonate, and $\frac{9}{16}$ oz of lemon juice. Order the amounts from least to greatest.

_____

Practice 2-7

Compare. Use <, >, or =.

1. $-\frac{2}{9}$ ☐ $-\frac{4}{9}$

2. $-\frac{1}{6}$ ☐ $-\frac{2}{3}$

3. $-\frac{5}{12}$ ☐ $-\frac{3}{4}$

4. -1.2 ☐ -2.1

5. -0.6 ☐ -0.52

6. -1.23 ☐ -1.25

7. -5.3 ☐ $-5.\overline{3}$

8. $-3\frac{1}{4}$ ☐ -3.25

9. $-4\frac{2}{5}$ ☐ -4.12

Order from least to greatest.

10. $\frac{5}{4}, 1.5, -\frac{3}{2}, -0.5$

11. $\frac{1}{11}, -0.9, 0.09, \frac{1}{10}$

_____

_____

12. $0.1\overline{2}, -\frac{11}{12}, -\frac{1}{6}, -0.1$

13. $\frac{2}{3}, 0.6, -\frac{5}{6}, -6.6$

_____

_____

14. $1.312, 1\frac{3}{8}, -1\frac{3}{10}, -1.33$

15. $1, \frac{4}{5}, -\frac{8}{9}, -1$

_____

_____

Evaluate. Write in simplest form.

16. $\frac{y}{z}$, for $y = -6$ and $z = -20$ _____

17. $\frac{2y}{-z}$, for $y = -5$ and $z = -12$ _____

18. $\frac{y + z}{2z}$, for $y = -4$ and $z = 8$ _____

19. $\frac{-2y + 1}{-z}$, for $y = 3$ and $z = 10$ _____

Compare.

20. The temperature at 3:00 A.M. was $-17.3°$F. By noon the temperature was $-17.8°$F. At what time was it the coldest?

_____

21. Samuel is $\frac{5}{8}$ in. taller than Jackie. Shelly is 0.7 in. taller than Jackie. Who is the tallest?

_____

2-7 • Guided Problem Solving

GPS Student Page 105, Exercise 29:

Animals About $\frac{1}{25}$ of a toad's eggs survive to adulthood. About 0.25 of a frog's eggs and $\frac{1}{5}$ of a green turtle's eggs survive to adulthood. Which animal's eggs have the highest survival rate?

Understand

1. Circle the information you will need to solve.

2. What are you being asked to do?

   _____

   _____

3. In order to find the greatest number, what must you do first?

   _____

Plan and Carry Out

4. Write $\frac{1}{25}$ as a decimal. _____

5. Write $\frac{1}{5}$ as a decimal. _____

6. Which is the largest decimal,
   0.04, 0.2, or 0.25? _____

7. Which animal's eggs have
   the highest survival rate? _____

Check

8. What fraction is 0.25 equal to? Is it the greatest value?

   _____

Solve Another Problem

9. In order to organize the nails in a garage, Anne and Jeff measured the nails. Anne used fractions to measure her 3 groups of nails and found that they were $\frac{3}{5}$ in., $\frac{7}{12}$ in., and $\frac{4}{9}$ in. Jeff used decimals to measure his two groups and found that they were 0.62 in., and 0.31 in. Which nail is the longest?

   _____

Practice 2-8

Scientific Notation

• •

Write each number in scientific notation.

1. 73,000,000

2. 4,300

3. 510

4. 56,870

_____

_____

_____

_____

5. 68,900

6. 98,000,000,000

7. 4,890,000

8. 38

_____

_____

_____

_____

9. 120,000

10. 543,000

11. 27

12. 54,000

_____

_____

_____

_____

Write in standard form.

13. 5.7×10^6

14. 2.45×10^8

15. 4.706×10^{11}

_____

_____

_____

16. 8×10^1

17. 7.2×10^3

18. 1.63×10^{12}

_____

_____

_____

19. 8.03×10^{14}

20. 3.26×10^4

21. 5.179×10^5

_____

_____

_____

Write each number in scientific notation.

22. One type of roundworm can lay 200,000 eggs each day.

_____

23. The nose of a German shepherd dog has about 220 million cells that are used in picking out smells.

_____

24. The brain contains about 100 trillion nerve connections.

_____

25. During an average life span, the human heart will beat about 2,800,000,000 times.

_____

26. The volume of the water behind the Grand Coulee Dam is about 10.6 million cubic yards.

_____

27. A second has been defined as the time it takes for an atom of a particular metal to vibrate 9,192,631,770 times.

_____

2-8 • Guided Problem Solving

GPS Student Page 109, Exercise 31:

Plants There are about 350,000 species of plants on Earth. Write this number in scientific notation.

Understand

1. What are you being asked to do?

    _____

    _____

2. How do you write a number in scientific notation?

    _____

    _____

    _____

    _____

Plan and Carry Out

3. How many places do you move the decimal point so that you obtain a factor greater than 1 and less than 10?

    _____

4. What is the exponent on the power of 10?

    _____

5. What are the two factors? _____

6. Write the number in scientific notation. _____

Check

7. Multiply $3.5 \times 100,000$. Does your answer check?

    _____

Solve Another Problem

8. In July 2002, the population of the United States was 287,509,286. Write this number in scientific notation.

    _____

2A: Graphic Organizer

Study Skill Develop consistent study habits. Block off the same amount of time each evening for schoolwork. Plan ahead by setting aside extra time when you have a big project or test coming up.

Write your answers.

1. What is the chapter title? _____

2. How many lessons are there in this chapter? _____

3. What is the topic of the Test-Taking Strategies page? _____

4. Complete the graphic organizer below as you work through the chapter.
   • In the center, write the title of the chapter.
   • When you begin a lesson, write the lesson name in a rectangle.
   • When you complete a lesson, write a skill or key concept in a circle linked to that lesson block.
   • When you complete the chapter, use this graphic organizer to help you review.

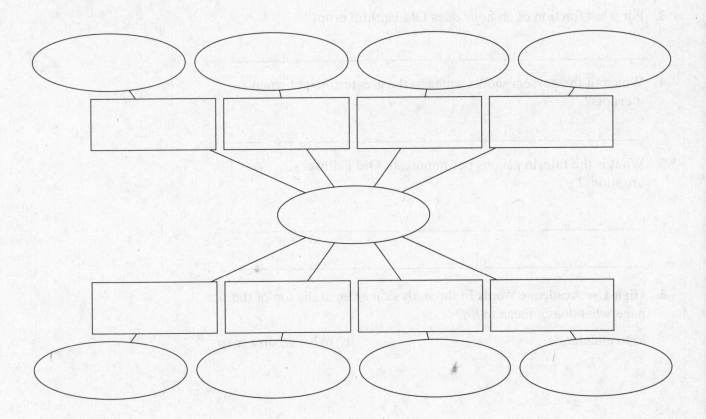

2B: Reading Comprehension

For use after Lesson 2-5

Study Skill Never go to class unprepared. List your assignments, books needed, and supplies to help you prepare.

Read the paragraph and answer the questions.

Old Faithful is the most famous geyser at Yellowstone National Park. It erupts approximately every $1\frac{1}{4}$ hours for up to 5 minutes. When it erupts, a mixture of water and steam shoots into the air as high as 170 feet. The amount of water expelled during each eruption ranges from 10,000 to 12,000 gallons. Giant Geyser and Steamboat Geyser, two other geysers at Yellowstone, shoot water to heights of 200 feet and 380 feet, respectively.

1. What is the paragraph about?

   _____

2. Which number in the paragraph is written as a mixed number?

   _____

3. For what fraction of an hour does Old Faithful erupt?

   _____

4. Which of the geysers shoots water to the greatest height when it erupts?

   _____

5. What is the rate, in gallons per minute, of Old Faithful's eruptions?

   _____

   _____

6. **High-Use Academic Words** In the study skill given at the top of the page, what does it mean to *list*?

   a. to enumerate   b. to locate on a map

Vocabulary and Study Skills

2C: Reading/Writing Math Symbols

For use after Lesson 2-7

Study Skill Use flashcards to help you memorize math symbols and their meanings.

Write each statement in words.

1. $-7 < 6$ _____

2. $4^3 = 64$ _____

3. $-3 > -5$ _____

4. $|-5| = 5$ _____

5. $3^2 = 9$ _____

6. $3.01 \approx 3$ _____

7. $\frac{8}{4} = 2$ _____

8. $\frac{1}{3} < \frac{3}{5}$ _____

9. $4.\overline{6} > 0$ _____

10. $5^4 = 625$ _____

Write each statement using mathematical symbols.

11. Three and seven tenths is less than 4 and one–half.

   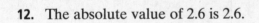

12. The absolute value of 2.6 is 2.6.

   _____

13. Negative three-fourths is greater than negative ten.

   _____

14. Four and three tenths is approximately equal to four point three repeating.

   _____

15. Two raised to the fifth power is thirty-two.

   _____

16. Six cubed is two hundred sixteen.

   _____

2D: Visual Vocabulary Practice

For use after Lesson 2-8

Study Skill Mathematics builds on itself, so build a strong foundation.

Concept List

equivalent fractions	greatest common factor	improper fraction
least common denominator	least common multiple	prime factorization
repeating decimal	scientific notation	simplest form

Write the concept that best describes each exercise. Choose from the concept list above.

1. $\dfrac{6}{4}$ _____	**2.** The number 24 represents this for the numbers 48 and 72. _____	**3.** $0.312312312\ldots = 0.\overline{312}$ _____
4. $\dfrac{1}{2} \quad = \quad \dfrac{3}{6}$ _____	**5.** The number 12 represents this for the fractions $\dfrac{1}{6}$ and $\dfrac{3}{4}$. _____	**6.** $0.00034 = 3.4 \times 10^{-4}$ _____
7. The number 60 represents this for the numbers 12 and 15. _____	**8.** $\dfrac{3}{20}$ _____	**9.** $108 = 2^2 \cdot 3^3$ _____

2E: Vocabulary Check

Study Skill Strengthen your vocabulary. Use these pages and add cues and summaries by applying the Cornell Notetaking style.

Write the definition for each word or term at the right. To check your work, fold the paper back along the dotted line to see the correct answers.

_____ exponent

_____

_____

_____ composite number

_____

_____

_____ mixed number

_____

_____

_____ terminating decimal

_____

_____

_____ simplest form

_____

_____

2E: Vocabulary Check (continued)

Write the vocabulary word or term for each definition. To check your work, fold the paper forward along the dotted line to see the correct answers.

how many times a number, or base, is used as a factor

_____

a whole number that has more than two factors

_____

the sum of a whole number and a fraction

_____

a decimal that stops, or terminates

_____

a fraction where the numerator and denominator have no common factors other than 1

_____

2F: Vocabulary Review Puzzle

For use with the Chapter Review

Study Skill Use a notebook or a section of a loose-leaf binder for math assignments. Review problems that gave you trouble.

Unscramble each of the key words from the chapter to help you fill in the famous quote by Lewis Carroll. Match the letters in the numbered cells with the numbered cells at the bottom.

NENPTEXO
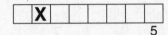

FECINCITSI NATNOOTI

OPWER

LORNIATA RUNMEB

SIVIEBIDL
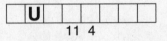

TARTEEGS COOMNM RAOFTC

MIEPLLUT

LESAT COOMNM METLULPI
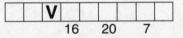

RIPME MUNREB

MIEDX MUEBRN

ROMPIERP FRTAINOC

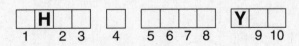

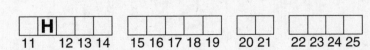

Practice 3-1

Estimating With Fractions and Mixed Numbers

Estimate each sum or difference.

1. $\frac{1}{6} + \frac{5}{8}$ _____

2. $\frac{7}{8} - \frac{1}{16}$ _____

3. $\frac{9}{10} + \frac{7}{8}$ _____

4. $\frac{1}{10} + \frac{5}{6}$ _____

5. $\frac{4}{5} - \frac{1}{6}$ _____

6. $\frac{11}{12} - \frac{5}{16}$ _____

7. $2\frac{1}{6} + 7\frac{1}{9}$ _____

8. $4\frac{9}{10} - 3\frac{5}{8}$ _____

9. $4\frac{7}{8} + 8\frac{1}{5}$ _____

10. $14\frac{3}{4} + 9\frac{7}{8}$ _____

11. $7\frac{11}{15} - 6\frac{7}{16}$ _____

12. $3\frac{11}{15} - 2\frac{9}{10}$ _____

Estimate each product or quotient.

13. $13\frac{1}{8} \div 6\frac{1}{5}$ _____

14. $5\frac{1}{6} \cdot 8\frac{4}{5}$ _____

15. $8\frac{1}{6} \div 1\frac{9}{10}$ _____

16. $27\frac{6}{7} \div 3\frac{2}{3}$ _____

17. $20\frac{4}{5} \cdot 2\frac{2}{7}$ _____

18. $9\frac{1}{3} \div 2\frac{7}{8}$ _____

19. $19\frac{4}{5} \div 4\frac{5}{8}$ _____

20. $9\frac{2}{13} \div 3\frac{1}{18}$ _____

21. $42\frac{1}{6} \div 6\frac{1}{16}$ _____

22. $15\frac{1}{20} \cdot 3\frac{1}{10}$ _____

23. $72\frac{2}{15} \div 8\frac{3}{4}$ _____

24. $3\frac{5}{6} \cdot 10\frac{1}{12}$ _____

Solve each problem.

25. Each dress for a wedding party requires $7\frac{1}{8}$ yd of material. Estimate the amount of material you would need to make 6 dresses.

_____

26. A fabric store has $80\frac{3}{8}$ yd of a particular fabric. About how many pairs of curtains could be made from this fabric if each pair requires $4\frac{1}{8}$ yd of fabric?

_____

27. Adam's car can hold $16\frac{1}{10}$ gal of gasoline. About how many gallons are left if he started with a full tank and has used $11\frac{9}{10}$ gal?

_____

28. Julia bought stock at $\$28\frac{1}{8}$ per share. The value of each stock increased by $\$6\frac{5}{8}$. About how much is each share of stock now worth?

_____

Estimate each answer.

29. $6\frac{2}{9} - 2\frac{7}{8}$ _____

30. $\frac{1}{8} + \frac{9}{10}$ _____

31. $8\frac{2}{9} \cdot 10\frac{4}{9}$ _____

32. $6\frac{1}{4} \div 2\frac{3}{11}$ _____

33. $5\frac{1}{11} \cdot 8\frac{13}{15}$ _____

34. $\frac{21}{40} - \frac{5}{89}$ _____

35. $\frac{81}{100} - \frac{1}{2}$ _____

36. $11\frac{5}{9} \div 2\frac{1}{2}$ _____

37. $\frac{3}{5} + \frac{7}{8}$ _____

Name _____ Class _____ Date _____

3-1 • Guided Problem Solving

GPS **Student Page 123, Exercise 43:**

Writing in Math You need $9\frac{9}{16}$ lb of chicken. The store sells chicken in half-pound packages. How much chicken should you order? Explain.

Understand

1. What are you being asked to do?

   _____

2. How do you know when to round up or when to round down with a fraction?

   _____

   _____

   _____

Plan and Carry Out

3. What is the numerator of the fraction? _____

4. What is half of the denominator of the fraction? _____

5. Is the numerator bigger or smaller than half of the denominator? _____

6. Do you round the fraction up or down? _____

7. How many pounds of chicken do you need? _____

8. How many packages of chicken will you need to buy? _____

Check

9. What is 9 ÷ 16? Round to the nearest whole number. Does your answer make sense?

   _____

   _____

   _____

Solve Another Problem

10. You are making curtains to cover the top of four windows. Each window is $15\frac{5}{8}$ in. wide. You buy material by the whole yard. How many yards should you buy?

   _____

Practice 3-2

Adding and Subtracting Fractions

Write a number statement for each model.

1.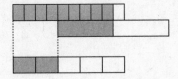

_____

2.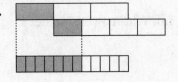

_____

3.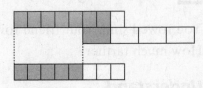

_____

Find each sum or difference.

4. $\frac{1}{6} + \frac{7}{8}$ _____

5. $\frac{9}{10} - \frac{1}{6}$ _____

6. $\frac{1}{6} + \frac{1}{6}$ _____

7. $\frac{1}{10} + \frac{2}{5}$ _____

8. $\frac{5}{6} + \frac{1}{12}$ _____

9. $\frac{2}{3} - \frac{1}{2}$ _____

10. $\frac{7}{9} - \frac{1}{3}$ _____

11. $\frac{3}{4} - \frac{1}{4}$ _____

12. $\frac{1}{5} + \frac{3}{4}$ _____

13. $\frac{1}{3} + \frac{1}{2}$ _____

14. $\frac{1}{8} + \frac{1}{12}$ _____

15. $\frac{7}{10} - \frac{1}{3}$ _____

Use the table at the right for Exercises 16–21. Tell which two snacks combine to make each amount.

Snack	Serving Amount
Raisins	$\frac{1}{4}$ c
Walnuts	$\frac{3}{8}$ c
Almonds	$\frac{1}{8}$ c
Sesame sticks	$\frac{2}{3}$ c
Mini pretzels	$\frac{5}{8}$ c
Dried apricots	$\frac{1}{6}$ c

16. $\frac{5}{6}$ c _____

17. $\frac{1}{2}$ c _____

18. $\frac{3}{4}$ c _____

19. $\frac{11}{12}$ c _____

20. 1 c _____

21. $\frac{19}{24}$ c _____

_____

Solve each equation.

22. $\frac{2}{3} + x = \frac{4}{6}$

_____

23. $s - \frac{1}{5} = \frac{2}{10}$

_____

24. $b - \frac{4}{12} = \frac{8}{12}$

_____

25. $c + \frac{1}{6} = \frac{5}{12}$

_____

26. $\frac{3}{8} + d = \frac{7}{8}$

_____

27. $f - \frac{1}{10} = \frac{2}{5}$

_____

Course 2 Lesson 3-2

3-2 • Guided Problem Solving

GPS **Student Page 129, Exercise 40:**

You rowed $\frac{2}{3}$ mi. Your friend rowed $\frac{8}{10}$ mi. Who rowed farther?
How much farther?

Understand

1. Circle the information you will need to solve.

2. What are you being asked to do?

   _____

   _____

3. In order to subtract fractions what needs to be true about the denominators?

   _____

Plan and Carry Out

4. How far did you row? _____

5. How far did your friend row? _____

6. What is the common denominator for
   the two fractions in Steps 4 and 5? _____

7. Write the two numbers with a common
   denominator. _____

8. Who rowed farther? _____

9. How much farther? _____

Check

10. Write a sum you can use to check the answer.

   _____

Solve Another Problem

11. A cherry cheesecake was cut into 15 pieces. You ate $\frac{4}{15}$ of the
   cheesecake and your brother ate $\frac{1}{3}$ of the cheesecake. How much
   was left?

   _____

   _____

Practice 3-3

Find each sum.

1. $5\frac{1}{3} + 3\frac{2}{3}$

2. $7\frac{1}{4} + 4\frac{3}{8}$

3. $2\frac{1}{8} + 6\frac{5}{8}$

_____

_____

_____

4. $8\frac{1}{5} + 4\frac{3}{10}$

5. $9\frac{1}{6} + 6\frac{1}{4}$

6. $3\frac{2}{3} + 10\frac{5}{6}$

_____

_____

_____

Find each difference.

7. $6\frac{11}{12} - 4\frac{5}{12}$

8. $12 - 5\frac{3}{10}$

9. $14\frac{1}{2} - 7\frac{1}{5}$

_____

_____

_____

10. $9 - 5\frac{5}{6}$

11. $13\frac{3}{4} - 10\frac{1}{2}$

12. $15\frac{1}{6} - 6\frac{5}{12}$

_____

_____

_____

Find each sum or difference.

13. $1\frac{1}{6} - \frac{3}{4}$

14. $4\frac{1}{2} - 2\frac{7}{8}$

15. $9\frac{3}{4} + 7\frac{7}{8}$

_____

_____

_____

16. $5\frac{1}{6} - 4\frac{7}{12}$

17. $9\frac{8}{15} + 11\frac{5}{12}$

18. $\frac{14}{15} - \frac{1}{2}$

_____

_____

_____

Write a mixed number for each time period. Be sure each fraction is in lowest terms.

19. 8:00 A.M. to 9:20 A.M.

20. 9:00 A.M. to 2:45 P.M.

_____

_____

21. 11:00 A.M. to 3:55 P.M.

22. 8:30 A.M. to 10:40 P.M.

_____

_____

3-3 • Guided Problem Solving

GPS **Student Page 133, Exercise 29:**

On Saturday you hiked $4\frac{3}{8}$ mi. On Sunday, you hiked $3\frac{1}{2}$ mi. How far did you hike during the weekend?

Understand

1. Circle the information you will need to solve.

2. What are you being asked to do?

   _____

3. Estimate the sum of the distances.

   _____

Plan and Carry Out

4. Add the whole numbers.   _____

5. In order to add $\frac{3}{8} + \frac{1}{2}$, what do you need to find first?

   _____

6. What is the common denominator for $\frac{3}{8} + \frac{1}{2}$? _____

7. Add. $\frac{3}{8} + \frac{1}{2}$ _____

8. Add. $7 + \frac{7}{8}$ _____

9. How far did you hike during the weekend?   _____

Check

10. Is your answer reasonable according to the estimate you made in Step 3?

    _____

    _____

Solve Another Problem

11. On a white-water rafting trip you paddled $1\frac{3}{4}$ mi the first day and $2\frac{3}{8}$ mi the second day. How many miles did you raft on both days?

    _____

Practice 3-4

Multiplying Fractions and Mixed Numbers

Find each product.

1. $\frac{5}{6} \cdot \frac{3}{5}$ _____

2. $\frac{7}{8} \cdot \frac{4}{5}$ _____

3. $\frac{9}{10} \cdot \frac{5}{12}$ _____

4. $\frac{5}{8} \cdot \frac{3}{5}$ _____

5. $\frac{1}{6}$ of 36 _____

6. $\frac{5}{9} \cdot 36$ _____

7. $\frac{3}{4} \cdot 36$ _____

8. $2 \cdot \frac{9}{10}$ _____

9. $8 \cdot \frac{9}{10}$ _____

10. $\frac{1}{3} \cdot 3\frac{1}{3}$ _____

11. $\frac{5}{6}$ of $1\frac{3}{5}$ _____

12. $\frac{1}{8}$ of $1\frac{4}{5}$ _____

13. $3 \cdot 4\frac{1}{2}$ _____

14. $5 \cdot 2\frac{1}{4}$ _____

15. $3 \cdot 2\frac{2}{3}$ _____

16. $3\frac{2}{3} \cdot 1\frac{1}{2}$ _____

17. $4\frac{1}{6} \cdot 2\frac{2}{5}$ _____

18. $3\frac{1}{4} \cdot 2\frac{1}{6}$ _____

Solve.

19. A sheet of plywood is $\frac{5}{8}$ in. thick. How tall is a stack of 21 sheets of plywood?

   _____

20. A poster measures 38 cm across. If a photocopy machine is used to make a copy that is $\frac{3}{5}$ of the original size, what is the width of the copy?

   _____

21. A one-kilogram object weighs about $2\frac{1}{5}$ pounds. Find the weight, in pounds, of a computer monitor with mass $7\frac{3}{8}$ kilograms.

   _____

22. The population of Sweden is about $1\frac{11}{16}$ times as great as the population of Denmark. Find the population of Sweden if the population of Denmark is about 5,190,000.

   _____

Course 2 Lesson 3-4

3-4 • Guided Problem Solving

GPS Student Page 139, Exercise 39:

The length of a track around a field is $\frac{1}{4}$ mi. You jog
$3\frac{1}{2}$ times around the track. How far do you jog?

Understand

1. Circle the information you will need to solve.

2. What are you being asked to do?

   _____

3. What operation will you use to solve the problem?

   _____

Plan and Carry Out

4. What is the length of the track?   _____

5. How many times did you run
   around the track?   _____

6. Write a multiplication expression
   to solve the problem.   _____

7. How far do you jog?

Check

8. How many times would you have to run around the track to run
   one mile? Is your answer reasonable? Explain.

   _____

   _____

Solve Another Problem

9. One can of paint covers $2\frac{1}{2}$ walls. You have $\frac{3}{4}$ of a can of paint.
   How many walls can you paint?

   _____

Practice 3-5

Dividing Fractions and Mixed Numbers

Find the reciprocal of each number.

1. $\frac{1}{2}$ _____

2. $\frac{9}{16}$ _____

3. $\frac{4}{5}$ _____

4. $1\frac{1}{4}$ _____

5. $2\frac{9}{10}$ _____

6. $3\frac{1}{6}$ _____

Find each quotient.

7. $\frac{3}{4} \div \frac{1}{4}$ _____

8. $\frac{5}{6} \div \frac{1}{12}$ _____

9. $\frac{1}{12} \div \frac{5}{6}$ _____

10. $6 \div \frac{3}{4}$ _____

11. $5 \div \frac{9}{10}$ _____

12. $\frac{4}{5} \div 2$ _____

13. $\frac{7}{8} \div 3$ _____

14. $\frac{4}{9} \div 8$ _____

15. $1\frac{1}{2} \div \frac{2}{3}$ _____

16. $\frac{3}{4} \div 1\frac{1}{3}$ _____

17. $2\frac{1}{2} \div 1\frac{1}{4}$ _____

18. $1\frac{3}{4} \div \frac{3}{4}$ _____

19. $1\frac{7}{10} \div \frac{1}{2}$ _____

20. $4\frac{1}{2} \div 2\frac{1}{2}$ _____

21. $6 \div 3\frac{4}{5}$ _____

22. $4\frac{3}{4} \div \frac{7}{8}$ _____

23. $5\frac{5}{6} \div 1\frac{1}{3}$ _____

24. $3\frac{3}{8} \div 1\frac{1}{4}$ _____

25. $6\frac{1}{2} \div 1\frac{1}{2}$ _____

26. $2\frac{9}{10} \div 1\frac{3}{4}$ _____

27. $3\frac{1}{4} \div 1\frac{1}{3}$ _____

Solve each problem.

28. Rosa makes $2\frac{1}{2}$ c of pudding. How many $\frac{1}{3}$ c servings can she get from the pudding?

_____

29. One type of lightning bug glows once every $1\frac{1}{2}$ s. How many times can it glow in 1 min?

_____

30. Bea can run $\frac{1}{6}$ mi in 2 min. How long should it take her to run 2 mi?

_____

31. Joe drives 20 mi in $\frac{1}{2}$ h. How long will it take him to drive 50 mi?

_____

3-5 • Guided Problem Solving

GPS Student Page 145, Exercise 44:

Biology A manatee can swim 5 mi in $1\frac{1}{4}$ h. If the manatee swims at the same average speed, how far can it swim in 1 h?

Understand

1. Circle the information you will need to solve.

2. What are you being asked to do?

_____

_____

Plan and Carry Out

3. Write a ratio comparing 5 miles to $1\frac{1}{4}$ hours.

_____

4. Write a ratio comparing *x* miles to 1 hour.

_____

5. Write a proportion comparing the ratios in Steps 3 and 4.

_____

6. How far can the manatee swim in 1 hour?

_____

Check

7. Will the manatee swim more or less than 5 miles in 1 hour? Is your answer reasonable? Explain.

_____

_____

Solve Another Problem

8. Glenda ran 8 miles in $2\frac{1}{2}$ hours. If she runs at the same average speed, how far can she run in 1 hour?

_____

_____

Practice 3-6

Tell whether you would multiply or divide to change from one unit of measure to the other.

1. tons to pounds

_____

2. pints to quarts

_____

3. feet to yards

_____

4. gallons to pints

_____

5. cups to quarts

_____

6. pounds to ounces

_____

Change each unit of length, capacity, or weight.

7. 9 qt = _____ gal

8. $2\frac{1}{4}$ t = _____ lb

9. $3\frac{1}{2}$ yd = _____ in.

10. 4 yd = _____ ft

11. 60 c = _____ qt

12. 246 in. = _____ ft

13. 1,750 oz = _____ lb

14. 84 ft = _____ yd

15. 198 in. = _____ yd

16. 480 fl oz = _____ pt

17. $\frac{1}{4}$ gal = _____ fl oz

18. $\frac{1}{2}$ mi = _____ ft

19. $\frac{1}{10}$ mi = _____ in.

20. 2 lb 6 oz = _____ lb

21. 2 qt 8 fl oz = _____ qt

Solve.

22. United States farms produced 2,460,000,000 bushels of soybeans in 1994. How many quarts is this? (A bushel is 32 quarts.)

_____

23. In 1994, Brian Berg built an 81-story "house" using playing cards. The house was $15\frac{2}{3}$ ft tall. How many inches is this?

_____

Choose an appropriate customary unit of measure.

24. capacity of a mug

_____

25. length of a family room

_____

26. distance between two capital cities

_____

27. capacity of a shampoo bottle

_____

3-6 • Guided Problem Solving

GPS **Student Page 151, Exercise 42:**

The length of the Amazon River in South America is about 4,000 mi.
How many feet is this?

Understand

1. Circle the information you will need to solve.

2. What are you being asked to do?

_____

_____

Plan and Carry Out

3. How many feet are there in 1 mile?

_____

4. Do you multiply or divide to find the number of feet in 4,000 miles?

_____

5. Write a multiplication expression to solve this problem.

_____

6. How many feet are there in 4,000 mi?

_____

Check

7. Should the number of feet in 4,000 miles be more or less than 4,000? Explain why.

_____

_____

Solve Another Problem

8. A fishing boat is working 90 miles from shore. How many feet from shore is this?

_____

Practice 3-7

Underline the more precise measurement.

1. 23 oz, 20.7 oz   2. 1,830 g, 2.5 kg   3. 63.7 L, 63.70 L

4. 3.7 t, 5,610 lb   5. 58.3 cm, 4.6 m   6. 12 L, 1,735 mL

7. 3,008 pt, 0.95 pt   8. 7.3 min, 516 sec   9. 2.7 mL, 12 mL

10. 26.4 cm, 8.39 cm   11. 216 ft, 3,106 in.   12. 4.1 lb, 6.123 lb

Find each sum or difference. Round your answer to match the less precise measurement.

13. 6.35 oz + 4.2 oz   14. 83 g − 1.8 g   15. 4.20 yd + 8.64 yd

_____   _____   _____

16. 21 cm + 53.60 cm   17. 5.382 m + 8 m   18. 6.4 ft + 4300 ft

_____   _____   _____

19. 2.713 mL + 8.4 mL   20. 50 lb − 4.6 lb   21. 6.83 km + 10.3 km

_____   _____   _____

22. Boundary Peak in Nevada is 13,000 ft high. Guadalupe Peak in Texas is 8,749.75 ft high. How much higher than Guadalupe Peak is Boundary Peak? Round your answer to match the less precise measurement.

_____

23. You measure the area of your garden as 9 yd wide by 11 yd long. Your brother measures the garden as $27\frac{1}{2}$ ft wide by $32\frac{3}{4}$ ft long. Whose measurement is more precise? Why?

_____

_____

_____

3-7 • Guided Problem Solving

GPS **Student Page 157, Exercise 35:**

A climber ascends 2,458.75 ft up a 3,000-ft mountainside. How much farther does the climber have to go to reach the top? Round your answer appropriately.

Understand

1. Circle the information you will need to solve.

2. What are you being asked to do?

   _____

   _____

3. Which measurement is the least precise? Explain.

   _____

4. What will you round to?

   _____

Plan and Carry Out

5. How far has the climber climbed? _____

6. How tall is the mountain? _____

7. What is the difference between
   3,000 ft and 2,458.75 ft? _____

8. Round the answer in Step 7
   to the least precise measurement. _____

Check

9. Round 2,458.75 ft to the nearest whole number. Subtract this from 3,000 ft. Is your answer reasonable?

   _____

   _____

Solve Another Problem

10. Aaron used 3.25 oz of peanut butter and 0.5 oz of marshmallow cream for a fruit dip. How many ounces did he use in total? Round your answer appropriately.

    _____

3A: Graphic Organizer

For use before Lesson 3-1

Study Skill You should fully understand the basic concepts in each chapter before moving on to more complex material. Be sure to ask questions when you are not comfortable with what you have learned.

Write your answers.

1. What is the chapter title? _____

2. How many lessons are there in this chapter? _____

3. What is the topic of the Test-Taking Strategies page? _____

4. Complete the graphic organizer below as you work through the chapter.
   • In the center, write the title of the chapter.
   • When you begin a lesson, write the lesson name in a rectangle.
   • When you complete a lesson, write a skill or key concept in a circle linked to that lesson block.
   • When you complete the chapter, use this graphic organizer to help you review.

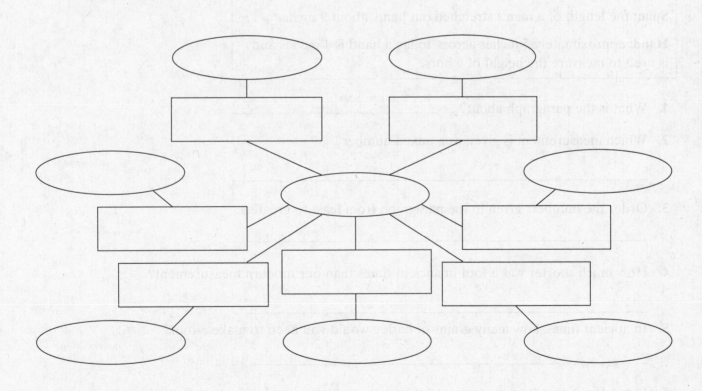

3B: Reading Comprehension

For use after Lesson 3-6

Study Skill Make a realistic study schedule. Set specific goals for yourself, rather than general ones. For example, read Chapter 2, do problems 1–20, or study for a math test before doing homework.

Read the paragraph below and answer the questions.

In ancient times, people measured things by comparing them to parts of the body. For example, a foot length or a finger width was considered an acceptable measurement. Later, other common objects were used to represent measurements. Below is a list of some common lengths and their early standards of measurement.

Inch: the width of a man's thumb, 3 grains of barley placed end to end

Foot: the length of an average man's foot, about $11\frac{1}{42}$ inches

Yard: the length of a man's belt, or the distance from a man's nose to the tip of his outstretched arm

Span: the length of a man's stretched out hand, about 9 inches

Hand: approximately 5 inches across, today a hand is 4 inches and is used to measure the height of a horse

1. What is the paragraph about? _____

2. Which measurement is given as a mixed number?

    _____

3. Order the numbers given in the paragraph from least to greatest.

    _____

4. How much shorter was a foot in ancient times than our modern measurement?

    _____

5. In ancient times, how many grains of barley would you need to make a foot?

    _____

6. In modern times, how many grains of barley would you need to make a foot?

    _____

7. **High-Use Academic Words** In question three, what does it mean to *order*?

    a. to arrange information in a sequence   b. to determine the value of

3C: Reading/Writing Math Symbols

For use after Lesson 3-6

Study Skill Read problems carefully. Pay special attention to units when working with measurements.

Match the abbreviation in Column A with its appropriate U.S. customary units in Column B.

Column A	Column B
1. lb	**A.** ounces
2. c	**B.** quarts
3. oz	**C.** pounds
4. yd	**D.** pints
5. pt	**E.** gallons
6. ft	**F.** yards
7. qt	**G.** feet
8. gal	**H.** cups

Write each of the following using appropriate mathematical symbols.

9. one hundred kilometers _____

10. forty-seven pounds _____

11. three and seven tenths ounces _____

12. two and five-tenths milliliters _____

13. five and thirty three hundredths grams _____

14. four and three-quarter inches _____

15. thirteen meters _____

16. five and one-third tons _____

3D: Visual Vocabulary Practice

For use after Lesson 3-5

High-Use Academic Words

Study Skill When learning a new concept, try to draw a picture to illustrate it.

Concept List

compare	table	estimate
equivalent	convert	define
order	figure	sum

Write the concept that best describes each exercise. Choose from the concept list above.

1. 3 yd = 9 ft _____	2. $-5 + 20 + 13 + (-2) = 26$ _____	3. Two numbers are *reciprocals* if their product is one. _____
4. 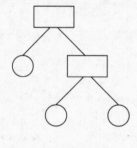 _____	5. $5^2 < 2^5$ _____	6. $\frac{2}{5}$ and $\frac{4}{10}$ _____
7. $-28, 4, \frac{1}{2}, -2, 0.1$ $-28, -2, 0.1, \frac{1}{2}, 4$ _____	8. $23.15 + 5.79 \approx 23 + 6$ _____	9. **Average Lifespan** | Insect	Weeks
---	---
Ant	4
Butterfly	2
Cockroach	104
Mosquito	2	 _____

Vocabulary and Study Skills

3E: Vocabulary Check

Study Skill Strengthen your vocabulary. Use these pages and add cues and summaries by applying the Cornell Notetaking style.

Write the definition for each word or term at the right. To check your work, fold the paper back along the dotted line to see the correct answers.

_____ benchmark

_____
_____

_____ precision
_____

_____
_____

_____ reciprocals
_____

_____
_____

_____ mean
_____

_____
_____

_____ opposites
_____

_____

Vocabulary and Study Skills

3E: Vocabulary Check (continued)　　For use after Lesson 3-7

Write the definition for each word or term at the right. To check your work, fold the paper forward along the dotted line to see the correct answers.

a convenient number used to replace fractions that are less than 1

_____

the exactness of a measurement, determined by the unit of measure

_____

two numbers whose product is 1

_____

the sum of the data divided by the number of data items

_____

two numbers that are the same distance from 0 on the number line, but in opposite directions

_____

3F: Vocabulary Review Puzzle

For use with the Chapter Review

Study Skill Take short breaks between assignments. You will be able to concentrate on a new assignment more easily if you take a brief "time out" before starting.

Complete the crossword puzzle using the words below. For help, use the glossary in your textbook.

improper fraction   denominator   numerator   benchmark   mode

mixed number   precision   composite   median   prime

ACROSS

4. number with more than two factors

7. number that is in the middle of a data set when the values are ranked in order from least to greatest

10. sum of a whole number and a fraction

DOWN

1. refers to the degree of exactness

2. value that can be used as a reference point

3. bottom number in a fraction

5. number with exactly two factors

6. numerator is greater than or equal to the denominator

8. top number in a fraction

9. number that occurs most often in a data set

Practice 4-1

Evaluating and Writing Algebraic Expressions

Evaluate each expression using the values $m = 7$, $r = 8$, and $t = 2$.

1. $5m - 6$

2. $4m + t$

3. $r \div t$

_____

4. $m \times t$

5. $5t + 2m$

6. $r \times m$

_____

7. $3m - 5t$

8. $(m \times r) \div t$

9. mrt

_____

10. Write an algebraic expression for the nth term of the table below.

A	0	1	2	3	4	5	n
B	3	5	7	9	11	13	?

_____

Write a word phrase for each algebraic expression.

11. $n + 16$

12. $3.2n$

13. $25.6 - n$

_____

14. $n \div 24$

15. $\frac{45}{n}$

16. $15.4 - n$

_____

Write an algebraic expression for each word phrase.

17. 12 more than m machines

18. six times the daily amount of fiber f in your diet

_____

19. your aunt's age a minus 25

20. the total number of seashells s divided by 10

_____

21. You and four friends plan a surprise party. Each of you contributes the same amount of money m for food.

   a. Write an algebraic expression for the total amount of money contributed for food. _____

   b. Evaluate your expression for $m = \$5.25$. _____

4-1 • Guided Problem Solving

GPS Student Page 172, Exercise 38:

Estimation This section of a page from a telephone directory shows a column with 11 names in 1 inch. Each page has four 10-inch columns. Write an algebraic expression for the approximate number of names in p pages of the directory.

6-4462	**Daalling V** 8 Everett All..........
2-3302	~~Daasin K 444 Crowley R~~..........
4-1775	**Dabady V** 94 Burnside All........
2-0014	**Dabagh L** 13 Lancaster R........
6-3356	**Dabagh W** Dr 521 Weston All...
4-7322	**Dabar G** 98 River All...............
6-1530	**Dabarera F** 34 Rosiland All......
2-2279	**Dabas M** 17 Riverside R...........
4-9978	**D'Abate D** 86 Moss Hill Rd All...
2-6745	**D'Abate G** 111 South Central R
4-5456	**Dabbous H** 670 Warren Dr All..
6-3064	**Dabbraccio F** 151 Century All..
6-2257	**Dabby D** 542 Walnut All...........
2-9987	................................Green R...
6-5643	**Dabcovich M** 72 Main All..........

Understand

1. What are you being asked to do?

_____

_____

2. What is an algebraic expression?

_____

_____

3. What does p represent?

_____

_____

Plan and Carry Out

4. How many names are in 1 in. of one column? _____

5. How many names are in one 10-in. column? _____

6. How many names are in four 10-in. columns? _____

7. How many names are listed on one page? _____

8. How many names are listed on p pages? _____

9. Write an algebraic expression for the approximate number of names in p pages of the directory. _____

Check

10. Substitute $p = 1, 2,$ and 3 in the expression and solve. Does your expression provide reasonable values?

_____

Solve Another Problem

11. The yearbook committee can fit 1 student picture in one inch of a row. If there are eight 6-inch rows on each page, write an expression for the approximate number of pictures that can fit on p pages.

_____

Practice 4-2

Using Number Sense to Solve Equations

Identify a solution for each equation from the given set of numbers.

1. $30p = 900$; 3, 20, 30, or 60

_____

2. $\frac{h}{9} = 11$; 3, 30, 72, or 99

_____

3. $t + 32.4 = 62$; 29.6, 31.4, or 18.6

_____

4. $r - 17 = 40$; 23, 57 or 63

_____

Solve each equation using mental math.

5. $5t = 25$

_____

6. $8w = 64$

_____

7. $p + 5 = 12$

_____

8. $a + 2 = 15$

_____

9. $\frac{h}{6} = 4$

_____

10. $\frac{g}{8} = 16$

_____

11. $y - 11 = 28$

_____

12. $d - 4 = 12$

_____

13. $w - 10 = 15$

_____

14. $18 - t = 14$

_____

15. $21 + y = 31.64$

_____

16. $18.43 + x = 123.4$

_____

17. The seventh-grade class has been collecting aluminum cans for recycling. The class has collected 210 cans. Their goal is to collect 520 cans. Write an equation and estimate the number of aluminum cans needed to reach their goal.

_____

18. A seamstress bought some bolts of fabric at $25.30 each. She spent a total of $227.70. Write an equation and estimate the number of bolts of fabric that she purchased.

_____

19. For your party you purchased balloons for $.79 each. You spent a total of $11.85. Write an equation and estimate the number of balloons purchased.

_____

4-2 • Guided Problem Solving

GPS **Student Page 176, Exercise 25:**

An elevator has a maximum lift of 2,000 lb. You are moving 55-lb boxes of books. Write an equation and estimate how many boxes you can safely place on the elevator.

Understand

1. Circle the information you will need to solve.

2. What are you being asked to do?

   _____

   _____

3. What will your variable represent?

   _____

   _____

Plan and Carry Out

4. How much weight does the elevator hold? _____

5. How much does each box weigh? _____

6. Write an equation to find how many boxes the elevator can hold.

   _____

7. Estimate how many boxes the elevator
   can safely hold at one time.   _____

Check

8. Determine if your answer to Step 7 times 55 lb each is less than 2,000.

   _____

   _____

Solve Another Problem

9. Laurie can type 65 words per minute. She has to write a 5,000-word paper for her Shakespeare class. Write an equation to calculate how long it will take Laurie to type her paper. Estimate the answer.

   _____

   _____

Practice 4-3

Solving Equations by Adding or Subtracting

Solve each equation. Check your answer.

1. $n + 2 = 5$

2. $x - 1 = -3$

3. $7 = a + 2$

4. $p + 2 = -6$

_____

_____

_____

_____

5. $-9 = -4 + a$

6. $-2 = c + 2$

7. $x - (-3) = 7$

8. $a + (-6) = 5$

_____

_____

_____

_____

9. $16 + s = 6$

10. $p + (-2) = 19$

11. $r - 7 = -13$

12. $25 = a - (-3)$

_____

_____

_____

_____

Use a calculator, paper and pencil, or mental math. Solve each equation.

13. $t + 43 = 28$

14. $-19 = r + 6$

15. $25 = r + 7$

16. $13 = 24 + c$

_____

_____

_____

_____

17. $d - 19 = -46$

18. $b + 27 = -18$

19. $46 = f - 19$

20. $z - 74 = -19$

_____

_____

_____

_____

21. The odometer on your family car reads 20,186.7 after going 62.3 miles. Write and solve an equation to determine how many miles were on the odometer before going 62.3 miles.

_____

22. Michael bought a $25.00 gift for a friend. After he bought the gift, Michael had $176.89. Write and solve an equation to calculate how much money Michael had before he bought the gift.

_____

23. This spring it rained a total of 11.5 inches. This was 3 inches less than last spring. Write and solve an equation to find the amount of rain last season.

_____

4-3 • Guided Problem Solving

GPS **Student Page 183, Exercise 24:**

Biology A student collects 12 ladybugs for a science project. This is 9 fewer than the number of ladybugs the student collected yesterday. Write and solve an equation to find the number of ladybugs the student collected yesterday.

Understand

1. Circle the information you will need to solve.

2. What are you being asked to do?

_____

_____

3. What will your variable represent?

_____

_____

Plan and Carry Out

4. How many ladybugs did the student
collect today? _____

5. Determine a variable for the number
of ladybugs the student collected yesterday. _____

6. Write an expression for the phrase;
*9 fewer than the number of ladybugs
the student collected yesterday.* _____

7. Write an equation that compares the answer
to step 4 with the answer to Step 6. _____

8. Solve the equation written in Step 7. _____

9. How many ladybugs did the student
collect yesterday? _____

Check

10. Substitute the answer to Step 9 into the equation for the variable
and solve.

_____

_____

Solve Another Problem

11. Jason is 72 in. tall. If Kenny is 15 in. shorter than Jason, write and
solve an equation for the height of Kenny.

_____

_____

Practice 4-4

Solving Equations by Multiplying or Dividing

Use a calculator, paper and pencil, or mental math. Solve each equation.

1. $9n = 126$

2. $\dfrac{d}{3} = -81$

3. $-2t = 56$

4. $\dfrac{k}{-3} = 6$

_____

_____

_____

_____

5. $-18 = \dfrac{y}{-2}$

6. $\dfrac{y}{16} = 3$

7. $-56 = 8r$

8. $9w = -63$

_____

_____

_____

_____

9. $-3v = -48$

10. $13 = \dfrac{x}{-4}$

11. $28 = -4a$

12. $\dfrac{t}{-42} = 3$

_____

_____

_____

_____

13. $24 = \dfrac{f}{-4}$

14. $15 = -3j$

15. $102k = 408$

16. $\dfrac{b}{-96} = -3$

_____

_____

_____

_____

Solve and check each equation.

17. $\dfrac{x}{19} = -21$

18. $\dfrac{x}{-22} = -63$

19. $-41x = 164$

_____

_____

_____

20. $\dfrac{x}{91} = -98$

21. $452 = -4x$

22. $50x = -2,500$

_____

_____

_____

Write and solve an equation to represent each situation.

23. One of the largest flowers, the Rafflesia, weighs about 15 lb. How many Rafflesia flowers can be placed in a container that can hold a maximum of 240 lb?

_____

24. "Heavy water" is a name given to a compound used in some nuclear reactors. Heavy water costs about $1,500 per gallon. If a nuclear plant spent $10,500 on heavy water, how many gallons of heavy water were bought?

_____

4-4 • Guided Problem Solving

GPS **Student Page 190, Exercise 45:**

Trees A growing tree absorbs about 26 lb of carbon dioxide each year. How many years will the tree take to absorb 390 lb of carbon dioxide?

Understand

1. Circle the information you will need to solve.

2. What are you being asked to do?

   _____

   _____

3. If 390 lb is on one side of the equation, what operation will be performed with the other two values? Explain.

   _____

   _____

   _____

Plan and Carry Out

4. How much carbon dioxide does a tree absorb each year? _____

5. How much carbon dioxide does a tree absorb in y years? _____

6. Write an equation that can be used to solve for y. _____

7. Solve the equation. _____

8. How many years will the tree take to absorb 390 lb of carbon dioxide? _____

Check

9. Substitute the answer in Step 8 into the equation for the variable and solve.

   _____

   _____

Solve Another Problem

10. Delila runs 8 mi every day at her health club. She earns a free month membership after she's run 1,000 mi. Write and solve an equation to determine how many days she has to run before she earns the free month.

    _____

    _____

Practice 4-5

Exploring Two-Step Problems

Define a variable and write an algebraic expression for each phrase.

1. six times the price of gas minus 20

_____

2. one-half the distance from Boston to New York minus 25

_____

3. two fewer than five times the number of eggs needed in the recipe

_____

4. 10 megabytes less than the number of megabytes in a computer, divided by 6

_____

Solve each equation using number sense.

5. $10 + 5h = 25$

_____

6. $8s - 8 = 64$

_____

7. $3y + 78 = 81$

_____

8. $2g + 4 = 12$

_____

9. $5j + 5 = 15$

_____

10. $3w + 8 = 20$

_____

11. $\frac{h}{2} + 1 = 4$

_____

12. $\frac{g}{8} + 12 = 16$

_____

13. $2 + \frac{b}{7} = 3$

_____

14. For a walk-a-thon a sponsor committed to give you a flat fee of $5 plus $2 for every mile you walk. Write an expression for the total amount you will collect from your sponsor at the end of the walk-a-thon. Then evaluate your expression for 20 miles walked.

_____

4-5 • Guided Problem Solving

GPS **Student Page 198, Exercise 39:**

Food You are helping to prepare food for a large family gathering. You can slice 2 zucchinis per minute. You need 30 sliced zucchinis. How long will it take you to finish, if you have already sliced 12 zucchinis?

Understand

1. Circle the information you will need to solve.

2. What are you being asked to do?

   _____

   _____

3. What will your variable represent?

   _____

Plan and Carry Out

4. How many sliced zucchinis do you need?   _____

5. How many sliced zucchinis do you
   already have?   _____

6. Write and simplify an expression for the
   number of zucchinis you still need to slice. _____

7. To calculate the number of minutes it will take
   to slice the remaining zucchinis, what number
   will you divide your answer to Step 7 by?   _____

8. Write an equation to solve the problem.   _____

9. How long will it take you to finish slicing
   the remaining zucchinis?   _____

Check

10. Multiply your answer to Step 9 by your answer to Step 7. Does
    your answer match your result from Step 6?

    _____

Solve Another Problem

11. Jordan skates 6 mi/h. Today she has already skated 8 miles. Her
    goal is to skate a total of 20 miles. How much longer does she
    have to skate to reach her goal?

    _____

Practice 4-6

Solve each equation. Then check your answer.

1. $7m + 8 = 71$

2. $\frac{y}{7} + 6 = 11$

3. $12y + 2 = 146$

4. $\frac{m}{9} - 17 = 21$

_____   _____   _____   _____

5. $\frac{y}{-12} + 1 = 6$

6. $2a - 1 = 19$

7. $\frac{c}{9} - 8 = 17$

8. $-4t + 16 = 24$

_____   _____   _____   _____

9. $\frac{b}{-2} - 8 = -6$

10. $3d + 14 = 11$

11. $\frac{z}{17} - 1 = 8$

12. $\frac{e}{5} - 14 = 21$

_____   _____   _____   _____

13. $\frac{f}{-9} + 4 = 2$

14. $-2y + 16 = 10$

15. $4w - 26 = 82$

16. $\frac{j}{19} - 2 = -5$

_____   _____   _____   _____

Solve each equation.

17. $3n - 8 = 4$

18. $\frac{n}{5} - 4 = 11$

_____   _____

19. $2n - 3 = 9$

20. $1 + \frac{n}{4} = 9$

_____   _____

Match each sentence with a two-step equation.

21. Half of the height of a tree minus five equals fifteen.

     _____

22. Two less than three times the number of feet of fencing required equals twelve feet.

     _____

23. Eight less than the quotient of Dave's golf score and four equals negative five.

     _____

24. Three times Gail's age increased by two years equals twelve years.

     _____

A. $3n - 2 = 12$

B. $3n + 2 = 12$

C. $\frac{n}{2} - 5 = 15$

D. $\frac{n}{4} - 8 = -5$

4-6 • Guided Problem Solving

GPS **Student Page 203, Exercise 32:**

Jobs You earn $20 per hour landscaping a yard. You pay $1.50 in bus fare each way. How many hours must you work to earn $117?

Understand

1. Circle the information you will need to solve.

2. What are you being asked to do?

   _____

   _____

3. How much do you spend in bus fare
   to go to and from work? _____

Plan and Carry Out

4. Write an expression for the amount of money you make after
   h hours.

   _____

5. Write an expression for the amount of money you have after you
   pay for bus fare.

   _____

6. How much money do you need to earn? _____

7. Write an equation that can be solved for h. _____

8. Solve the equation. _____

9. How many hours must you work to earn $117? _____

Check

10. Substitute the answer in Step 9 into the equation for the variable
    and solve.

    _____

Solve Another Problem

11. You charge $6 per hour to babysit one child. You charge an
    additional $2 per hour for each additional child. The Taylors have
    4 children. How many hours would you have to babysit the
    Taylors' children to earn $84?

    _____

Practice 4-7

Graphing and Writing Inequalities

Graph the solution of each inequality on a number line.

1. $x \le 3$ <———|———|———|———|———|———|———|———|———|———> x
$\quad\quad\quad -4\ -3\ -2\ -1\ \ 0\ \ 1\ \ 2\ \ 3\ \ 4$

2. $t > 1$ <———|———|———|———|———|———|———|———|———|———> t
$\quad\quad\quad -4\ -3\ -2\ -1\ \ 0\ \ 1\ \ 2\ \ 3\ \ 4$

3. $q \ge -10$ <———|———|———|———|———|———> q
$\quad\quad\quad\quad -20\quad -10\quad 0\quad 10\quad 20$

4. $m < 50$ 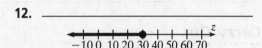 m
$\quad\quad\quad\quad -10\ 0\ 10\ 20\ 30\ 40\ 50\ 60\ 70$

For each inequality, tell whether the number in bold is a solution.

5. $x < 7; \mathbf{7}$ _____

6. $p > -3; \mathbf{3}$ _____

7. $k \ge 5; \mathbf{0}$ _____

8. $3z \le 12; \mathbf{4}$ _____

9. $n - 5 > 3; \mathbf{6}$ _____

10. $2g + 8 \ge 3; \mathbf{-1}$ _____

Write an inequality for each graph.

11. _____

<———|———|———○———|———|———|———|———|———> x
$-4\ -3\ -2\ -1\ 0\ 1\ 2\ 3\ 4$

12. _____

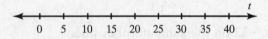 z
$-10\ 0\ 10\ 20\ 30\ 40\ 50\ 60\ 70$

Write an inequality for each statement. Graph each solution on the number line shown.

13. You can walk there in 20 minutes or less.

_____

<———|———|———|———|———|———|———|———|———|———> t
$\quad 0\ \ \ 5\ \ 10\ \ 15\ \ 20\ \ 25\ \ 30\ \ 35\ \ 40$

14. Each prize is worth over $150.

_____

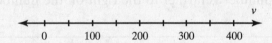 v
$\quad 0\quad\quad 100\quad\quad 200\quad\quad 300\quad\quad 400$

15. A species of catfish, *malapterurus electricus,* can generate up to 350 volts of electricity.

a. Write an inequality to represent the amount of electricity generated by the catfish.

_____

b. Draw a graph of the inequality you wrote in **a.**

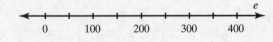 e
$\quad 0\quad\quad 100\quad\quad 200\quad\quad 300\quad\quad 400$

4-7 • Guided Problem Solving

GPS **Student Page 208, Exercise 30:**

Reasoning Explain why $-17 > -22$.

Understand

1. What are you being asked to do?

   _____

   _____

2. What visual representation can you use to help your explanation?

   _____

Plan and Carry Out

3. Graph -17 on a number line.

4. Graph -22 on the same number line.

5. Which number is farther to the right on the number line?

   _____

6. Why is $-17 > -22$?

   _____

   _____

Check

7. Which mathematical definition did you use to explain that $-17 > -22$?

   _____

   _____

Solve Another Problem

8. Explain why $-8 < -5$.

   _____

   _____

Practice 4-8

Solving Inequalities by Adding and Subtracting

Solve each inequality. Graph each solution.

1. $w + 4 < -2$

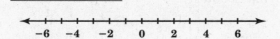

2. $a - 4 \geq 0$

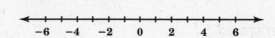

3. $a + 19 > 13$

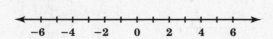

4. $x + 7 \leq 12$

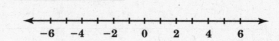

5. $a + 2 > -3$

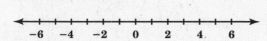

6. $t - 6 < 3$

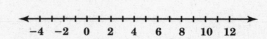

7. $r - 3.4 \leq 2.6$

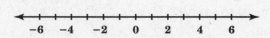

8. $a + 5.7 \geq -2.3$

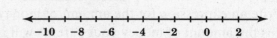

9. $h - 4.9 > -0.9$

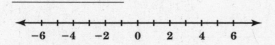

10. $y + 3.4 < -4.6$

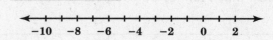

Write an inequality for each problem. Solve the inequality.

11. The school record for the most points scored in a football season is 85. Lawrence has 44 points so far this season. How many more points does he need to break the record?

_____

_____

12. The maximum weight limit for a fully loaded truck is 16,000 pounds. The truck you are loading currently weighs 12,500 pounds. How much more weight can be added and not exceed the weight limit?

_____

_____

_____

4-8 • Guided Problem Solving

GPS **Student Page 212, Exercise 25:**

Consumer Issues Your parents give you $35 for a scooter that costs at least $100. How much money do you have to save to buy the scooter?

Understand

1. Circle the information you will need to solve.

2. What are you being asked to do?

   _____

   _____

3. What expression would you use to represent the phrase "*at least* $100?"

   _____

Plan and Carry Out

Suppose the scooter costs *at least* $100.

4. Write an expression for the amount of money you need to save, *s,* plus the amount of money your parents will give you.

   _____

5. How much money do you need to buy the scooter?

   _____

6. Write an inequality to solve for *s.* _____

7. Solve the inequality. _____

8. How much money do you have to save for the scooter?

   _____

Check

9. If you save $65, how much money will you have? _____

Solve Another Problem

10. You have to be at least 42 in. tall to ride the big roller coasters at the amusement park. You are 36 in. tall right now. How much more do you have to grow? Write and solve an inequality.

    _____

Name _____ Class _____ Date _____

Practice 4-9

Solving Inequalities by Multiplying and Dividing

Solve each inequality. Graph each solution.

1. $6w \leq 36$

_____

2. $10a \geq 40$

_____

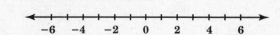

3. $\frac{f}{3} \leq -2$

_____

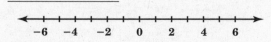

4. $\frac{v}{4} > 2$

_____

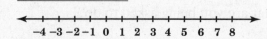

5. $7a > -28$

_____

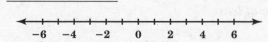

6. $\frac{c}{-3} \geq 3$

_____

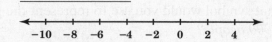

7. $\frac{f}{2} > -1$

_____

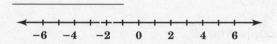

8. $9a \leq 63$

_____

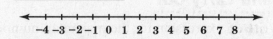

9. $4w \geq -12$

_____

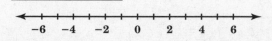

10. $\frac{h}{-2} \geq -5$

_____

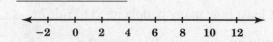

Write an inequality to solve each problem. Then solve the inequality.

11. Marcus wants to buy 5 baseballs. He has $35. What is the most each baseball can cost?

_____

_____

12. Melinda charges $4 per hour for babysitting. Mrs. Garden does not want to spend more than $25 for babysitting. What is the maximum number of hours that she can have Melinda babysit?

_____

_____

4-9 • Guided Problem Solving

GPS **Student Page 217, Exercise 32:**

Rides A roller coaster can carry 36 people per run. At least how many times does the roller coaster have to run to allow 10,000 people to ride?

Understand

1. Circle the information you will need to solve.

2. What are you being asked to do?

   _____

   _____

3. What symbol would you use to represent the phrase *at least 10,000 people*?

   _____

Plan and Carry Out

4. Write an expression for the maximum number of people who could ride the roller coaster in *r* runs.

   _____

5. At least how many people need to ride? _____

6. Write an inequality to solve for *r*. _____

7. Solve the inequality. _____

8 How many times does the roller coaster
   need to run?   _____

Check

9. If the roller coaster runs 278 times, how many people will it have carried? Use a calculator to check your answer.

   _____

Solve Another Problem

10. Chicken is on sale for $1.99 per pound. You can only spend up to $20, and you must buy a whole number of pounds. How many pounds of chicken can you buy?

   _____

4A Graphic Organizer

Study Skill Take notes when your teacher presents new material in class and when you read the lesson yourself. Organize these notes as a way to study, reviewing them as you go.

Write your answers.

1. What is the chapter title? _____

2. How many lessons are there in this chapter? _____

3. What is the topic of the Test-Taking Strategies page? _____

4. Complete the graphic organizer below as you work through the chapter.
   • In the center, write the title of the chapter.
   • When you begin a lesson, write the lesson name in a rectangle.
   • When you complete a lesson, write a skill or key concept in a circle linked to that lesson block.
   • When you complete the chapter, use this graphic organizer to help you review.

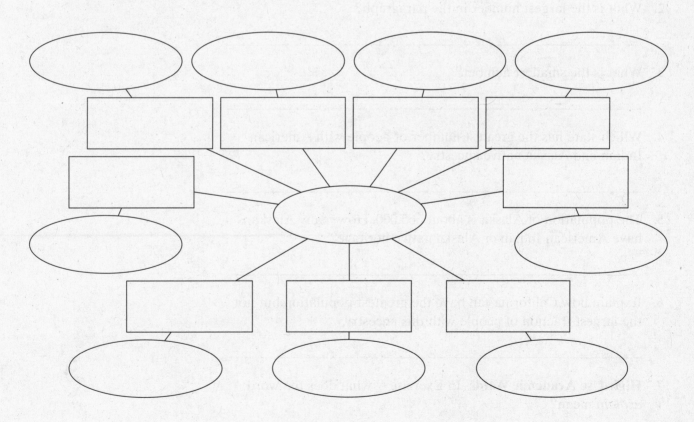

4B: Reading Comprehension

Study Skill As you learn more vocabulary, more concepts are within your reach.

Read the paragraph below and answer the questions that follow.

> November is American Indian and Alaska Native Heritage Month. According to the U.S. Census Bureau, more than 4 million people in the United States identified themselves as American Indian or Alaska native in 2004. That is 1.5% of the total U.S. population. About 687,000 people with this heritage live in California, giving it the largest American Indian and Alaska native population of any state. However, $\frac{1}{5}$ of the Alaska population is American Indian or Alaska native. This is a much greater fraction than in California.

1. What is the subject of this paragraph?

   _____

2. What is the largest number in the paragraph?

   _____

3. What is the smallest number?

   _____

4. Which state has the greatest number of people with American Indian and Alaska native ancestry?

   _____

5. The population of Alaska is about 665,000. How many Alaskans have American Indian or Alaska native heritage?

   _____

6. Explain how California can have the greatest population but not the largest fraction of people with this ancestry.

   _____

7. **High-Use Academic Words** In Exercise 6, what does the word *explain* mean?

   a. to put or use in place of something else

   b. to give facts and details that make an idea easier to understand

4C: Reading/Writing Math Symbols

For use after Lesson 4-3

Study Skill Mathematics builds on itself, so build a strong foundation.

Match each expression with its word form.

1. $x - 3$
2. $4m$
3. $\frac{7}{x}$
4. $m + 6$
5. $m \div 5$

A. six more than a number
B. the quotient of a number and five
C. a number decreased by three
D. seven divided by a number
E. four multiplied by a number

Write a mathematical expression or equation for each word description.

6. nine less than the product of eleven and x

7. a number plus four equals thirteen

8. the quotient of x and 4

9. the absolute value of a number

Write two different word phrases for each of the following expressions.

10. $x - 10$

11. $5m$

12. $3^2 + m$

Vocabulary and Study Skills

4D: Visual Vocabulary Practice

Study Skill Making sense of mathematical symbols is like reading a foreign language that uses different letters.

Concept List

Addition Property of Equality	Subtraction Property of Inequality
Division Property of Equality	Multiplication Property of Inequality
variable	solution of an equation
open sentence	solution of an inequality
inequality	

Write the concept that best describes each exercise. Choose from the concept list above.

1. If $5 - y = 2 - 3y$, then $5 - y + 3y = 2 - 3y + 3y$. _____	2. $8 + x \geq 2x$ _____	3. $-2(3x + 5) = 14$ $3x + 5 = -7$ $3x = -12$ $x = -4$ -4 represents this for $-2(3x + 5) = 14$. _____
4. z in the equation $\frac{2z}{5} = 12$ _____	5. If $7m < 1 + 2m$, then $7m - 2m < 1 + 2m - 2m$. _____	6. $3z + \frac{1}{4} = 21$ _____
7. If $5b = 3$, then $\frac{5b}{5} = \frac{3}{5}$. _____	8. $-2x + 1 < 4$ $-2x < 3$ $x > -\frac{3}{2}$ 0 represents this for $-2x + 1 < 4$. _____	9. If $\frac{1}{9}z < 8$, then $9 \times \left(\frac{1}{9}z\right) < 9 \times 8$. _____

4E: Vocabulary Check

Study Skill Strengthen your vocabulary. Use these pages and add cues and summaries by applying the Cornell Notetaking style.

Write the definition for each word or term at the right. To check your work, fold the paper back along the dotted line to see the correct answers.

variable

algebraic expression

equation

open sentence

inverse operations

4E: Vocabulary Check (continued)

Write the vocabulary word or term for each definition. To check your work, fold the paper forward along the dotted line to see the correct answers.

a symbol that represents one or more numbers

_____

a mathematical expression with at least one variable

_____

a mathematical sentence with an equal sign

_____

an equation with one or more variables

_____

operations that undo each other

_____

4F: Vocabulary Review

Study Skill: Review notes that you have taken in class as soon as possible to clarify any points you missed and to refresh your memory.

Circle the word that best completes the sentence.

1. A (*variable, expression*) is a letter that stands for a number.

2. An (*expression, equation*) is a mathematical statement with an equal sign.

3. A (*solution, sentence*) is a value for a variable that makes an equation true.

4. To solve an equation, use (*inverse, variable*) operations.

5. A mathematical statement that contains $<$ or $>$ is called an (*equation, inequality*).

6. The statement $4 + (9 + 3) = (4 + 9) + 3$ is an example of the (*Commutative Property of Addition, Associative Property of Addition*).

7. The (*opposite, absolute value*) of 15 is -15.

8. The (*mean, median*) is the middle number in a data set when the data is arranged from least to greatest.

9. You can use the (*commutative, identity*) property to change the order in an expression.

10. The statement $a + 0 = a$ is an example of the (*Identity Property of Zero, Identity Property of Multiplication*).

11. The (*absolute value, opposite*) of a number is its distance from 0 on a number line.

12. (*Rational numbers, Integers*) are the set of whole numbers, their opposites, and zero.

13. Two numbers whose sum is 0 are (*additive, opposite*) inverses.

14. A(n) (*outlier, range*) is a data value that is much greater or less than the other values in the data set.

15. Using the (*distributive property, order of operations*), you can calculate that $12 + 5 \cdot 2$ equals 22.

Practice 5-1

Write a ratio for each situation in three ways.

1. Ten years ago in Louisiana, schools averaged 182 pupils for every 10 teachers.

    _____

2. Between 1899 and 1900, 284 out of 1,000 people in the United States were 5–17 years old.

    _____

Use the chart below for Exercises 3–4.

Three seventh-grade classes were asked whether they wanted chicken or pasta served at their awards banquet.

Room Number	Chicken	Pasta
201	10	12
202	8	17
203	16	10

3. In room 201, what is the ratio of students who prefer chicken to students who prefer pasta?

    _____

4. Combine the totals for all three rooms. What is the ratio of the number of students who prefer pasta to the number of students who prefer chicken?

    _____

Write each ratio as a fraction in simplest form.

5. 12 to 18 _____   6. 81 : 27 _____   7. $\frac{6}{28}$ _____

Tell whether the ratios are *equivalent* or *not equivalent*.

8. 12 : 24, 50 : 100 _____

9. $\frac{22}{1}$, $\frac{1}{22}$ _____

10. 2 to 3, 24 to 36 _____

11. A bag contains green, yellow, and orange marbles. The ratio of green marbles to yellow marbles is 2 : 5. The ratio of yellow marbles to orange marbles is 3 : 4. What is the ratio of green marbles to orange marbles?

    _____

5-1 • Guided Problem Solving

GPS **Student Page 230, Exercise 27:**

Cooking To make pancakes, you need 2 cups of water for every 3 cups of flour. Write an equivalent ratio to find how much water you will need with 9 cups of flour.

Understand

1. Circle the information you will need to solve.

2. What are you being asked to do?

   _____

   _____

3. Why will a ratio help you to solve the problem?

   _____

   _____

Plan and Carry Out

4. What is the ratio of the cups of water
   to the cups of flour?   _____

5. How many cups of flour are you using?   _____

6. Write an equivalent ratio to use 9 cups of flour. _____

7. How many cups of water are
   needed for 9 cups of flour?   _____

Check

8. Why is the number of cups of water triple the number of cups
   needed for 3 cups of flour?

   _____

   _____

Solve Another Problem

9. Rebecca is laying tile in her bathroom. She needs 4 black tiles for
   every 16 white tiles. How many black tiles are needed if she uses
   128 white tiles?

   _____

   _____

Practice 5-2

Unit Rates and Proportional Reasoning

Write the unit rate for each situation.

1. travel 250 mi in 5 h

   _____

2. earn $75.20 in 8 h

   _____

3. read 80 pages in 2 h

   _____

4. type 8,580 words in 2 h 45 min

   _____

5. manufacture 2,488 parts in 8 h

   _____

6. 50 copies of a book on 2 shelves

   _____

Find each unit price. Then determine the better buy.

7. paper: 100 sheets for $.99
   500 sheets for $4.29

   _____

   _____

8. peanuts: 1 lb for $1.29
   12 oz for $.95

   _____

   _____

9. crackers: 15 oz for $1.79
   12 oz for $1.49

   _____

   _____

10. apples: 3 lb for $1.89
    5 lb for $2.49

    _____

    _____

11. mechanical pencils: 4 for $1.25
    25 for $5.69

    _____

    _____

12. bagels: 4 for $.89
    6 for $1.39

    _____

    _____

13. **a.** Yolanda and Yoko ran in a 100-yd dash. When Yolanda
    crossed the finish line, Yoko was 10 yd behind her. The girls
    then repeated the race, with Yolanda starting 10 yd behind the
    starting line. If each girl ran at the same rate as before, who
    won the race? By how many yards?

    _____

    b. Assuming the girls run at the same rate as before, how far
    behind the starting line should Yolanda be in order for the
    two to finish in a tie?

    _____

5-2 • Guided Problem Solving

GPS Student Page 235, Exercise 27a:

Geography Population density is the number of people per unit of area. Alaska has the lowest population density of any state in the United States. It has 626,932 people in 570,374 mi^2. What is its population density? Round to the nearest person per square mile.

Understand

1. What is *population density*?

   _____

   _____

2. What are you being asked to do?

   _____

3. What does the phrase *people per unit of area* imply?

   _____

   _____

   _____

Plan and Carry Out

4. What is the population of Alaska?   _____

5. What is the area of Alaska?   _____

6. Write a division expression for
   the population density.   _____

7. What is its population density?   _____

8. Round to the nearest person
   per square mile.   _____

Check

9. Why is the population density only about 1 person/mi^2?

   _____

   _____

Solve Another Problem

10. Mr. Boyle is buying pizza for the percussion band. The bill is $56.82 for 5 pizzas. If there are 12 members of the band, how much does the pizza cost per member? Round to the nearest cent.

   _____

Practice 5-3 .... **Proportions**

Determine if the ratios in each pair are proportional.

1. $\frac{12}{16}, \frac{30}{40}$ _____

2. $\frac{8}{12}, \frac{15}{21}$ _____

3. $\frac{27}{21}, \frac{81}{56}$ _____

4. $\frac{45}{24}, \frac{75}{40}$ _____

5. $\frac{5}{9}, \frac{80}{117}$ _____

6. $\frac{15}{25}, \frac{75}{125}$ _____

7. $\frac{2}{14}, \frac{20}{35}$ _____

8. $\frac{9}{6}, \frac{21}{14}$ _____

9. $\frac{24}{15}, \frac{16}{10}$ _____

10. $\frac{3}{4}, \frac{8}{10}$ _____

11. $\frac{20}{4}, \frac{17}{3}$ _____

12. $\frac{25}{6}, \frac{9}{8}$ _____

Decide if each pair of ratios is proportional.

13. $\frac{14}{10} \stackrel{?}{=} \frac{9}{7}$

_____

14. $\frac{18}{8} \stackrel{?}{=} \frac{36}{16}$

_____

15. $\frac{6}{10} \stackrel{?}{=} \frac{15}{25}$

_____

16. $\frac{7}{16} \stackrel{?}{=} \frac{4}{9}$

_____

17. $\frac{6}{4} \stackrel{?}{=} \frac{12}{8}$

_____

18. $\frac{19}{3} \stackrel{?}{=} \frac{114}{8}$

_____

19. $\frac{5}{14} \stackrel{?}{=} \frac{6}{15}$

_____

20. $\frac{6}{27} \stackrel{?}{=} \frac{8}{36}$

_____

21. $\frac{27}{15} \stackrel{?}{=} \frac{45}{25}$

_____

22. $\frac{3}{18} \stackrel{?}{=} \frac{4}{20}$

_____

23. $\frac{5}{2} \stackrel{?}{=} \frac{15}{6}$

_____

24. $\frac{20}{15} \stackrel{?}{=} \frac{4}{3}$

_____

Solve.

25. During the breaststroke competitions of the 1992 Olympics, Nelson Diebel swam 100 meters in 62 seconds, and Mike Bowerman swam 200 meters in 130 seconds. Are the rates proportional?

   _____

26. During a vacation, the Vasquez family traveled 174 miles in 3 hours on Monday, and 290 miles in 5 hours on Tuesday. Are the rates proportional?

   _____

5-3 • Guided Problem Solving

GPS Student Page 240, Exercise 29:

Decorating A certain shade of green paint requires 4 parts blue to 5 parts yellow. If you mix 16 quarts of blue paint with 25 quarts of yellow paint, will you get the desired shade of green? Explain.

Understand

1. Circle the information you will need to solve.

2. What are you being asked to do?

   _____

   _____

3. Will a ratio help you to solve the problem? Explain.

   _____

   _____

Plan and Carry Out

4. What is the ratio of blue parts to yellow parts? _____

5. What is the ratio of blue quarts to yellow quarts? _____

6. Check to see if the cross products of the two ratios are equal.

   _____

7. Are the ratios the same? _____

8. Will you get the desired shade of green? Explain.

   _____

   _____

Check

9. How do you know that the ratios are not the same?

   _____

Solve Another Problem

10. There are 15 boys and 12 girls in your math class. There are 5 boys and 3 girls in your study group. Determine if the boy to girl ratio is the same in study group as it is in your math class. Explain.

    _____

    _____

Practice 5-4

Solving Proportions

Use mental math to solve for each value of *n*.

1. $\frac{n}{14} = \frac{20}{35}$ _____

2. $\frac{9}{6} = \frac{21}{n}$ _____

3. $\frac{24}{n} = \frac{16}{10}$ _____

4. $\frac{3}{4} = \frac{n}{10}$ _____

Solve each proportion using cross products.

5. $\frac{k}{8} = \frac{14}{4}$

   $k =$ _____

6. $\frac{u}{3} = \frac{10}{5}$

   $u =$ _____

7. $\frac{14}{6} = \frac{d}{15}$

   $d =$ _____

8. $\frac{5}{1} = \frac{m}{4}$

   $m =$ _____

9. $\frac{36}{32} = \frac{n}{8}$

   $n =$ _____

10. $\frac{5}{30} = \frac{1}{x}$

    $x =$ _____

11. $\frac{t}{4} = \frac{5}{10}$

    $t =$ _____

12. $\frac{9}{2} = \frac{v}{4}$

    $v =$ _____

Solve.

13. A contractor estimates it will cost \$2,400 to build a deck
    to a customer's specifications. How much would it cost to
    build five similar decks?

    _____

14. A recipe requires 3 c of flour to make 27 dinner rolls. How much flour is needed
    to make 9 rolls?

    _____

Solve using a calculator, paper and pencil, or mental math.

15. Mandy runs 4 km in 18 min. She plans to run in a 15 km race.
    How long will it take her to complete the race?

    _____

16. Ken's new car can go 26 miles per gallon of gasoline. The car's gasoline
    tank holds 14 gal. How far will he be able to go on a full tank?

    _____

17. Eleanor can complete two skirts in 15 days. How long will it take
    her to complete eight skirts?

    _____

18. Three eggs are required to make two dozen muffins. How many
    eggs are needed to make 12 dozen muffins?

    _____

5-4 • Guided Problem Solving

GPS Student Page 247, Exercise 28:

There are 450 students and 15 teachers in a school. The school hires 2 new teachers. To keep the student-to-teacher ratio the same, how many students in all should attend the school?

Understand

1. What are you being asked to do?

   _____

   _____

2. Will a proportion help you to solve the problem? Explain.

   _____

   _____

   _____

Plan and Carry Out

3. Write a ratio for the current student-to-teacher ratio. _____

4. Write a ratio for the new student-to-teacher ratio. _____

5. Write a proportion using the ratios in Steps 3 and 4. _____

6. How many total students should attend the school?

   _____

Check

7. Are the two ratios equivalent? Explain.

   _____

   _____

Solve Another Problem

8. There are 6 black marbles and 4 red marbles in a jar. If you add 4 red marbles to the jar, how many black marbles do you need to add to keep the ratio of black marbles to red marbles the same?

   _____

Guided Problem Solving

Practice 5-5

△ *MNO* ~ △ *JKL*. **Complete each statement.**

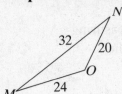

1. ∠*M* corresponds to _____.

2. ∠*L* corresponds to _____.

3. $\overline{JL}$ corresponds to _____.

4. $\overline{MN}$ corresponds to _____.

5. What is the ratio of the lengths of the corresponding sides? _____

The pairs of figures below are similar. Find the value of each variable.

6. 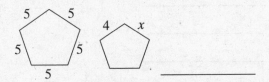 _____

7. 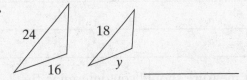 _____

8. 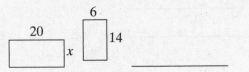 _____

9. 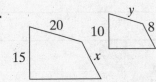 _____

10. 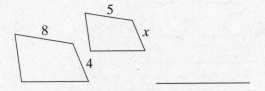 _____

11. _____

12. On a sunny day, if a 36-inch yardstick casts a 21-inch shadow, how tall is a building whose shadow is 168 ft?

_____

13. Oregon is about 400 miles from west to east, and 300 miles from north to south. If a map of Oregon is 15 inches tall (from north to south), about how wide is the map?

_____

5-5 • Guided Problem Solving

GPS Student Page 254, Exercise 13:

Geometry A rectangle with an area of 32 in.^{2} has one side measuring
4 in. A similar rectangle has an area of 288 in.^{2}. How long is the
longer side in the larger rectangle?

Understand

1. What are you being asked to do?

   _____

   _____

2. Will a proportion that equates the ratio of the areas to the ratio of the
   shorter sides result in the desired answer? Explain.

   _____

   _____

   _____

3. What measure should you determine first?

   _____

   _____

Plan and Carry Out

4. What is the length of the longer side of the rectangle
   whose area is 32 in.^{2} and whose shorter side is 4 in.?   _____

5. What is the ratio of the longer side to the shorter side?   _____

6. What pairs of factors multiply to equal 288?   _____

   _____

7. Which pair of factors has a ratio of $\frac{2}{1}$?   _____

8. What is the length of the longer side?   _____

Check

9. Why must the ratio between the factors be $\frac{2}{1}$?

   _____

   _____

Solve Another Problem

10. A triangle with perimeter 26 in. has two sides that
    are 8 in. long. What is the length of the third side of
    a similar triangle which has two sides that are 12 in. long?   _____

Practice 5-6

· ·

The scale of a map is 2 cm : 21 km. Find the actual distances for the following map distances.

1. 9 cm _____   **2.** 12.5 cm _____   **3.** 14 mm _____

4. 3.6 m _____   **5.** 4.5 cm _____   **6.** 7.1 cm _____

A scale drawing has a scale of $\frac{1}{4}$ in. : 12 ft. Find the length on the drawing for each actual length.

7. 8 ft _____   **8.** 30 ft _____   **9.** 15 ft _____

10. 18 ft _____   **11.** 20 ft _____   **12.** 40 ft _____

Use a metric ruler to find the approximate distance between the towns.

13. Hickokburg to Kidville _____

14. Dodgetown to Earp City _____

15. Dodgetown to Kidville _____

16. Kidville to Earp City _____

17. Dodgetown to Hickokburg _____

18. Earp City to Hickokburg _____

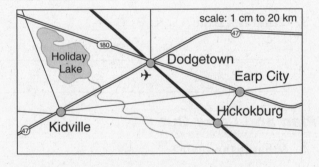

Solve.

19. The scale drawing shows a two-bedroom apartment. The master bedroom is 9 ft × 12 ft. Use an inch ruler to measure the drawing.

   a. The scale is _____ .

   b. Write the actual dimensions in place of the scale dimensions.

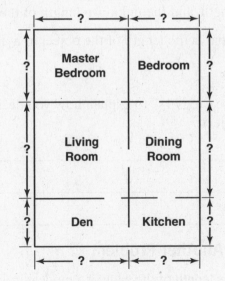

· ·

5-6 • Guided Problem Solving

GPS **Student Page 263, Exercise 24:**

Writing in Math You are making a scale drawing with a scale of
2 in. = 17 ft. Explain how you find the length of the drawing of an
object that has an actual length of 51 ft.

Understand

1. What are you being asked to do?

   _____

   _____

2. What points should you include in your explanation?

   _____

   _____

3. What is a scale?

   _____

   _____

Plan and Carry Out

4. What is the scale? _____

5. What is the actual length of the object? _____

6. Write a proportion using the scale, the actual
   length, and the unknown length of the drawing. _____

7. What is the length of the object in a drawing? _____

Check

8. Use Steps 4–7 to explain how you decided how long to draw the
   object.

   _____

   _____

   _____

Solve Another Problem

9. The length of the wing of a model airplane is 3 in.
   If the scale of the model to the actual plane is
   1 in. = 25 ft, what is the length of the actual wing? _____

5A: Graphic Organizer

For use before Lesson 5-1

Study Skill As you read over the material in the chapter, keep a paper and pencil handy to write down notes and questions in your math notebook. Review notes taken in class as soon as possible.

Write your answers.

1. What is the chapter title? _____

2. How many lessons are there in this chapter? _____

3. What is the topic of the Test-Taking Strategies page? _____

4. Complete the graphic organizer below as you work through the chapter.
   • In the center, write the title of the chapter.
   • When you begin a lesson, write the lesson name in a rectangle.
   • When you complete a lesson, write a skill or key concept in a circle linked to that lesson block.
   • When you complete the chapter, use this graphic organizer to help you review.

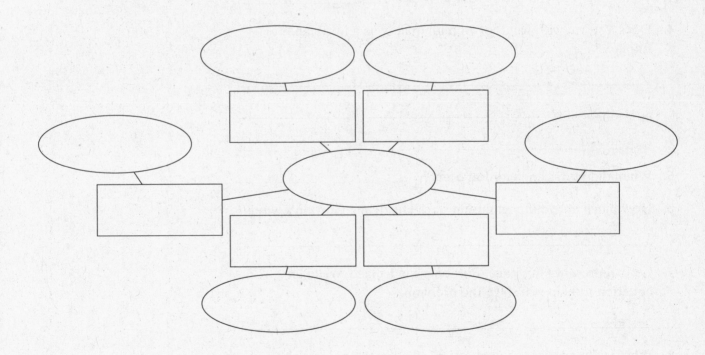

5B: Reading Comprehension

Study Skill When you read mathematics, look for words like "more than," "less than," "above," "times as many," "divided by." These clues will help you decide what operation you need to solve a problem.

Read the paragraph and answer the questions that follow.

> A tropical storm is classified as a hurricane when it has wind speeds in excess of 74 mi/h. The winds of Hurricane Gordon (1994) reached 12.4 mi/h above the minimum. How fast were the winds of Hurricane Gordon?

1. What numbers are in the paragraph? _____

2. What question are you asked to answer? _____

   _____

3. What units will you use in your answer? _____

4. Does a storm with winds of 74 mi/h qualify as a hurricane? Explain.

   _____

   _____

   _____

5. When did Hurricane Gordon occur? _____

6. How much above the minimum were Hurricane Gordon's winds?

   _____

7. Let x represent Hurricane Gordon's wind speed. Write an equation to help you solve the problem.

   _____

8. What is the answer to the question asked in the paragraph?

   _____

9. **High-Use Academic Words** In Exercise 7, what does it mean to *solve*?

   a. to find an answer for   b. to keep something going

5C: Reading/Writing Math Symbols

For use after Lesson 5-4

Study Skill When you take notes in any subject, use abbreviations and symbols whenever possible.

Write each statement or expression using the appropriate mathematical symbols.

1. the ratio of a to b _____

2. x to 4 is less than 5 to 2 _____

3. 4 more than 5 times n _____

4. $5 : 24$ is not equal to $1 : 5$ _____

Write each mathematical statement in words.

5. $x \leq 25$

6. $|-20| > |15|$

7. $1 \text{ oz} \approx 28 \text{ g}$

8. $\frac{1}{3} = \frac{4}{12}$

Match the symbolic statement or expression in Column A with its written form in Column B.

Column A	Column B
9. $k < 12$	**A.** 12 times x
10. $\lvert -5 \rvert$	**B.** negative 2 plus negative 4 is p
11. $n \geq 15$	**C.** the ratio of 4 to 8
12. $x = -4 + 5$	**D.** k is less than 12
13. $4 : 8$	**E.** the quotient of x and 9
14. $12x$	**F.** x equals negative 4 plus 5
15. $-2 + (-4) = p$	**G.** the absolute value of negative 5
16. $x \div 9$	**H.** n is greater than or equal to 15

5D: Visual Vocabulary Practice

For use after Lesson 5-6

Study Skill When you come across something you don't understand, view it as an opportunity to increase your brain power.

Concept List

cross products	equivalent ratios	indirect measurement
proportion	rate	scale
similar polygons	unit cost	unit rate

Write the concept that best describes each exercise. Choose from the concept list above.

1. $\frac{18}{16}$ and 4.5 : 4	**2.** A 6-ft-tall person standing near a building has a shadow that is 60 ft long. This can be used to determine the height of the building.	**3.** A bakery sells a dozen donuts for $3.15. This can also be represented as $\frac{\$3.15}{12 \text{ donuts}}$.
4. The expression "45 words per minute" represents this.	**5.** $\frac{30}{75} = \frac{2}{5}$	**6.** For the equation $\frac{15}{16} = \frac{3z}{4}$, these are represented by 15×4 and $3z \times 16$.
7. The equation $\frac{1}{2}$ in. = 50 mi represents this on a map.	**8.** $\frac{\$4.25}{5 \text{ lb}} = \$0.85/\text{lb}$	**9.** 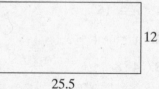

5E: Vocabulary Check

For use after Lesson 5-6

Study Skill Strengthen your vocabulary. Use these pages and add cues and summaries by applying the Cornell Notetaking style.

Write the definition for each word or term at the right. To check your work, fold the paper back along the dotted line to see the correct answers.

_____

_____ polygon

_____

_____

_____

_____ proportion

_____

_____

_____ unit rate

_____

_____

_____ ratio

_____

_____

_____ scale drawing

_____

_____

5E: Vocabulary Check (continued)

For use after Lesson 5-6

Write the vocabulary word or term for each definition. To check your work, fold the paper forward along the dotted line to see the correct answers.

a closed figure formed by three or more line segments that do not cross

_____

an equation stating that two ratios are equal

_____

the rate for one unit of a given quantity

_____

a comparison of two quantities by division

_____

an enlarged or reduced drawing of an object that is similar to the actual object

_____

5F: Vocabulary Review Puzzle

For use with the Chapter Review

Study Skill Use a special notebook or section of a loose-leaf binder for math.

Complete the crossword puzzle. For help, use the Glossary in your textbook.

Here are the words you will use to complete this crossword puzzle:

equation	factor	figures	fraction
inequality	mixed number	prime	proportion
ratio	scale drawing		

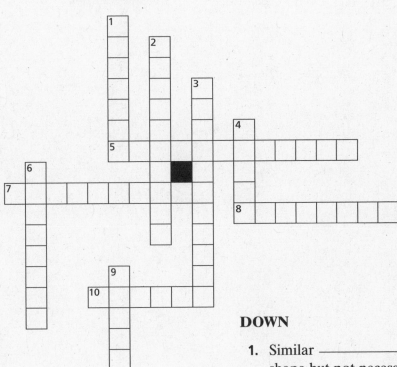

ACROSS

5. enlarged or reduced drawing of an object

7. equation stating two ratios are equal

8. a statement of two equal expressions

10. a whole number that divides another whole number evenly

DOWN

1. Similar _____ have the same shape but not necessarily the same size.

2. a statement that two expressions are not equal

3. a number made up of a nonzero whole number and a fraction

4. a number with only two factors, one and itself

6. a number in the form $\frac{a}{b}$

9. a comparison of two numbers by division

Name _____ Class _____ Date _____

Practice 6-1

Shade each grid to represent each of the following percents.

1. 53%

2. 23%

3. 71%

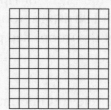

Write each ratio as a percent.

4. $\frac{4}{5}$ _____

5. $\frac{3}{5}$ _____

6. $\frac{9}{10}$ _____

7. $\frac{3}{10}$ _____

8. $\frac{6}{25}$ _____

9. $\frac{7}{100}$ _____

10. $\frac{9}{50}$ _____

11. $\frac{9}{25}$ _____

12. $\frac{2}{5}$ _____

13. $\frac{7}{10}$ _____

14. $\frac{4}{25}$ _____

15. $\frac{16}{25}$ _____

16. $\frac{11}{20}$ _____

17. $\frac{19}{20}$ _____

18. $\frac{27}{50}$ _____

19. 41 : 50 _____

Write a percent for each shaded figure.

20.

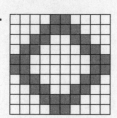

_____

21.

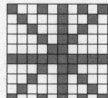

_____

22.

_____

Complete the following.

Ancient Egyptians did not write the fraction $\frac{4}{5}$ as "$\frac{4}{5}$". Instead, they used *unit fractions*. The numerator of a unit fraction is always 1. No denominator used to represent a given fraction can be repeated. For this reason, Egyptians would have written $\frac{4}{5}$ as $\frac{1}{2} + \frac{1}{5} + \frac{1}{10}$ and not as $\frac{1}{2} + \frac{1}{10} + \frac{1}{10} + \frac{1}{10}$. Write each of the following as a sum of unit fractions.

23. $\frac{3}{4}$ _____

24. $\frac{5}{8}$ _____

25. $\frac{9}{10}$ _____

26. $\frac{7}{12}$ _____

Course 2 Lesson 6-1

6-1 • Guided Problem Solving

GPS Student Page 277, Exercise 30:

History Before the Battle of Tippecanoe, nineteen twentieths of General William Harrison's troops had never before been in a battle. What percent of the troops had previously been in a battle?

Understand

1. What is the relevant information?

   _____

   _____

2. What are you being asked to do?

   _____

Plan and Carry Out

3. What fraction of the troops had never before been in a battle? _____

4. What fraction of the troops had previously been in a battle? _____

5. To write a number as a percent, first write an equivalent ratio with a denominator of what number? _____

6. Write an equivalent ratio of $\frac{1}{20}$. _____

7. Convert the fraction to a percent. _____

Check

8. What percent is nineteen twentieths? Does the sum of the percent you found in Step 7 and the equivalent percent of nineteen twentieths equal 100%?

   _____

   _____

Solve Another Problem

9. A marathon runner has run two fifths of the race. What percent of the race is left to run?

   _____

   _____

Practice 6-2

Percents, Fractions, and Decimals

Write each percent as a fraction in simplest form and as a decimal.

1. 65% _____   2. 37.5% _____   3. 80% _____   4. 25% _____

5. 18% _____   6. 46% _____   7. 87% _____   8. 8% _____

9. 43% _____   10. 55% _____   11. 94% _____   12. 36% _____

Write each number as a percent. Round to the nearest tenth of a percent where necessary.

13. $\frac{8}{15}$ _____   14. $\frac{7}{50}$ _____   15. 0.56 _____

16. 0.0413 _____   17. $\frac{3}{8}$ _____   18. $\frac{7}{12}$ _____

19. 0.387 _____   20. 0.283 _____   21. $\frac{2}{9}$ _____

Write each number as a percent. Place the number into the puzzle without using the percent sign or decimal point.

22.

Across

1. 0.134

3. $\frac{53}{100}$

5. 0.565

7. $1\frac{7}{50}$

9. 0.456

10. 0.63

11. $\frac{11}{200}$

13. 0.58

14. $\frac{191}{200}$

16. 0.605

Down

2. 0.346

4. 0.324

5. $\frac{1}{2}$

6. 0.515

8. $\frac{33}{200}$

9. 0.4385

10. $\frac{659}{1,000}$

12. $\frac{1,087}{20,000}$

15. $\frac{14}{25}$

6-2 • Guided Problem Solving

GPS Student Page 283, Exercise 35:

Your teacher uses different methods of grading quizzes. Your quiz grades are 85%, $\frac{9}{10}$, $\frac{16}{20}$, 92%, $\frac{21}{25}$, and 79%.

a. Write your quiz grades in order from least to greatest.

b. Find the average percent grade of your quizzes.

Understand

1. What are you being asked to do in part (a)?

   _____

   _____

2. In order to compare the grades, what should you do first?

   _____

   _____

3. Besides knowing the grades of the quizzes, explain what else is needed to find the average.

   _____

Plan and Carry Out

4. What are all your grades in percent form?

   _____

5. Order the grades from smallest to largest.

   _____

6. What is the total of all your grades? _____

7. Find the average percent grade of your six quizzes. _____

Check

8. Does the average grade fall between the smallest and largest grade?

   _____

Solve Another Problem

9. Your classmate had quiz grades of 75%, $\frac{13}{20}$, $\frac{15}{25}$, 89%, $\frac{8}{10}$, and 81%. Order the grades from least to greatest and find the average.

   _____

Practice 6-3

Percents Greater Than 100% or Less Than 1%

Classify each of the following as: (A) less than 1%, (B) greater than 100%, or (C) between 1% and 100%.

1. $\frac{1}{2}$ _____

2. $\frac{4}{3}$ _____

3. $\frac{2}{300}$ _____

4. $\frac{3}{10}$ _____

5. 1.03 _____

6. 0.009 _____

7. 0.635 _____

8. 0.0053 _____

Use > , < , or = to compare the numbers in each pair.

9. $\frac{1}{4}$ ☐ 20%

10. $\frac{1}{2}$% ☐ 50

11. 0.008 ☐ 8%

12. 150% ☐ $\frac{5}{4}$

13. 3 ☐ 300%

14. $\frac{7}{250}$ ☐ 0.3%

Write each fraction as a percent. Round to the nearest tenth of a percent if necessary.

15. $\frac{7}{5}$ _____

16. $\frac{137}{100}$ _____

17. $\frac{0.8}{100}$ _____

18. $\frac{21}{4}$ _____

19. $\frac{17}{10}$ _____

20. $\frac{65}{40}$ _____

21. $\frac{37}{20}$ _____

22. $\frac{7}{500}$ _____

23. $\frac{9}{8}$ _____

Write each decimal as a percent.

24. 0.003 _____

25. 1.8 _____

26. 0.0025 _____

27. 5.3 _____

28. 0.0041 _____

29. 0.083 _____

30. 0.0009 _____

31. 0.83 _____

32. 20 _____

Write each percent as a decimal and as a fraction in simplest form.

33. 175% _____

34. 120% _____

35. $\frac{2}{5}$% _____

_____

_____

_____

36. $\frac{5}{8}$% _____

37. 750% _____

38. $8\frac{1}{4}$% _____

_____

_____

_____

39. In 1990, the population of Kansas was 2,477,574, which included 21,965 Native Americans. What percent of the people living in Kansas were Native Americans?

_____

40. The mass of Earth is $\frac{1}{318}$ of the mass of Jupiter. What percent is this?

_____

6-3 • Guided Problem Solving

GPS **Student Page 287, Exercise 40:**

Write the percent as a decimal and as a fraction in simplest form.

Weather On March 1, the snowpack in the Northern Great Basin of Nevada was 126% of the average snowpack.

Understand

1. What is the relevant information?

   _____

   _____

2. What are you being asked to do?

   _____

3. How do you convert a percent to a decimal?

   _____

Plan and Carry Out

4. When changing 126% to a fraction, what
   will be your numerator and denominator? _____

5. Write this fraction as a mixed number in simplest form.

   _____

6. Convert 126% to a decimal. _____

Check

7. Multiply the answer to Step 6 by 100. Does it equal the percent?

   _____

Solve Another Problem

Write the percent as a decimal and as a fraction in simplest form.

8. Of the students in a class, 66% are female.

   _____

Practice 6-4

Finding a Percent of a Number

Find each answer.

1. 20% of 560

2. 42% of 200

3. 9% of 50

_____

_____

_____

4. 40% of 70

5. 25% of 80

6. 50% of 80

_____

_____

_____

7. 40% of 200

8. 5% of 80

9. 75% of 200

_____

_____

_____

Find each answer using mental math.

10. 14% of 120

11. 30% of 180

12. 62.5% of 24

_____

_____

_____

13. 34% of 50

14. 25% of 240

15. 85.5% of 23

_____

_____

_____

16. 120% of 56

17. 80% of 90

18. 42% of 120

_____

_____

_____

Solve.

19. A farmer grew a watermelon that weighed 20 lb. From his
experience with growing watermelons, he estimated that 95% of
the watermelon's weight is water.

a. How much of the watermelon is water? _____

b. How much of the watermelon is not water? _____

c. The watermelon was shipped off to market, where it sat
until it had dehydrated (lost water). If the watermelon
is still 90% water, what percent of it is not water? _____

d. The solid part of the watermelon still weighs the same.
What was the weight of the watermelon at this point? _____

20. A bicycle goes on sale at 75% of its original price of $160.
What is its sale price?

_____

6-4 • Guided Problem Solving

GPS **Student Page 293, Exercise 41:**

Forestry Russia had 17,000 forest fires in 2001. Aircraft put out 40% of the fires. How many of the fires were put out by aircraft?

Understand

1. What is the relevant information in the problem?

   _____

2. What are you being asked to do?

   _____

   _____

3. How will changing 40% to an equivalent decimal help you solve the problem?

   _____

   _____

Plan and Carry Out

4. What is the percent of fires in Russian forests that were put out by aircraft?

   _____

   _____

5. Write 40% as a decimal. _____

6. What is the total number of Russian forest fires? _____

7. Multiply your decimal answer from Step 5 by 17,000.

   _____

8. How many of the fires were put out by aircraft? _____

Check

9. What is 50% of 17,000? Is the number of fires put out by aircraft less than this?

   _____

Solve Another Problem

10. Your mother says that 80% of your shirts are dirty. If you have 30 shirts, how many are dirty?

    _____

Guided Problem Solving

Name _____ Class _____ Date _____

Practice 6-5

Solving Percent Problems Using Proportions

Use a proportion to solve.

1. 48 is 60% of what number?

2. What is 175% of 85?

3. What percent of 90 is 50?

4. 76 is 80% of what number?

5. What is 50% of 42.88?

6. 96 is 160% of what number?

7. What percent of 24 is 72?

8. What is 85% of 120?

9. What is 80% of 12?

10. 56 is 75% of what number?

Solve.

11. The sale price of a bicycle is $120. This is 75% of the original price. Find the original price.

12. The attendance at a family reunion was 160 people. This was 125% of last year's attendance. How many people attended the reunion last year?

13. A company has 875 employees. On "Half-Price Wednesday," 64% of the employees eat lunch at the company cafeteria. How many employees eat lunch at the cafeteria on Wednesdays?

14. There are 1,295 students attending a small university. There are 714 women enrolled. What percentage of students are women?

Course 2 Lesson 6-5

6-5 • Guided Problem Solving

GPS Student Page 297, Exercise 34:

At the library, you find 9 books on a certain topic. The librarian tells you that 55% of the books on this topic have been signed out. How many books does the library have on the topic?

Understand

1. Circle the information you will need to solve.

2. What are you being asked to do?

   _____

   _____

3. If 55% of the books have been signed out, what percent of the books have *not* been signed out?

   _____

Plan and Carry Out

4. Choose a variable to represent the total number of books the

   library has on the topic. _____

5. How many books did you find on the topic? _____

6. Write a proportion comparing the percent of books in the library

   to the number of books in the library. _____

7. Solve the proportion. _____

8. How many books does the library have on the topic? _____

Check

9. Is 55% of your answer plus 9 equal to your answer?

   _____

Solve Another Problem

10. There are 12,000 people attending a concert. You learn that 20% of the people who bought tickets to the concert did not attend. How many people bought tickets to the concert?

    _____

    _____

Practice 6-6

Solving Percent Problems Using Equations

Write and solve an equation. Round answers to the nearest tenth.

1. What percent of 64 is 48?

_____

_____

2. 16% of 130 is what number?

_____

_____

3. 25% of what number is 24?

_____

_____

4. What percent of 18 is 12?

_____

_____

5. 48% of 83 is what number?

_____

_____

6. 40% of what number is 136?

_____

_____

7. What percent of 530 is 107?

_____

_____

8. 74% of 643 is what number?

_____

_____

9. 62% of what number is 84?

_____

_____

10. What percent of 84 is 50?

_____

_____

11. 37% of 245 is what number?

_____

_____

12. 12% of what number is 105?

_____

_____

Solve.

13. A cafe offers senior citizens a 15% discount off its regular price of $8.95 for the dinner buffet.

    a. What percent of the regular price is the price for senior citizens? _____

    b. What is the price for senior citizens? _____

14. In 1990, 12.5% of the people in Oregon did not have health insurance. If the population of Oregon was 2,880,000, how many people were uninsured?

_____

6-6 • Guided Problem Solving

GPS **Student Page 301, Exercise 28:**

Food You make 72 cookies for a bake sale. This is 20% of the cookies at the bake sale. How many cookies are at the bake sale?

Understand

1. Circle the information you will need to solve.

2. What are you being asked to do?

   _____

3. What word indicates an equal sign?

   _____

Plan and Carry Out

4. Choose a variable to represent the number of cookies at the bake sale. _____

5. What number is 20% of the cookies at the bake sale? _____

6. Write an expression for the phrase,
   20% of the cookies at the bake sale. _____

7. Write an equation using what you wrote in Steps 5 and 6 to find the number of cookies at the bake sale.

   _____

8. Solve the equation. _____

9. How many cookies are at the bake sale? _____

Check

10. Find 20% of your answer. Does it equal 72?

    _____

Solve Another Problem

11. You collect trading cards and so far you have 12 different cards. If this is 30% of the possible cards, how many cards are there to collect?

    _____

Name _____ Class _____ Date _____

Practice 6-7

Find the total cost.

1. $17.50 with a 7% sales tax

   _____

2. $21.95 with a 4.25% sales tax

   _____

3. $52.25 with an 8% sales tax

   _____

4. $206.88 with a 5.75% sales tax

   _____

5. The price of a pair of shoes is $85.99 before sales tax.
   The sales tax is 7.5%. Find the total cost of the shoes. _____

Estimate a 15% tip for each amount.

6. $12.68

   _____

7. $18.25

   _____

8. $15.00

   _____

Find each commission.

9. 2% on $1,500 in sales

   _____

10. 8% on $80,000 in sales

    _____

11. 5% on $600 in sales

    _____

12. 12% on $3,200 in sales

    _____

Find the total earnings when given the salary, commission rate, and sales.

13. $1,000 plus 6% on sales of $2,000

    _____

14. $500 plus 10% on sales of $1,400

    _____

15. $850 plus 8% on sales of $8,000

    _____

16. $1,200 plus 4.5% on sales of $6,500

    _____

17. To recover a large chair in your home, you purchase $9\frac{1}{2}$ yards of
    upholstery fabric at $11.00 per yard. If there is a 7% sales tax,
    what is the total cost of the fabric?

    _____

18. You and your sister rake and pick up leaves from your
    grandmother's yard. She says she'll pay you $35.00 for the job.
    Upon completion of your work, she also decides to add a
    separate 20% tip for each of you. You and your sister each keep
    your individual tips, and you decide to split your other earnings
    in half. How much will each of you earn from the job?

    _____

6-7 • Guided Problem Solving

GPS **Student Page 307, Exercise 26:**

Sales A store pays a 6% commision on the first $500 in sales and 8% on sales over $500. Find the commission on an $800 sale.

Understand

1. Circle the information you will need to solve.

2. Define commission.

_____

_____

3. Which operations do you need to use to solve this problem?

_____

Plan and Carry Out

4. $800 = $500 + __?__   _____

5. What is 6% of $500?   _____

6. What is 8% of $300?   _____

7. What is the commission on a $800 sale? _____

Check

8. Find 10% of $500 and 10% of $300. Since 6% is a little more than half of 10%, what is half of 10% of 500? Add this with 10% of 30, since 8% is close to 10%. Does your answer make sense?

_____

Solve Another Problem

9. Dan's uncle asks him to come work for him at his men's clothing store. He will pay him 5% on his first $1,000 in sales and 8% on sales above $1,000. How much will Dan earn if he sells $2,500 in merchandise?

_____

_____

Practice 6-8

Find each percent of change. State whether the change is an increase or a decrease.

1. A $50 coat is put on sale for $35.

   _____

   _____

2. Mayelle earns $18,000 a year. After a raise, she earns $19,500.

   _____

   _____

3. Last year Anthony earned $24,000. After a brief lay-off this year, Anthony's income is $18,500.

   _____

   _____

4. In 1981, about $1.1 million was lost due to fires. In 1988, the loss was about $9.6 million.

   _____

   _____

5. In a recent year, certain colleges and universities received about $268 million in aid. Ten years later, they received about $94 million.

   _____

   _____

6. A coat regularly costing $125 is put on sale for $75.

   _____

   _____

7. Complete the table.

Enrollment in Center City Schools From 1995 to 2000

Year	Enrollment	Change from Last Year (number of students)	Change from Last Year (%)	Increase or Decrease
1995	18,500	—	—	—
1996	19,300			
1997	19,700			
1998	19,500			
1999	19,870			
2000	19,200			

6-8 • Guided Problem Solving

GPS **Student Page 313, Exercise 29:**

Sports A football player gained 1,200 yd last season and 900 yd this season. Find the percent of change. State whether the change is an increase or a decrease.

Understand

1. What two numbers will you be comparing?

   _____

2. Did the football player gain more yards last season or this season?

   _____

3. What are you being asked to do?

   _____

   _____

Plan and Carry Out

4. What is the difference in the number of yards gained last season and this season? _____

5. Write a proportion comparing the difference and the percent of change. _____

6. What are the cross products? _____

7. What number do you divide each side by? _____

8. What is the percent of change? _____

9. Is it a decrease or increase? _____

Check

10. Explain your answer to step 9.

    _____

    _____

    _____

Solve Another Problem

11. In a previous game the school's star basketball player scored 25 points. In today's game he scored 40 points. What was the percent of change in the player's scoring? Is the change an increase or decrease?

    _____

6A: Graphic Organizer

Study Skill As you read over the material in the chapter, keep a paper and pencil handy to write down notes and questions that you have.

Write your answers.

1. What is the chapter title? _____

2. How many lessons are there in this chapter? _____

3. What is the topic of the Test-Taking Strategies page? _____

4. Complete the graphic organizer below as you work through the chapter.
   • In the center, write the title of the chapter.
   • When you begin a lesson, write the lesson name in a rectangle.
   • When you complete a lesson, write a skill or key concept in a circle linked to that lesson block.
   • When you complete the chapter, use this graphic organizer to help you review.

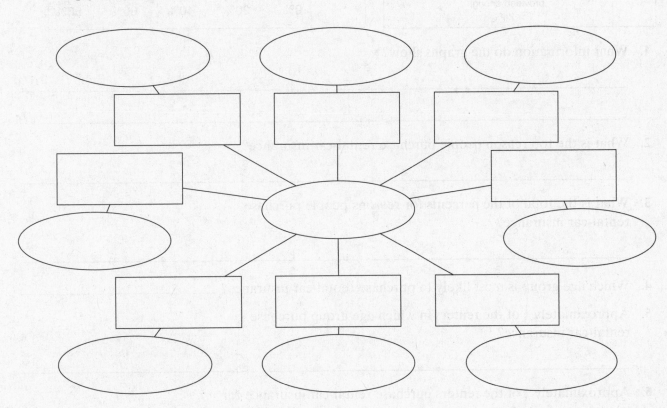

6B: Reading Comprehension

Study Skill Use a special notebook (or section of a loose-leaf binder) for your math handouts and homework. Keep your notebook neat and organized by reviewing its contents often.

Use the graphs shown below to answer the questions that follow.

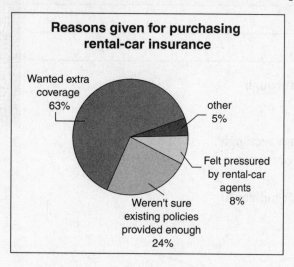

Reasons given for purchasing rental-car insurance

Wanted extra coverage 63%

other 5%

Felt pressured by rental-car agents 8%

Weren't sure existing policies provided enough 24%

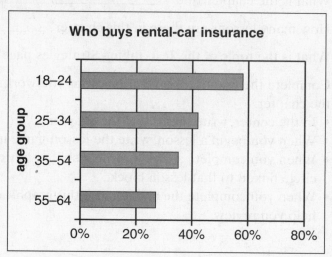

Who buys rental-car insurance

age group

18–24

25–34

35–54

55–64

0%   20%   40%   60%   80%

1. What information do the graphs show?

_____

_____

2. What is the top reason people purchase rental-car insurance?

_____

3. What is the total of the percents for reasons people purchase rental-car insurance?

_____

4. Which age group is most likely to purchase rental-car insurance? _____

5. Approximately $\frac{1}{3}$ of the renters in which age group purchase rental-car insurance?

_____

6. Approximately $\frac{1}{4}$ of the renters purchase rental-car insurance for what reason?

_____

7. **High-Use Academic Words** In Exercise 1, what does the word *show* mean?

a. to display   b. to put in a sequence

Vocabulary and Study Skills

6C: Reading/Writing Math Symbols

For use after Lesson 6-4

Study Skill When working on your math homework, use a pencil and have an eraser nearby.

Write each of the following using appropriate mathematical symbols and abbreviations.

1. 3 feet to 1 yard _____

2. 47 and 6 tenths percent _____

3. 37 percent is greater than $\frac{1}{3}$ _____

4. 1 meter to 100 centimeters _____

5. 106 percent _____

6. $\frac{1}{4}$ is less than 26% _____

7. 8 quarts to 2 gallons _____

8. 93 and 32 hundredths percent _____

9. the absolute value of negative 16 _____

10. 78 out of 100 _____

Write each of the following in words.

11. $|-7.3| = 7.3$

_____

12. 30.08%

_____

13. $50\% > \frac{2}{5}$

_____

14. 2 h : 120 min

_____

15. $\frac{55}{100}$

_____

16. $\frac{1}{10} < 12\%$

_____

6D: Visual Vocabulary Practice

For use after Lesson 6-7

High-Use Academic Words

Study Skill When making a sketch, make it simple but make it complete.

Concept List

represent	graph	solve
model	explain	pattern
substitute	calculate	verify

Write the concept that best describes each exercise. Choose from the concept list above

1. 35% of 70 is $0.35 \times 70 = 24.5$ _____	**2.** $\overset{\longleftarrow}{\underset{-3 \quad -2 \quad -1 \quad 0 \quad 1}{\rule{3cm}{0.4pt}}}$ _____	**3.** $5 : 7$ 5 to 7 $\frac{5}{7}$ _____
4. $n + 76 \geq 64$ $n + 76 - 76 \geq 64 - 76$ $n \geq -12$ _____	**5.** Sales tax is a percent of a purchase price you must pay when buying certain items. The formula for sales tax is sales tax = tax rate × purchase price. _____	**6.** If $\frac{t}{18} = \frac{7}{126}$, then $t = 1$. Check: $1 \times 126 = 7 \times 18$ _____
7. 	A	B
---	---
3	15
6	30
9	45
12	60
15	75 | _____	**8.** $7a = 161$; a is either 23 or 26 $7(21) \overset{?}{=} 147$ False $7(23) \overset{?}{=} 161$ True _____	**9.** 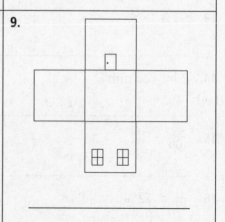 _____

Vocabulary and Study Skills

6E: Vocabulary Check

Study Skill Strengthen your vocabulary. Use these pages and add cues and summaries by applying the Cornell Notetaking style.

Write the definition for each word or term at the right. To check your work, fold the paper back along the dotted line to see the correct answers.

_____   commission

_____

_____

_____   discount

_____

_____

_____   markup

_____

_____

_____   percent

_____

_____

_____   percent of change

_____

_____

6E: Vocabulary Check (continued)

For use after Lesson 6-8

Write the vocabulary word or term for each definition. To check your work, fold the paper back along the dotted line to see the correct answers.

pay that is equal to a percent of sales

_____

the difference between the original price and the sale price of an item

_____

the difference between the selling price and the original cost

_____

a ratio that compares a number to 100

_____

the percent a quantity increases or decreases from its original amount

_____

6F: Vocabulary Review

For use with the Chapter Review

Study Skill When you have to match words and descriptions from two columns, read the list of words and the definitions carefully and completely so you can quickly find the obvious matches. Then do the rest, one at a time. Cross out words and definitions as you use them.

Match the word in Column A with its definition in Column B.

Column A	Column B
1. percent	**A.** difference between the original price and the sale price
2. factor	**B.** equation stating two ratios are equal
3. discount	**C.** whole number that divides into another whole number evenly
4. ratio	**D.** difference between the selling price and the original cost of an item
5. proportion	**E.** comparison of two numbers by division
6. markup	**F.** ratio comparing a number to 100

Match the word in Column A with its definition in Column B.

Column A	Column B
7. mode	**G.** percent a quantity increases or decreases from its original amount
8. equation	**H.** enlarged or reduced drawing of an object
9. commission	**J.** statement that two expressions are equal
10. tip	**K.** number that occurs most often in a data set
11. scale drawing	**L.** percent of sales
12. percent of change	**M.** percent of a bill that you give to a person for providing a service

Name _____ Class _____ Date _____

Practice 7-1

Lines and Planes

Describe the lines or line segments as *parallel* or *intersecting*.

1. the rows on a spreadsheet _____

2. the marks left by a skidding car _____

3. sidewalks on opposite sides of a street _____

4. the cut sides of a wedge of apple pie _____

5. the wires suspended between telephone poles _____

6. the hands of a clock at 7:00 P.M. _____

7. the trunks of grown trees in a forest _____

Use the diagram below for exercises 8–12.

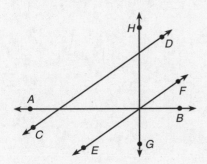

8. Name a pair of parallel lines. _____

9. Name a segment. _____

10. Name three points. _____

11. Name two rays. _____

12. Name a pair of intersecting lines. _____

Use a straightedge to draw each figure.

13. a line parallel to $\overline{UV}$ **14.** a line intersecting $\overline{XY}$

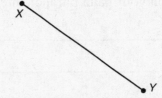

7-1 • Guided Problem Solving

GPS **Student Page 327, Exercise 23:**

Are the rungs on a ladder parallel, intersecting, or skew?

Understand

1. What is a ladder? Draw a sketch of one.

_____

_____

2. What are the rungs of a ladder? Circle the rungs on your sketch.

_____

_____

3. What are you being asked to do?

_____

_____

Plan and Carry Out

4. Do the rungs have any points in common? _____

5. Are the rungs in the same plane? _____

6. Are the rungs intersecting? _____

7. Are the rungs skew? _____

8. Are the rungs parallel? _____

Check

9. Define *parallel*. Does this describe the rungs?

_____

_____

Solve Another Problem

10. Are the lines on your palm parallel, intersecting, or skew?

_____

_____

_____

Practice 7-2

Identifying and Classifying Angles

In exercises 1–6, classify each angle as *acute, right, obtuse,* or *straight.*

1. _____

2. _____

3. _____

4. $m\angle A = 180°$ _____

5. $m\angle B = 43°$ _____

6. $m\angle D = 90°$ _____

Use the figure at the right to name the following.

7. two lines _____

8. three segments _____

9. a pair of congruent angles _____

10. four right angles

11. two pairs of obtuse vertical angles

_____

_____

12. two pairs of adjacent supplementary angles

13. two pairs of complementary angles

_____

Solve.

14. If $m\angle A = 23°$, what is the measure of its complement?

_____

15. If $m\angle T = 163°$, what is the measure of its supplement?

_____

16. If a 67° angle is complementary to $\angle Q$, what is the measure of $\angle Q$?

_____

17. Use the dot grid to draw two supplementary angles, one of which is 45°. Do *not* use a protractor.

7-2 • Guided Problem Solving

GPS **Student Page 334, Exercise 26:**

Writing in Math Can an angle ever have the same measure as its complement? Explain.

Understand

1. What are you being asked to do?

   _____

   _____

2. What do you have to do to explain your answer?

   _____

   _____

Plan and Carry Out

3. What is the definition of complementary angles?

   _____

4. If an angle and its complement have the same measure, explain the relationship between the angle and 90°.

   _____

   _____

5. Determine the measure of the angle. _____

6. Can an angle ever have the same measure as its complement? _____

Check

7. Explain your answer.

   _____

   _____

Solve Another Problem

8. Can an angle ever have the same measure as its supplement? Explain.

   _____

   _____

Practice 7-3

Triangles

Find the value of *x* in each triangle.

1.
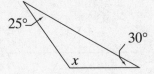

_____

2.

_____

3.

_____

4.
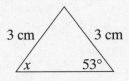

_____

5.
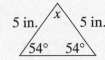

_____

6.
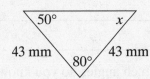

_____

Classify each triangle.

7. The measures of two angles are 53° and 76°.

_____

8. Two sides have the same length.

_____

9. The measure of one angle is 90°.

_____

10. All three sides have the same length.

_____

11. The measures of the angles of a triangle are 40°, 50°, and 90°.

   a. Classify the triangle by its angles. _____

   b. Can the triangle be equilateral? Why or why not? _____

   _____

   c. Can the triangle be isosceles? Why or why not? _____

   _____

   d. Can you classify the triangle by its sides? Why or why not? _____

   _____

7-3 • Guided Problem Solving

GPS Student Page 339, Exercise 19:

Writing in Math What is the measure of $\angle E$? Show your work and justify your steps.

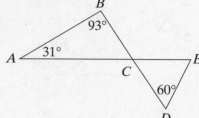

Understand

1. What are you being asked to do?

   _____

   _____

2. Which angles do you know the measure of? What is their measure?

   _____

Plan and Carry Out

3. What is the sum of the measures of the angles in a triangle?

   _____

4. What is the sum of the measures of angles A and B?

   _____

5. Use the results from Steps 3 and 4 to determine the measure of $\angle ACB$. What is the measure of $\angle ECD$?

   _____

6. What is the sum of the measures of angles $\angle ECD$ and $\angle D$?

   _____

7. Use the results from Steps 3 and 6 to determine $m\angle E$.

   _____

Check

8. How do you justify using 180° to find the measure of the unknown angles?

   _____

Solve Another Problem

9. Suppose $m\angle A = 62°$, $m\angle B = 43°$, and $m\angle D = 73°$. Find the measure of $\angle E$.

   _____

   _____

Name _____ Class _____ Date _____

Practice 7-4

Quadrilaterals and Other Polygons

Identify each polygon and classify it as *regular* or *irregular*.

1.

_____

_____

2.

_____

_____

3.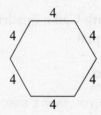

_____

_____

State all correct names for each quadrilateral. Then circle the best name.

4.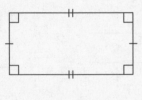

_____

_____

5.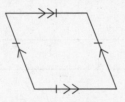

_____

_____

6.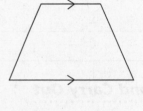

_____

_____

Use dot paper to draw each quadrilateral.

7. a rectangle that is not a square

8. a rhombus with two right angles

9. a trapezoid with no right angles

10. List all additional side lengths and angle measures you can find for the trapezoid *JKLM*, where $\overline{KL}$ is parallel to $\overline{JM}$, ∠*K* is a right angle, and the length of $\overline{LM}$ is 10 cm.

_____

7-4 • Guided Problem Solving

GPS **Student Page 344, Exercise 22:**

Writing in Math Can a quadrilateral be both a rhombus and a rectangle? Explain.

Understand

1. What are you being asked to do?

_____

_____

2. In order to answer this question, what definitions do you need to know?

_____

_____

_____

Plan and Carry Out

3. What is a quadrilateral?

_____

4. What is a rhombus?

_____

5. What is a rectangle?

_____

6. Can a quadrilateral be both a rhombus and a rectangle?

_____

Check

7. Explain your answer to Step 6 by giving an example of a shape that is both a rhombus and a rectangle.

_____

_____

_____

Solve Another Problem

8. If all squares are types of rectangles, are all rhombuses types of rectangles? Explain.

_____

_____

Practice 7-5

Congruent Figures

Are the figures *congruent* or *not congruent*? Explain.

1.
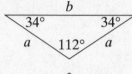

2.
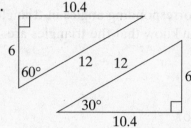

3.
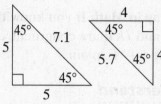

_____ _____ _____

_____ _____ _____

_____ _____ _____

_____ _____ _____

Complete each congruence statement.

4. $\triangle ABC \cong$ _____

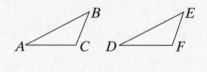

5. $\triangle ABC \cong$ _____

6. $\triangle ABC \cong$ _____

Write six congruences involving corresponding sides and angles for each pair of triangles.

7. $\triangle ABC \cong \triangle DEF$

_____

_____

_____

8. $\triangle JKL \cong \triangle MNO$

_____

_____

_____

Use the diagram at the right to complete each of the following.

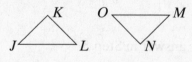

9. a. $\angle ABC \cong$ _____

   b. $\overline{AB} \cong$ _____

   c. $\angle F \cong$ _____

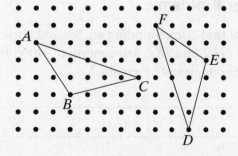

7-5 • Guided Problem Solving

GPS Student Page 349, Exercise 13:

Writing in Math If you know that corresponding angles in triangles *GHI* and *JKL* are congruent, do you know that the triangles are congruent? Explain.

Understand

1. What are you being asked to do?

   _____

   _____

2. What proves that two triangles are congruent?

   _____

   _____

Plan and Carry Out

3. What do you know about triangles *GHI* and *JKL*?

   _____

4. What do you know about the corresponding sides of triangles *GHI* and *JKL*?

   _____

5. Do you know that the two triangles are congruent?

   _____

Check

6. Explain your answer in Step 5.

   _____

   _____

   _____

Solve Another Problem

7. If you know that corresponding angles and corresponding sides in triangles *GHI* and *JKL* are congruent, do you know that the triangles are congruent? Explain.

   _____

   _____

Practice 7-6

Name each of the following for circle *O*.

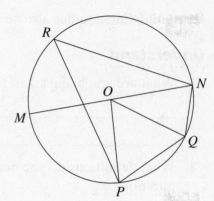

1. two chords

   _____

2. three radii

   _____

3. a diameter

   _____

4. a central angle

   _____

5. a semicircle

   _____

6. two arcs

   _____

7. the longest chord

   _____

8. the shortest chord

   _____

Name all of the indicated arcs for circle *Q*.

9. all arcs shorter than a semicircle _____

10. all arcs longer than a semicircle _____ _____ _____

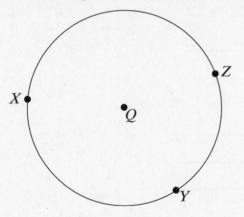

11. Use a compass to draw and label a circle *Q*. Label a semicircle
    $\overset{\frown}{ABC}$ and an arc $\overset{\frown}{AX}$.

7-6 • Guided Problem Solving

GPS **Student Page 352, Exercise 25:**

Reasoning Can a radius also be a chord? Explain.

Understand

1. What are you being asked to do?

   _____

   _____

2. What definitions do you need to know in order to answer the question?

   _____

Plan and Carry Out

3. What is a radius?

   _____

   _____

4. Where are the endpoints of a radius?

   _____

   _____

5. What is a chord?

   _____

   _____

6. Can a radius also be a chord? _____

Check

7. Explain your answer in Step 6.

   _____

   _____

   _____

Solve Another Problem

8. Can a diameter also be a chord? Explain.

   _____

   _____

Practice 7-7

Use the information in each table to create a circle graph.

1. The data show the total number of space vehicles that either successfully reached or exceeded orbit around Earth.

Years	Number of Successful United States Space Launches
1957–1959	15
1960–1969	470
1970–1979	258
1980–1989	153
1990–1995	146

2. The data represent the percent of private schools in the United States that have an annual tuition in each of the given ranges.

Annual Tuition	% of Private Schools
Less than $500	13
$500–$1,000	28
$1,001–$1,500	26
$1,501–$2,500	15
More than $2,500	18

3. The data represent a poll taken in a seventh-grade class.

Favorite Color for a Car	Number of Seventh Graders
Red	14
Blue	9
White	3
Green	1

a. What percent of seventh graders like blue cars? _____

b. What percent of seventh graders like green cars? _____

c. What percent of seventh graders like either red *or* blue cars?

_____

d. What percent of seventh graders like a car color *other than* white?

_____

7-7 • Guided Problem Solving

GPS **Student Page 357, Exercise 17:**

The table shows how many days each week students do volunteer work. Use the table to make a circle graph.

Days	1	2	3	4	5
Students	11	5	5	2	2

Understand

1. What are you being asked to do?

   _____

2. How many students total volunteered?

   _____

Plan and Carry Out

3. Use a proportion to find the angle of measure for the number of students who volunteered on Day 1.

   _____

4. Repeat Step 3 for Day 2.

   _____

5. Repeat Step 3 for Day 3.

   _____

6. Repeat Step 3 for Day 4.

   _____

7. Repeat Step 3 for Day 5.

   _____

8. Use the central angles you found in Steps 3–7 to draw the circle graph.

Check

9. Does the section for 1 day take up a large portion of the circle?

   _____

Solve Another Problem

10. You are in charge of the activities page in the school yearbook. You want to show how many students are participating in each activity. Use the data in the table to make a circle graph.

Activity	Sports	Band	Student Council	Horticulture	Clubs
Students	28	15	5	3	10

Practice 7-8

Construct the perpendicular bisector of each segment.

1.

2.

Construct a congruent segment.

3.

4.

Construct each angle or segment.

5. Construct a segment with measure $\frac{3}{4}$ that of $\overline{TU}$.

6. Construct the perpendicular bisector of $\overline{XY}$. Then make the perpendicular bisector congruent to segment $\overline{XY}$.

Point _D_ is the midpoint of $\overline{BC}$. Complete.

7. $\overline{BC}$ = 10 in., $\overline{CD}$ = _____

8. $\overline{DC}$ = 9 mm, $\overline{BD}$ = _____

9. $\overline{BD}$ = 2 cm, $\overline{BC}$ = _____

10. $\overline{BC}$ = 12 yd, $\overline{DC}$ = _____

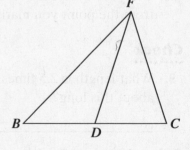

7-8 • Guided Problem Solving

GPS Student Page 363, Exercise 16:

Draw $\overline{MN}$ about 4 in. long. Then construct $\overline{JK}$ two and one half times as long as $\overline{MN}$.

Understand

1. How many times as long as $\overline{MN}$ is $\overline{JK}$?

   _____

2. What two constructions will you need to know how to perform to draw $\overline{JK}$?

   _____

Plan and Carry Out

3. Draw $\overline{MN}$ so that it is about 4 inches long.

4. Next, draw a ray with endpoint J that looks at least two and one half times as long as $\overline{MN}$.

5. Use your compass to mark a point on your ray that is exactly the length of $\overline{MN}$ from J.

6. Now use your compass to mark a point the length of $\overline{MN}$ away from the point you marked in Step 5.

7. Construct the bisector for $\overline{MN}$. Use this to find half the length of $\overline{MN}$.

8. Use your compass to mark endpoint K half the length of $\overline{MN}$ away from the point you marked in Step 6.

Check

9. What length is 2.5 times as long as 4 in.? Is your line segment about this long?

   _____

Solve Another Problem

10. Draw $\overline{AB}$ about 1.5 in. long. Then construct $\overline{CD}$ two and one half times as long as $\overline{AB}$.

7A: Graphic Organizer

For use before Lesson 7-1

Study Skill Take notes while you study. Writing something down might help you remember it better. Go back and review your notes when you study for quizzes and tests.

Write your answers.

1. What is the chapter title? _____

2. How many lessons are there in this chapter? _____

3. What is the topic of the Test-Taking Strategies page? _____

4. Complete the graphic organizer below as you work through the chapter.
   - In the center, write the title of the chapter.
   - When you begin a lesson, write the lesson name in a rectangle.
   - When you complete a lesson, write a skill or key concept in a circle linked to that lesson block.
   - When you complete the chapter, use this graphic organizer to help you review.

7B: Reading Comprehension

For use after Lesson 7-7

Study Skill Review notes that you have taken in class as soon as possible to clarify any points you missed. Be sure to ask questions if you need extra help.

Here is a circle graph for a monthly household budget. Use the graph to answer the questions that follow.

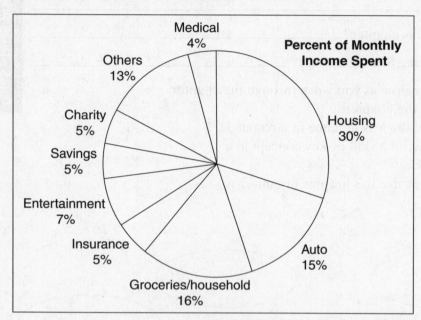

Percent of Monthly Income Spent

1. On which category was the largest percent of income spent? _____

2. On which category was the smallest percent of income spent? _____

3. Why are the insurance, savings, and charity sectors the same size?

    _____

4. What is the total of the percents listed in the circle graph? _____

5. If the monthly income is $2,400, how much should be spent on an automobile?

    _____

6. How much of a $1,900 monthly income should be saved? _____

7. If $60 is the amount budgeted for entertainment, what is the monthly income?

    _____

8. **High-Use Academic Words** What does it mean to *review,* as mentioned in the study skill?

    a. to put in order   b. to study again

7C: Reading/Writing Math Symbols   For use after Lesson 7-5

Study Skill When you take notes, use abbreviations and symbols such as @ (at), # (number), and w/ (with) to save time and reduce writing.

Match the symbol in Column A with its meaning in Column B.

Column A	Column B
1. $\angle ABC$	**A.** the measure of angle ABC
2. $\overline{AB}$	**B.** the length of segment AB
3. $\overleftrightarrow{AB}$	**C.** triangle ABC
4. AB	**D.** segment AB
5. $\overrightarrow{AB}$	**E.** ray starting at A and passing through B
6. $m\angle ABC$	**F.** ray starting at B and passing through A
7. $\overrightarrow{BA}$	**G.** line AB
8. $\triangle ABC$	**H.** angle ABC

Write the meaning of each of the following mathematical statements.

9. $m\angle B = 80°$

_____

10. $\triangle ABC \cong \triangle HIJ$

_____

11. $\angle XYZ \cong \angle MNP$

_____

12. $BC = 4$

_____

13. $\overline{DJ} \cong \overline{KL}$

_____

14. $DJ = KL$

_____

15. $m\angle P = m\angle R$

_____

16. $BC = \frac{1}{2}TU$

_____

7D: Visual Vocabulary Practice

For use after Lesson 7-8

Study Skill Use Venn Diagrams to understand the relationship between words whose meanings overlap, such as squares, rectangles, and quadrilaterals or real numbers, integers, and counting numbers.

Concept List

obtuse angle	right triangle	adjacent angles
chord	equilateral triangle	perpendicular bisector
midpoint	hexagon	pentagon

Write the concept that best describes each exercise. Choose from the concept list above.

1. 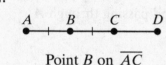 Point *B* on $\overline{AC}$	**2.** 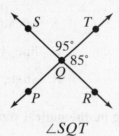 ∠*SQT*	**3.** 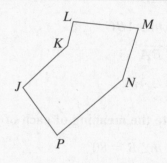
4. 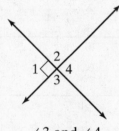 ∠3 and ∠4	**5.** 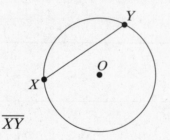 $\overline{XY}$	**6.** 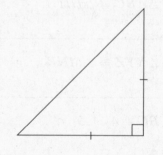
7. 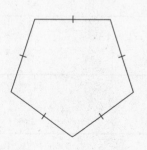	**8.** 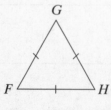 $\overline{FG} \cong \overline{GH} \cong \overline{FH}$	**9.** 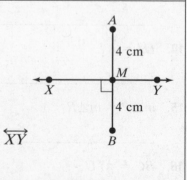 $\overleftrightarrow{XY}$

Vocabulary and Study Skills

7E: Vocabulary Check

Study Skill Strengthen your vocabulary. Use these pages and add cues and summaries by applying the Cornell Notetaking style.

Write the definition for each word or term at the right. To check your work, fold the paper back along the dotted line to see the correct answers.

_____ polygon

_____

_____

_____ parallel lines

_____

_____

_____ trapezoid

_____

_____

_____ acute angle

_____

_____

_____ circle

_____

_____

Vocabulary and Study Skills

7E: Vocabulary Check (continued)

For use after Lesson 7-6

Write the vocabulary word or term for each definition. To check your work, fold the paper forward along the dotted line to see the correct answers.

a closed figure with sides formed
by three or more line segments

_____

lines in the same plane that never
intersect

_____

a quadrilateral with exactly
one pair of parallel sides

_____

an angle with measure between
0 and 90 degrees

_____

the set of all points in the plane
that are the same distance from
a given point

_____

7F: Vocabulary Review Puzzle

For use with the Chapter Review

Study Skill Write assignments down; do not rely only on your memory.

Below is a list of clues grouped by the number of letters in the answer. Identify the word each clue represents, and fit each word into the puzzle grid.

7 letters
- tool used to draw circles and arcs
- polygon with 10 sides
- type of triangle with no congruent sides
- polygon with all sides and angles congruent

8 letters
- point that divides a segment into two segments of equal length
- polygon with 5 sides

9 letters
- sides that have the same length
- type of triangle with at least two sides congruent
- parallelogram with four right angles
- quadrilateral with exacly one pair of parallel sides

11 letters
- triangle with three congruent sides

12 letters
- lines that have exactly one point in common

13 letters
- two angles whose sum is 180°
- two angles whose sum is 90°

3 letters
- part of a circle

5 letters
- angle that measures between 0° and 90°
- formed by two rays with a common endpoint
- segment that has both endpoints on the circle
- flat surface that extends indefinitely in all directions

6 letters
- point of intersection of two sides on an angle or figure
- set of all points in a plane that are the same distance from a given point
- angle that measures between 90° and 180°

Practice 8-1

Estimate the perimeter of each figure. The length of one side of each square represents 1 yd.

1.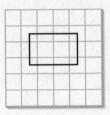

2.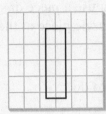

3.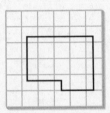

4.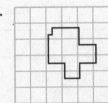

Choose a reasonable estimate. Explain your choice.

5. height of a truck cab: 12 in. or 12 ft _____

6. width of a book: 8 in. or 8 ft _____

7. diameter of a pizza: 8 in. or 8 ft _____

8. depth of a bathtub: 2 ft or 2 yd _____

Suppose each square on the grids below is 1 cm by 1 cm. Estimate the area of each figure.

9.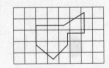

10.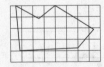

11.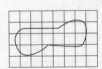

12.

Choose the unit of measure you would use to estimate the given length or area.

13. the height of a tree: in., ft, yd, mi

14. the perimeter of the cover of a book: in., ft, yd, mi

15. the area of an ocean: ft^2, yd^2, $in.^2$, mi^2

_____   _____   _____

8-1 • Guided Problem Solving

Writing in Math How could you use a piece of string to
estimate the perimeter of the puzzle piece at the right?

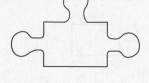

Understand

1. What are you being asked to do?

   _____

   _____

2. Define *perimeter*.

   _____

   _____

   _____

Plan and Carry Out

3. What do you have to do with the string?

   _____

4. How do you use the string to get a measurement?

   _____

   _____

5. Why would the measurement be an estimate?

   _____

   _____

Check

6. Why might using a piece of string to measure the perimeter of
   the puzzle piece be a good idea?

   _____

   _____

Solve Another Problem

7. How could you estimate the area of the puzzle piece with
   the string?

   _____

   _____

   _____

Practice 8-2

Find the area of each parallelogram.

1.

4 m

4 m

_____

2.
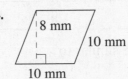
5 cm

23 cm

_____

3.
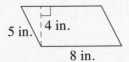
5 in. 4 in.

8 in.

_____

4.

8 mm

10 mm

10 mm

_____

Find the area of each parallelogram with base *b* and height *h*.

5. $b = 16$ mm, $h = 12$ mm

_____

6. $b = 23$ km, $h = 14$ km

_____

7. $b = 65$ mi, $h = 48$ mi

_____

8. $b = 19$ in., $h = 15$ in.

_____

Solve.

9. The area of a parallelogram is 6 square units. Both the height and the length of the base are whole numbers. What are the possible lengths and heights?

_____

10. The perimeter of a rectangle is 72 m. The width of the rectangle is 16 m. What is the area of the rectangle?

_____

11. The area of a certain rectangle is 288 yd². The perimeter is 68 yd. If you double the length and width, what will be the area and perimeter of the new rectangle?

_____

12. If you have 36 ft of fencing, what are the areas of the different rectangles you could enclose with the fencing? Consider only whole-number dimensions.

_____

8-2 • Guided Problem Solving

 **Student Page 383, Exercise 22:**

Geography The shape of the state of Tennesee is similar to a parallelogram. Estimate the area of Tennessee.

110 mi

380 mi

Understand

1. What are you being asked to do?

_____

_____

2. What shape is Tennessee similar to?

_____

_____

3. How do you find the area of a parallelogram?

_____

_____

_____

Plan and Carry Out

4. What is the height of Tennessee? _____

5. What is the length of the base of Tennessee? _____

6. Substitute the values into the formula $A = bh$. _____

7. What is the approximate area of Tennessee? _____

Check

8. Is this estimate more or less than the actual area of Tennessee? Explain.

_____

_____

Solve Another Problem

9. Tamika's yard is similar to the shape of a parallelogram. Estimate the area of Tamika's yard.

_____

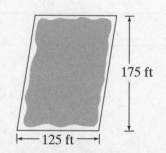

175 ft

125 ft

Practice 8-3

Perimeter and Area of a Triangle

Find the perimeter of each triangle.

1.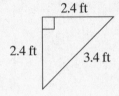
   2.4 ft
   2.4 ft
   3.4 ft

_____

2.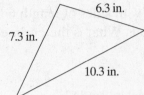
   6.3 in.
   7.3 in.
   10.3 in.

_____

3.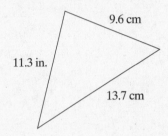
   9.6 cm
   11.3 in.
   13.7 cm

_____

4.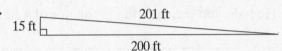
   15 ft
   201 ft
   200 ft

_____

Find the area of each triangle.

5.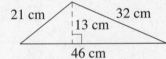
   21 cm
   32 cm
   13 cm
   46 cm

_____

6.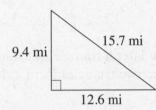
   9.4 mi
   15.7 mi
   12.6 mi

_____

7.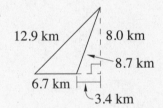
   12.9 km
   8.0 km
   8.7 km
   6.7 km
   3.4 km

_____

8.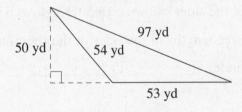
   50 yd
   97 yd
   54 yd
   53 yd

_____

Solve.

9. The perimeter of an isosceles triangle is 12 in. What are the possible whole-number lengths of the legs?

_____

10. The side of an equilateral triangle has a length of 5.4 m. The height of the triangle is approximately 4.7 m. What are the perimeter and area of this triangle? Round your answers to the nearest tenth.

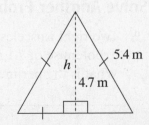
5.4 m
h
4.7 m

_____

8-3 • Guided Problem Solving

GPS **Student Page 387, Exercise 26:**

Two equilateral triangles with sides of length 6 inches are joined together to form a rhombus. What is the perimeter of the rhombus?

Understand

1. What are you being asked to do? _____

_____

2. How do you measure the perimeter of a figure?

_____

3. What is an equilateral triangle? _____

_____

Plan and Carry Out

4. In the space to the right, draw an equilateral triangle. Label all of its sides as 6 in.

5. Draw another equilateral triangle touching the first equilateral triangle so that the two triangles form a rhombus.

6. Label the sides of the second triangle as 6 in.

7. Add the lengths of the sides of the rhombus to find the

perimeter. _____

Check

8. Count the number of sides that the rhombus has. Multiply this number by the length of the sides. Is this number the same as your answer? _____

_____

Solve Another Problem

9. Two right isosceles triangles with legs of 5 in. length and a hypotenuse of 7.1 in. are joined together to make a square. What is the perimeter of the square?

_____

Name _____ Class _____ Date _____

Practice 8-4

Areas of Other Figures

Find the area of each trapezoid.

1.
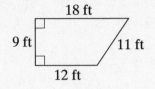
18 ft
9 ft   11 ft
12 ft

2.
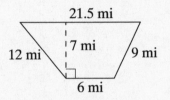
16.4 mm
10.6 mm   9.7 mm   10.6 mm
24.8 mm

3.
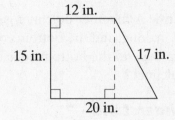
12 in.
15 in.   17 in.
20 in.

_____   _____   _____

4.
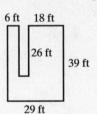
21.5 mi
12 mi   7 mi   9 mi
6 mi

5.
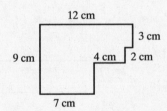
8 m
8 m   10 m
14 m

6.
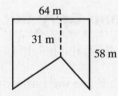
18 in.
17 in.   12 in.
6 in.

_____   _____   _____

Find the area of each irregular figure.

7.
6 ft   18 ft
26 ft
39 ft
29 ft

8.
12 cm
9 cm   3 cm
4 cm   2 cm
7 cm

9.
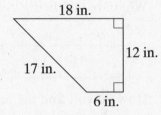
64 m
31 m   58 m

_____   _____   _____

Solve.

10. The flag of Switzerland features a white cross on a red background.

a. Each of the 12 sides of the cross has a length of 15 cm.
Find the area of the white cross.   _____

b. The flag has dimensions 60 cm by 60 cm.
Find the area of the red region.   _____

11. A trapezoid has an area of 4 square units, and a height of 1 unit.
What are the possible whole-number lengths for the bases?   _____

8-4 • Guided Problem Solving

Student Page 392, Exercise 17:

Music A hammer dulcimer is shaped like a trapezoid. The top edge is 17 in. long, and the bottom edge is 39 in. long. The distance from the top edge to the bottom edge is 16 in. What is the area of the dulcimer?

Understand

1. Circle the information you will need to solve the problem.

2. What are you being asked to do?

   _____

   _____

3. How do you find the area of a trapezoid?

   _____

   _____

Plan and Carry Out

4. What is the height of the dulcimer? _____

5. What are the bases of the dulcimer? _____

6. Substitute the values for the bases and
   the height into the formula for area. _____

7. What is the area of the dulcimer? _____

Check

8. Explain how you chose which measurements are the bases.

   _____

   _____

Solve Another Problem

9. Suppose the dulcimer had bases of 20 in. and 36 in. with the
   same height. What would be the area of the dulcimer? How
   do the areas compare? Explain.

   _____

   _____

Practice 8-5

Circumference and Area of a Circle

Find the circumference and area of each circle. Round your answers
to the nearest tenth.

1.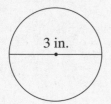

3 in.

_____

2.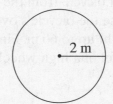

2 m

_____

3.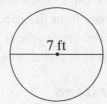

7 ft

_____

4.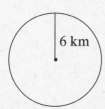

6 km

_____

5.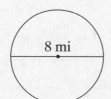

8 mi

_____

6.

15 in.

_____

7.

15.6 m

_____

8.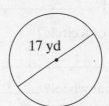

17 yd

_____

9.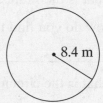

8.4 m

_____

Estimate the radius of each circle with the given circumference.
Round your answer to the nearest tenth.

10. 80 km

_____

11. 92 ft

_____

12. 420 in.

_____

13. In the diagram at the right, the radius of the large circle is 8 in.
The radius of each of the smaller circles is 1 in. Find the area of
the shaded region to the nearest square unit.

_____

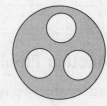

8-5 • Guided Problem Solving

Bicycles The front wheel of a high-wheel bicycle from the late 1800s was larger than the rear wheel to increase the bicycle's overall speed. The front wheel measured in height up to 60 in. Find the circumference and area of the front wheel of a high-wheel bicycle.

Understand

1. Circle the information you will need to solve.

2. In the space to the right, draw a sketch of the bicycle that the problem is discussing.

3. What are you being asked to do?

   _____

   _____

Plan and Carry Out

4. What is the diameter of the front wheel? _____

5. What is the radius of the front wheel? _____

6. How do you find the circumference of a circle?

   _____

7. What is the circumference of the front wheel? _____

8. How do you find the area of a circle?

   _____

9. What is the area of the front wheel? _____

Check

10. How do you determine the radius if you know the area and circumference of a circle?

    _____

    _____

Solve Another Problem

11. The diameter of a normal front wheel on a bicycle is 24 in. Find the circumference and area of the front wheel.

    _____

Practice 8-6

Square Roots and Irrational Numbers

Simplify each square root.

1. $\sqrt{64}$ _____

2. $\sqrt{81}$ _____

3. $\sqrt{100}$ _____

4. $\sqrt{121}$ _____

5. $\sqrt{1}$ _____

6. $\sqrt{36}$ _____

7. $\sqrt{25}$ _____

8. $\sqrt{16}$ _____

9. $\sqrt{256}$ _____

10. $\sqrt{196}$ _____

11. $\sqrt{49}$ _____

12. $\sqrt{225}$ _____

Identify each number as rational or irrational.

13. $0.363636\ldots$

14. $\sqrt{10}$

15. $-\frac{1}{9}$

_____

_____

_____

For each number, write all the sets to which it belongs. Choose from rational number, irrational number, whole number, and integer.

16. $\frac{3}{8}$

17. $\sqrt{49}$

18. $\sqrt{98}$

_____

_____

_____

Find the length of the side of a square with the given area.

19. 64 km^2

20. 81 m^2

21. 121 ft^2

_____

_____

_____

22. 225 in.^2

23. 196 yd^2

24. 169 cm^2

_____

_____

_____

Solve.

25. The square of a certain number is the same as three times the number. What is the number?

26. The area of a square lawn is 196 yd^2. What is the perimeter of the lawn?

_____

_____

Find two consecutive whole numbers that each number is between.

27. $\sqrt{80}$

28. $\sqrt{56}$

29. $\sqrt{130}$

_____

_____

_____

30. $\sqrt{70}$

31. $\sqrt{190}$

32. $\sqrt{204}$

_____

_____

_____

8-6 • Guided Problem Solving

GPS **Student Page 402, Exercise 32:**

Open-Ended Write three irrational numbers between 4 and 5.

Understand

1. What are you being asked to do?

   _____

   _____

2. What is an irrational number?

   _____

   _____

   _____

Plan and Carry Out

3. Find 4^2 and 5^2. Use these values to find an irrational number between 4 and 5 using square roots.

   _____

4. Name a decimal between 4 and 5 that has a pattern but does not repeat.

   _____

5. Based on Step 3 or Step 4, write one more irrational number between 4 and 5.

   _____

   _____

6. How many irrational numbers do you think there are between 4 and 5?

   _____

Check

7. Is the number you chose in Step 3 irrational? Do the decimals you chose repeat or terminate? _____

Solve Another Problem

8. Write three irrational numbers between 2 and 3.

   _____

   _____

Practice 8-7

The Pythagorean Theorem

The lengths of two sides of a right triangle are given. Find the length of the third side to the nearest tenth of a unit.

1. legs: 5 ft and 12 ft

_____

2. legs: 13 cm and 9 cm

_____

3. leg: 7 m; hypotenuse: 14 m

_____

Find each missing length. Round to the nearest tenth of a unit, if necessary.

4.
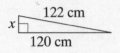

_____

5.
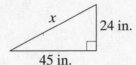

_____

6.
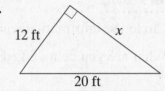

_____

7.
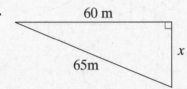

_____

8.
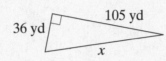

_____

9.
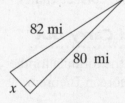

_____

10.

_____

11.
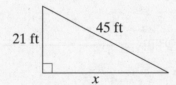

_____

12.
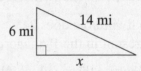

_____

Solve.

13. A playground is 50 yd by 50 yd. Amy walked across the playground from one corner to the opposite corner. How far did she walk?

_____

14. A 70-ft ladder is mounted 10 ft above the ground on a fire truck. The bottom of the ladder is 40 ft from the wall of a building. The top of the ladder is touching the building. How high off the ground is the top of the ladder?

_____

8-7 • Guided Problem Solving

GPS Student Page 408, Exercise 21:

Camping A large tent has an adjustable center pole. A rope 26 ft long connects the top of the pole to a peg 24 ft from the bottom of the pole. What is the height of the pole? Round to the nearest hundredth if necessary.

Understand

1. Circle the information you will need to solve.

2. What are you being asked to do?

   _____

3. The right triangle shown models the tent pole and rope. Label it with the correct values.

Plan and Carry Out

4. Write the formula for the Pythagorean Theorem.   _____

5. What variable does 26 ft represent in the Pythagorean Theorem?   _____

6. What variable does 24 ft represent in the Pythagorean Theorem?   _____

7. Substitute these values into the Pythagorean Theorem formula and find the height of the pole.   _____

Check

8. Substitute your answer from Step 7 and 24 ft into the Pythagorean Theorem formula for a and b. Do you get a true statement?

   _____

Solve Another Problem

9. You're building a right-triangular brace for a basketball hoop. You have the piece for the hypotenuse and for one of the legs. The hypotenuse measures 10 in. long, and the leg measures 6 in. long. How long must the other leg of the brace be?

   _____

Practice 8-8

Describe the base and name the figure.

1.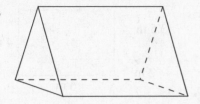

_____

_____

2.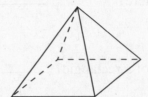

_____

_____

3.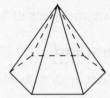

_____

_____

4.

_____

_____

5.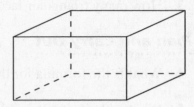

_____

_____

6.

_____

_____

Draw each figure named.

7. a triangular pyramid

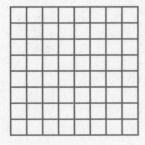

8. a square prism

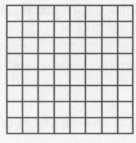

9. a cone

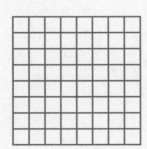

10. a pentagonal pyramid

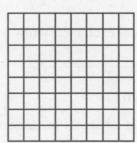

8-8 • Guided Problem Solving

GPS Student Page 413, Exercise 23:

What are the areas of all the faces of the figure at the right?

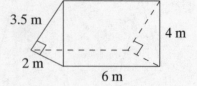

Understand

1. What are you being asked to do?

_____

2. How many rectangular faces are there? _____

3. How many triangular faces are there? _____

Plan and Carry Out

4. What is the formula for the area of a rectangle? _____

5. What is the formula for the area of a triangle? _____

6. What are the dimensions of the triangular faces?

_____

7. What is the area of one triangular face? _____

8. What is the area of all the triangular faces? _____

9. What are the dimensions of each rectangular face?

_____

10. What is the area of each rectangular face?

_____

11. Find the total area of the base and faces of the figure.

_____

Check

12. Did you find the area of each face? How many faces are there?

_____

Solve Another Problem

13. A rectangular solid has a base 11 in., height 15 in., and a length of 6 in. Find the total area of all faces.

_____

_____

Practice 8-9

Surface Areas of Prisms and Cylinders

Find the surface area of each prism.

1.

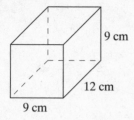

9 cm
12 cm
9 cm

_____

2.

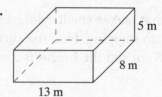

5 m
8 m
13 m

_____

3.

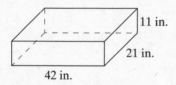

11 in.
21 in.
42 in.

_____

4.

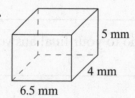

5 mm
4 mm
6.5 mm

_____

Find the surface area of each cylinder. Round to the nearest whole number.

5.

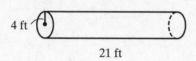

4 ft
21 ft

_____

6.

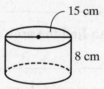

15 cm
8 cm

_____

7.

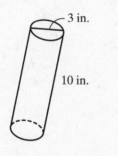

3 in.
10 in.

_____

8.

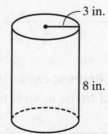

2 m
9 m

_____

Draw a net for each three-dimensional figure.

9.

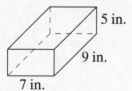

5 in.
9 in.
7 in.

10.

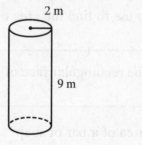

3 in.
8 in.

8-9 • Guided Problem Solving

GPS Student Page 418, Exercise 22:

A cosmetics company that makes small cylindrical bars of soap wraps the bars in plastic prior to shipping. Find the surface area of a bar of soap if the diameter is 5 cm and the height is 2 cm. Round to the nearest tenth.

Understand

1. What are you being asked to do?

   _____

2. What do you need to do to your final answer?

   _____

Plan and Carry Out

3. How do you find the surface area of a cylinder?

   _____

   _____

4. What formula do you use to find the area of a circular face?

   _____

5. What is the total area of the circular faces of a bar of soap?

   _____

6. What formula do you use to find the area of the rectangular face?

   _____

7. What is the area of the rectangular face of a bar of soap?

   _____

8. What is the surface area of a bar of soap? _____

Check

9. Did you find the area of all the surfaces of a bar of soap? Does your answer check?

   _____

Solve Another Problem

10. Find the surface area of a cylindrical candle if the diameter is 6 in. and the height is 8 in. Round to the nearest tenth.

    _____

Practice 8-10

Find each volume. Round to the nearest cubic unit.

1.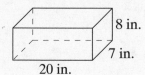
8 in.
7 in.
20 in.

2.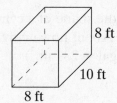
8 ft
10 ft
8 ft

3.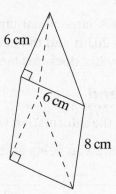
6 cm
6 cm
8 cm

_____

4.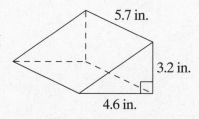
5.7 in.
3.2 in.
4.6 in.

5.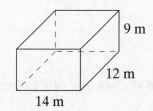
9 m
12 m
14 m

6.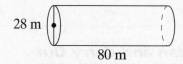
28 m
80 m

_____

7.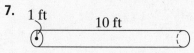
1 ft   10 ft

8.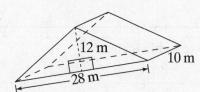
12 m
10 m
28 m

9.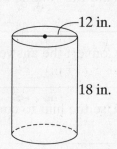
12 in.
18 in.

_____

Find the height of each rectangular prism given the volume, length, and width.

10. $V = 122{,}500 \text{ cm}^3$
$l = 50 \text{ cm}$
$w = 35 \text{ cm}$

11. $V = 22.05 \text{ ft}^3$
$l = 3.5 \text{ ft}$
$w = 4.2 \text{ ft}$

12. $V = 3{,}375 \text{ m}^3$
$l = 15 \text{ m}$
$w = 15 \text{ m}$

_____

8-10 • Guided Problem Solving

GPS Student Page 425, Exercise 21:

Aquariums A large aquarium is built in the shape of a cylinder. The diameter is 203 ft and the height is 25 ft. About how many million gallons of water does this tank hold? (1 gal ≈ 231 in.^{3})

Understand

1. Circle the information you will need to solve.

2. What are you being asked to do?

   _____

   _____

3. What do you need to do to the units in your final answer?

   _____

Plan and Carry Out

4. Write the formula you use to find the volume of a cylinder.

   _____

5. Find the volume of the aquarium in cubic feet.

   _____

6. Convert the answer in Step 4 to cubic inches.

   _____

7. Use the hint to convert the answer in Step 5 to gallons.

   _____

8. About how many million gallons does the tank hold?

   _____

Check

9. Estimate the answer by using 3 for π, 200 ft for the diameter, and 1 gal ≈ 230 in.^{3} Does your answer make sense? Check.

   _____

   _____

Solve Another Problem

10. The diameter of a tank is 26 cm, and the height is 58 cm. About how many liters of fuel oil can this steel tank hold? (1,000 cm^3 = 1L)

   _____

8A: Graphic Organizer

For use before Lesson 8-1

Vocabulary and Study Skills

Study Skill Take a few minutes to relax before and after studying. Your mind will absorb and retain more information if you alternate studying with brief rest intervals.

Write your answers.

1. What is the chapter title? _____

2. How many lessons are there in this chapter? _____

3. What is the topic of the Test-Taking Strategies page? _____

4. Complete the graphic organizer below as you work through the chapter.
   • In the center, write the title of the chapter.
   • When you begin a lesson, write the lesson name in a rectangle.
   • When you complete a lesson, write a skill or key concept in a circle linked to that lesson block.
   • When you complete the chapter, use this graphic organizer to help you review.

8B: Reading Comprehension

For use after Lesson 8-9

Study Skill Learning to read for detail takes practice. As you read your notes, underline or highlight important information.

Read the paragraph and answer the questions.

> The Grand Canyon was formed by the Colorado River in Arizona. It is estimated to be nearly 10 million years old. With a length of 277 miles, the Grand Canyon is nearly 18 miles wide at its widest point and one mile deep in some places. Arizona, called the Grand Canyon State, has a total land area of approximately 113,000 square miles.

1. What is the paragraph about?

   _____

2. How old is the Grand Canyon?

   _____

3. What dimensions are given for the Grand Canyon?

   _____

4. Use these dimensions to calculate the approximate area of the bottom of the Grand Canyon.

   _____

5. What percent of the land area in Arizona is occupied by the Grand Canyon?

   _____

6. Why is the area determined in Exercise 4 a maximum area?

   _____

   _____

7. What is the approximate volume of the Grand Canyon?

   _____

8. **High-Use Academic Words** In Exercise 4, what does it mean to *calculate?*

   a. to determine by mathematical processes   b. to show that you recognize something

8C: Reading/Writing Math Symbols

For use after Lesson 8-10

Study Skill After completing an assignment, take a break. Then, come back and check your work.

State whether each of the following units represents length, area or volume.

1. cm^2 _____

2. $in.^3$ _____

3. mi _____

4. ft^2 _____

5. km _____

6. mm^3 _____

State whether each expression can be used to calculate length, area, or volume and to what shapes they apply.

7. $\frac{1}{2}bh$ _____

8. lwh _____

9. bh _____

10. πd _____

11. πr^2 _____

12. s^2 _____

13. $\sqrt{a^2 + b^2}$ _____

14. $\frac{1}{2}h(b_1 + b_2)$ _____

15. $\pi r^2 h$ _____

16. $2\pi r$ _____

8D: Visual Vocabulary Practice

For use after Lesson 8-8

Study Skill When interpreting an illustration, look for the most specific concept represented.

Concept List

circumference	base	cone
Pythagorean Theorem	perfect square	edges
vertices	prism	pyramid

Write the concept that best describes each exercise. Choose from the concept list above.

1. $AB^2 = 6^2 + 8^2$ $AB^2 = 36 + 64 = 100$ $AB = \sqrt{100} = 10$ 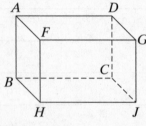	**2.** 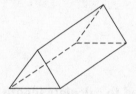	**3.** 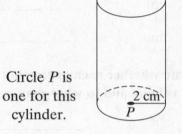 Circle P is one for this cylinder.
4. 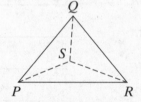 $\overline{AB}$ and $\overline{CJ}$ are examples.	**5.**	**6.** There are four of these in this three-dimensional figure.
7. 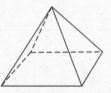	**8.** 576, since $24^2 = 576$.	**9.** 4 cm P $C \approx 25.1$ cm

8E: Vocabulary Check

Study Skill Strengthen your vocabulary. Use these pages and add cues and summaries by applying the Cornell Notetaking style.

Write the definition for each word or term at the right. To check your work, fold the paper back along the dotted line to see the correct answers.

_____ irrational numbers

_____

_____

_____ face

_____

_____

_____ area

_____

_____ volume

_____

_____

_____ prism

_____

8E: Vocabulary Check (continued)

Write the vocabulary word or term for each definition. To check your
work, fold the paper forward along the dotted line to see the correct
answers.

a number that cannot be written
as the ratio of two integers

_____

a flat surface of a three-
dimensional figure that is shaped
like a polygon

_____

the number of square units a
figure encloses

_____

the number of cubic units needed
to fill the space inside a three-
dimensional figure

_____

a three-dimensional figure with
two parallel and congruent
polygonal faces, called bases

_____

8F: Vocabulary Review

For use with the Chapter Review

Study Skill Participating in class discussions will help you remember new material. Do not be afraid to express your thoughts when your teacher asks for questions, answers, or discussion.

Circle the word that best completes the sentence.

1. The longest side of a right triangle is the (*leg, hypotenuse*).

2. (*Parallel, Perpendicular*) lines lie in the same plane and do not intersect.

3. A (*solution, statement*) is a value of a variable that makes an equation true.

4. Figures that are the same size and shape are (*similar, congruent*).

5. (*Complementary, Supplementary*) angles are two angles whose sum is 90°.

6. A (*circle, sphere*) is the set of all points in space that are the same distance from a center point.

7. The perimeter of a circle is the (*circumference, circumcenter*).

8. The (*area, volume*) of a figure is the number of square units it encloses.

9. A(n) (*isosceles, scalene*) triangle has no congruent sides.

10. A (*rhombus, square*) is a parallelogram with four right angles and four congruent sides.

11. A number that is the square of an integer is a (*perfect square, square root*).

12. A (*pyramid, prism*) is a three-dimensional figure with triangular faces that meet at one point.

13. A speed limit of 65 mi/h is an example of a (*ratio, rate*).

14. A (*cone, cylinder*) has two congruent parallel bases that are circles.

Vocabulary and Study Skills

Practice 9-1

1. The table shows the costs of packages containing writable CDs. Graph the data in the table.

Number of CDs	10	20	50	100	200
Cost ($)	10	15	25	40	75

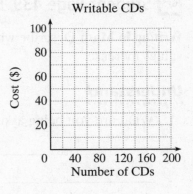

Writable CDs

The graph shows the 2005 median income of some year-round workers and the number of years of school. The trend line is shown. Use this graph for Exercises 2–3.

2. Predict the median income for the workers who have spent 20 years in school.

_____

3. Do you think you can use this graph to predict the median salary for workers who have spent less than 8 years in school? Explain.

_____

_____

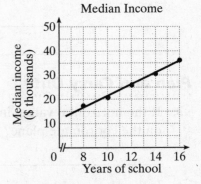

Median Income

The table shows average monthly temperatures in degrees Fahrenheit for American cities in January and July. Use this information for Exercises 4–5.

City	Seattle	Boise	Chicago	LA	New York	Anchorage
Jan.	39.1	29.9	21.4	56.0	31.8	13.0
Jul.	64.8	74.6	73.0	69.0	76.4	58.1

4. Graph the data in the table.

5. Use your graph to estimate the July temperature of a city whose average January temperature is 10°F.

_____

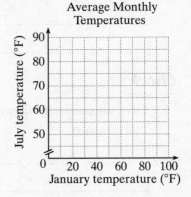

Average Monthly Temperatures

9-1 • Guided Problem Solving

GPS **Student Page 439, Exercise 13:**

Writing in Math Describe what a graph looks like when both sets of values increase.

Understand

1. What are you being asked to do?

_____

_____

2. What does the phrase *both sets of values* mean?

_____

_____

Plan and Carry Out

3. If the horizontal values increase, or get bigger, where are the points on the coordinate plane?

_____

4. If the vertical values increase, or get bigger, where are the points on the coordinate plane?

_____

5. Describe what a graph looks like when both sets of values increase.

_____

_____

Check

6. Give an example of two quantities that would have this relationship.

_____

_____

Solve Another Problem

7. Describe what a graph looks like when only the vertical values decrease.

_____

_____

Guided Problem Solving

Practice 9-2

**Identify each sequence as *arithmetic*, *geometric*, or *neither*.
Write a rule for each sequence.**

1. 2, 6, 18, 54, . . .

_____

_____

2. 5, −10, 20, −40, . . .

_____

_____

3. 3, 5, 7, 9, . . .

_____

_____

4. 5, 6, 8, 11, 15, . . .

_____

_____

5. 1, 2, 6, 24, . . .

_____

_____

6. 17, 16, 15, 14, . . .

_____

_____

7. 50, −50, 50, −50, . . .

_____

_____

8. 1, 2, 4, 5, 10, 11, 22, . . .

_____

_____

Find the next three terms in each sequence.

9. 15, −14, 13, −12, . . .

_____

10. 243, 81, 27, . . .

_____

11. 5, 12, 26, . . .

_____

12. 2, 5, 9, 14, . . .

_____

**Write the first five terms in the sequence described by the rule.
Identify the sequence as *arithmetic*, *geometric*, or *neither*.**

13. Start with 2 and multiply by −3 repeatedly.

_____

14. Start with 27 and add −9 repeatedly.

_____

15. Start with 18 and multiply by 0.1, then by 0.2, then by 0.3, and so on.

_____

9-2 • Guided Problem Solving

GPS Student Page 444, Exercise 21:

Running Mario can run a mile in 9 min. After 4 months of training,
he hopes to run a mile in 8 min. His time decreases by 15 s each month.
What would you tell Mario about his conjecture?

Understand

1. What is a conjecture?

   _____

   _____

2. What is Mario's conjecture?

   _____

   _____

3. What are you being asked to do?

   _____

Plan and Carry Out

4. After 1 month of training, how fast can Mario run a mile?

   _____

5. After 2 months of training, how fast can Mario run a mile? After 3
   months? After 4 months?

   _____

6. Is Mario's conjecture valid? _____

Check

7. How could you have worked the problem another way?

   _____

   _____

Solve Another Problem

8. Linda can walk a mile in 12 min. After 6 months of training, she
   hopes to walk a mile in 10 min 30 s. Her time decreases by 10 s
   each month. What would you tell Linda about her conjecture?

   _____

   _____

Practice 9-3

Patterns and Tables

Complete each table.

1.

Time (h)	1	2	3	4	7
Distance cycled (mi)	8	16	24	32	

2.

Time (min)	1	2	3	4	7
Distance from surface of water (yd)	−3	−2	−1	0	

Write a variable expression to describe the rule for each sequence. Then find the 100th term.

3. 35, 36, 37, . . .

Expression: _____

100th term: _____

4. 8, 10, 12, 14, . . .

Expression: _____

100th term: _____

Find the values of the missing entries in each table.

5.

m	4	6		10
n	24	26	28	

6.

p	2		10	14
q	1	13	25	

7. A pattern of squares is shown.

a. Sketch the 4th and 5th figure in this pattern. _____

b. Make a table comparing the figure number to the number of squares. Write an expression for the number of squares in the *n*th figure.

c. How many squares would there be in the 80th figure? _____

Write a variable expression to describe the rule for each sequence. Then find the 20th term.

8. 6, 12, 18, 24, . . .

Expression: _____

20th term: _____

9. 3, 6, 9, 12, . . .

Expression: _____

20th term: _____

10. One month's average price for ground beef is $2.39 per pound. Using this relationship, make a table that shows the price for 1, 2, 3, and 4 pounds of ground beef.

9-3 • Guided Problem Solving

GPS Student Page 448, Exercise 20:

Music The table shows costs for violin lessons. Complete the table.

Time (h)	0.5	1	1.5	2
Cost ($)	12.50			

Understand

1. In which row is the cost of a violin lesson?

   _____

2. What information is given in the first column of the table?

   _____

3. What are you being asked to do?

   _____

Plan and Carry Out

4. How much is a 0.5-hour lesson? _____

5. What is the relationship between 0.5 and 1? _____

6. Use the same relationship you found in
   Step 5 to find the cost of a 1-hour lesson. _____

7. What amount should you add to the answer
   in Step 6 to find the cost of a 1.5-hour lesson? _____

8. How much does a 1.5-hour lesson cost? _____

9. How much does a 2-hour lesson cost? _____

Check

10. Explain how you could use multiplication in this problem.

    _____

    _____

    _____

Solve Another Problem

11. The table shows costs for math tutoring. Complete the table.

Time (h)	0.5	1	1.5	2
Cost ($)	15.75			

Practice 9-4

Function Rules

Use each function rule. Find *y* for *x* = 1, 2, 3, and 4.

1. $y = 2x$

2. $y = x + 4$

3. $y = x^2 - 1$

_____

_____

_____

4. $y = -2x$

5. $y = 3x + 1$

6. $y = 8 - 3x$

_____

_____

_____

7. $y = 6 + 4x$

8. $y = x - 5$

9. $y = 2x + 7$

_____

_____

_____

Write a rule for the function represented by each table.

10.

x	y
1	6
2	7
3	8
4	9

11.

x	y
1	4
2	8
3	12
4	16

12.

x	y
1	−6
2	−9
3	−12
4	−15

_____

_____

_____

13.

x	y
1	5
2	7
3	9
4	11

14.

x	y
1	4
2	7
3	10
4	13

15.

x	y
1	−1
2	−3
3	−5
4	−7

_____

_____

_____

16. A typist types 45 words per minute.

a. Write a function rule to represent the relationship between the number of typed words and the time in which they are typed.

_____

b. How many words can the typist type in 25 minutes?

_____

c. How long would it take the typist to type 20,025 words?

_____

9-4 • Guided Problem Solving

GPS Student Page 454, Exercise 21:

Money Suppose you put $.50 in a piggy bank on July 1, $1.00 on July 2, $1.50 on July 3, and so on. Use n to represent the date. Write a function rule for the amount you put in for any date in July.

Understand

1. What is a function rule?

_____

_____

2. What are you being asked to do?

_____

_____

Plan and Carry Out

3. What are the inputs? _____

4. What are the outputs?

_____

5. What variable represents the inputs? _____

6. What is the relationship between the amount of money you put in the piggy bank on the first day and number of the day, July 1? July 2?

_____

7. What do you do to n to figure out how much money to put in the piggy bank? _____

8. Write a function rule for the amount, a, you put in for *any* date in July. _____

Check

9. Check that your rule works with days July 1, 2, and 3.

_____

Solve Another Problem

10. Suppose your parents paid you $.10 on December 1, $.20 on December 2, $.30 on December 3, and so on. Use n to represent the date. Write a function rule for the amount your parents will pay you for any date in December.

_____

Name _____ Class _____ Date _____

Practice 9-5

The graph at the right shows the relationship between distance and time for a car driven at a constant speed.

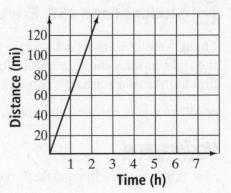

1. What is the speed? _____

2. Is this a function relationship? _____

3. If this is a function, write a rule to represent it.

    _____

4. Make a table for the function, listing six input/output pairs.

Graph each function. Use input values of 1, 2, 3, 4, and 5.

5. $y = -\frac{1}{2}x$

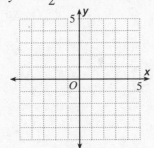

6. $y = -2x + 4$

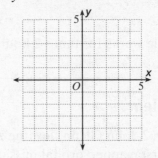

7. The relationship between the amount of time a zebra runs at maximum speed and the distance it covers is shown.

Time (min)	3	6	9	12	15
Distance (mi)	2	4	6	8	10

a. Write an equation to describe this relationship.

    _____

b. Use the equation to find the distance the zebra would travel in 48 minutes.

    _____

9-5 • Guided Problem Solving

GPS **Student Page 459, Exercise 20a:**

Flight Amelia Earhart set several flight speed records. The table at the right models the relationship between distance and time for a flight at Amelia Earhart's record speed.

a. Write a rule for the relationship represented by the table.

Amelia Earhart's Flight

Time (h)	Distance (mi)
2	362
4	724
6	1,086
8	1,448

Understand

1. What are you being asked to do?

   _____

   _____

Plan and Carry Out

2. How many miles did Earhart travel in 2 h? _____

3. How many miles did Earhart travel in 1 h? _____

4. What are the inputs? What are the outputs? _____

   _____

5. Use *d* to represent distance and *t* to represent time. Write a rule for the relationship represented by the table. _____

Check

6. Check that your rule works for times 2 hours, 4 hours, and 6 hours.

   _____

Solve Another Problem

7. On February 20, 1962, John Glenn flew the *Friendship 7* spacecraft on the first manned orbital mission of the United States. He completed three orbits around the earth, reaching a maximum orbital velocity of approximately 17,500 miles per hour. Write a rule for the relationship of Glenn's distance *d* and time *t* at this speed.

   _____

Practice 9-6

Graphs I through VI represent one of the six situations described below. Match each graph with the situation that describes it.

I. 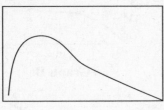 II. 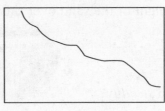 III.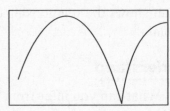

IV. 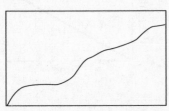 V. 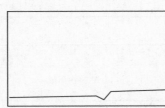 VI.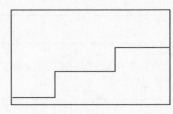

1. temperature as the weather changes from rainy to snowy

   _____

2. number of fish caught per hour on a bad fishing day _____

3. total rainfall during a rainy day _____

4. speed of a car starting from a stop sign and then approaching a

   stoplight _____

5. height of a cricket as it jumps _____

6. total amount of money spent over time during a trip to the mall

   _____

Sketch a graph for each situation.

7. The speed of a runner in a 1-mi race.

8. The height above ground of the air valve on a tire of a bicycle ridden on flat ground. (You can model this using a coin.)

9-6 • Guided Problem Solving

GPS Student Page 464, Exercise 10:

Suppose you steadily pour sand into the bowl below. Which graph better shows the relationship of the height of the sand over time? Explain.

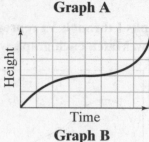

Graph A

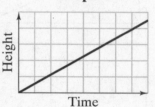

Graph B

Understand

1. What can you infer from the word *steadily*?

_____

_____

2. What are you being asked to do?

_____

_____

Plan and Carry Out

3. Describe the shape of the bowl.

_____

4. How is the bowl different from a cylinder?

_____

5. Will the height of the sand increase at a constant rate?

_____

6. Which graph better shows the relationship of the height of the sand with the amount you have poured? _____

Check

7. Explain your reasoning for Step 6.

_____

_____

Solve Another Problem

8. Suppose you are steadily pouring sand into the bowl at the right. Which graph above better shows the relationship of the height of the sand over time? Explain.

_____

_____

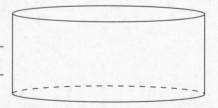

Guided Problem Solving

Practice 9-7

Simple and Compound Interest

Graph the total _simple_ interest earned for each account over 5 years.

1. $1,300 at 6.9%   **2.** $11,500 at 12.50%   **3.** $450 at 3%

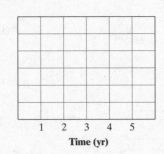 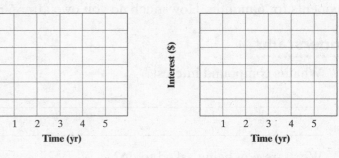

Find the simple interest earned in each account.

4. $2,000 at 4% for 6 months   **5.** $10,000 at 10% for 2 years

_____   _____

6. $500 at 3% for 3 months   **7.** $25,000 at 4.25% for 5 years

_____   _____

Find the balance in each _compound_ interest account.

8. $800 principal   **9.** $5,200 principal   **10.** $3,500 principal
6% interest rate   5% interest rate   4.5% interest rate
9 years   4 years   10 years

_____   _____   _____

Solve.

11. You borrow $600. You pay 5% interest compounded annually.
How much do you owe at the end of 4 years?

_____

12. You deposit $2,000 in an account that pays 6% interest
compounded annually. How much money is in the account
at the end of 12 years?

_____

13. You invest $5,000 in an account earning simple interest. The
balance after 6 years is $6,200. What is the interest rate?

_____

9-7 • Guided Problem Solving

GPS **Student Page 470, Exercise 21:**

You borrow $500 at 18% annual compound interest. You make no payments for 6 months. How much do you owe after 6 months?

Understand

1. What is compound interest?

   _____

   _____

2. What are you being asked to do?

   _____

Plan and Carry Out

3. What is the formula for compound interest? _____

4. What is the original principal? _____

5. What is the interest rate? _____

6. How much time in years has passed
   since the money was borrowed? _____

7. Substitute the values into the formula.

   _____

8. How much do you owe after 6 months? _____

Check

9. Find the total simple interest on the account after six months. Add
   the simple interest to the principal. How should this number compare
   to your answer?

   _____

   _____

   _____

Solve Another Problem

10. You borrow $1,050 at 16% annual compound interest. You make
    no payments for 9 months. How much do you owe after 9 months?

    _____

Practice 9-8

Solve each formula for the indicated variable.

1. $d = rt$, for r _____

2. $P = 4s$, for s _____

3. $K = C + 273$, for C _____

4. $S = 180(n - 2)$, for n _____

5. $m = \dfrac{a + b + c}{3}$, for a _____

6. $P = 2b + 2h$, for b _____

7. $V = \dfrac{1}{3}Bh$, for B _____

8. $A = 2(\ell w + wh + \ell h)$, for ℓ, given $w = 5, h = 3$, and $A = 158$

_____

9. $C = \dfrac{5}{9}(F - 32)$, for F, given $C = 25$

_____

10. $F = ma$, for m, given $a = 9.8$ and $F = 117.6$

_____

Solve.

11. In 1989, Dutch ice skater Dries van Wijhe skated 200 km at an average speed of 35.27 km/hr. How long was he skating?

_____

12. A roofer calculates his bid price using the formula $P = 1.85s + 4.2f$, where s is the area of the roof in square feet and f is the length of the fascia in feet. Find the area of the roof with 190 feet of fascia and a price of $4,148.

_____

9-8 • Guided Problem Solving

GPS **Student Page 475, Exercise 27:**

Construction Bricklayers use the formula $N = 7\ell h$ to estimate the number of bricks needed to cover a wall. N is the number of bricks, ℓ is the length of the wall in feet, and h is the height. If 980 bricks are used to build a wall 20 ft long, how high is the wall?

Understand

1. Circle the information you will need to solve.

2. What are you being asked to do?

   _____

3. What units will your final answer be in?

   _____

Plan and Carry Out

4. What formula are you to use? _____

5. How many bricks are used? _____

6. How long is the wall? _____

7. Substitute the values in the formula. _____

8. Solve the equation. _____

9. How tall is the wall? _____

Check

10. Substitute your answer into the formula. Does your answer check?

    _____

Solve Another Problem

11. The formula used to find your target heart rate while exercising is $h = 220 - 0.6a$. The target heart rate in heartbeats per minute is h, and a is the age in years of the person exercising. What is the target heart rate for a 26-year-old person?

    _____

    _____

9A: Graphic Organizer

For use before Lesson 9-1

Study Skill Many skills build on each other, particularly in mathematics. Before you begin a new lesson, do a quick review of the material you covered in earlier lessons. Make sure you ask for help when there are concepts you did not understand or do not remember.

Write your answers.

1. What is the chapter title? _____

2. How many lessons are there in this chapter? _____

3. What is the topic of the Test-Taking Strategies page? _____

4. Complete the graphic organizer below as you work through the chapter.
   • In the center, write the title of the chapter.
   • When you begin a lesson, write the lesson name in a rectangle.
   • When you complete a lesson, write a skill or key concept in a circle linked to that lesson block.
   • When you complete the chapter, use this graphic organizer to help you review.

9B: Reading Comprehension

For use after Lesson 9-3

Study Skill Use tables when you need to organize complex information. The columns and rows allow you to display different types of information in a way that is easy to read. Make sure you include appropriate headings.

Use the table below to answer the questions.

Top-Grossing Movies for the Weekend

Movie	Weekend Box Office Receipts (in millions)	Total Receipts (in millions)	Percent Change from Last Week	Weeks Movie Has Played
Movie A	$19.2	$62.3	−38%	2
Movie B	$16.2	16.2	New	1
Movie C	$14.0	$255.1	−33%	4
Movie D	$11.0	11.0	New	1
Movie E	$10.3	$370.4	−28%	6

1. What information does the table display?

   _____

2. What is the greatest number in the table? _____

3. What does a negative value in the Percent Change column indicate?

   _____

4. Why does Movie B have no value in the Percent Change
   column?

   _____

5. Which movie has been shown for six weeks? _____

6. Which movie had the greatest box office receipts for the weekend? _____

7. Movie E grossed a total of $370.4 million dollars in 6 weeks.
   What was the average amount of money it grossed per week?

   _____

8. **High-Use Academic Words** What does it mean to *organize,* as
   mentioned in the study skill at the top of the page?

   a. to exclude   b. to arrange

9C: Reading/Writing Math Symbols   **For use after Lesson 9-4**

Study Skill Using mathematical symbols is a great way to take notes more quickly. Other symbols are helpful as well, such as these: @ (at), w/ (with), # (number), and = (equal).

Write each mathematical statement in words.

1. $x \leq 3$

_____

_____

2. $MN = 3$

_____

_____

3. $y = 3x$

_____

_____

4. $(4 + (-7)) = -3$

_____

_____

5. $4 : 5 = 8 : 10$

_____

_____

6. $\triangle EFG \cong \triangle KLM$

_____

_____

7. $x > 3$

_____

_____

8. $\overline{MN} \cong \overline{AB}$

_____

_____

9. $60\% = \frac{60}{100}$

_____

_____

10. $5^2 = 25$

_____

_____

11. $\triangle EFG \sim \triangle KLM$

_____

_____

12. $\sqrt{17} \approx 4$

_____

_____

13. $y = x + 4$

_____

_____

14. $\frac{3}{5} \neq \frac{4}{6}$

_____

_____

Vocabulary and Study Skills

9D: Visual Vocabulary Practice

High-Use Academic Words

For use after Lesson 9-5

Study Skill When you feel you're getting frustrated, take a break.

Concept List

name	classify	acronym
measure	rule	symbolize
dimensions	abbreviate	property

Write the concept that best describes each exercise. Choose from the concept list above.

1. $a + b = b + a$ _____	**2.** 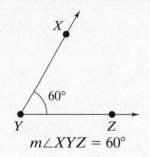 $m\angle XYZ = 60°$ _____	**3.** Trapezoids, rectangles, and parallelograms are all quadrilaterals; circles and octagons are not. _____
4. $l \times w \times h$ _____	**5.** Write oz for ounces. _____	**6.** is equal to $\quad$ = is similar to $\quad$ ~ is congruent to $\quad$ ≅ _____
7. 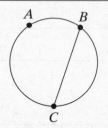 Three arcs are $\overset{\frown}{AB}$, $\overset{\frown}{ABC}$, and $\overset{\frown}{BC}$. _____	**8.** $f(x) = 2x + 1$ _____	**9.** Write GCF for greatest common factor. _____

9E: Vocabulary Check

Study Skill Strengthen your vocabulary. Use these pages and add cues and summaries by applying the Cornell Notetaking style.

Write the definition for each word or term at the right. To check your work, fold the paper back along the dotted line to see the correct answers.

_____

_____

_____   principal

_____

_____

_____   simple interest

_____

_____

_____   balance

_____

_____

_____   function

_____

_____

_____   arithmetic sequence

_____

_____

9E: Vocabulary Check (continued)

For use after Lesson 9-7

Write the vocabulary word or term for each definition. To check your work, fold the paper forward along the dotted line to see the correct answers.

the original amount deposited
or borrowed

_____

interest calculated only on the
principal

_____

the principal plus the interest
earned

_____

a relationship that assigns exactly
one output value to each input
value

_____

a sequence where each term
is the result of adding a fixed
number to the previous term

_____

9F: Vocabulary Review Puzzle

For use with the Chapter Review

Study Skill Have a dictionary or a textbook's glossary available while you are studying. Look up any unknown words.

Find the words in the puzzle from the definitions. Circle them. Words can be forwards, backwards, up, down, or diagonally.

```
Y  R  A  T  N  E  M  E  L  P  M  O  C  I  P  I  A  U  D
B  X  T  F  Q  X  E  L  A  P  I  C  N  I  R  P  B  Y  L
F  S  N  Y  E  Q  D  P  C  O  N  J  E  C  T  U  R  E  X
C  I  X  Z  G  C  T  A  O  L  W  X  H  R  M  V  F  P  A
Q  M  Y  N  A  M  N  S  F  I  P  B  B  O  M  U  P  I  R
B  P  S  D  J  R  F  E  S  U  N  E  T  O  P  Y  H  D  I
U  L  L  M  G  O  U  N  R  H  A  C  C  O  U  Q  Q  T  T
V  E  A  E  R  C  N  G  P  E  E  O  R  U  J  F  P  S  H
T  H  W  L  H  O  C  I  C  E  F  C  G  O  C  W  U  E  M
N  V  W  Y  Q  M  T  L  O  H  Y  M  N  A  P  Z  D  Q  E
I  G  E  U  P  P  I  X  N  Z  L  I  U  A  X  T  D  U  T
O  T  L  D  X  O  O  D  G  G  V  P  L  C  L  E  W  E  I
P  P  C  R  J  U  N  I  R  U  I  M  L  C  R  A  H  N  C
D  V  R  O  N  N  K  M  U  J  S  O  Z  R  O  I  B  C  Z
I  U  I  H  O  D  R  A  E  X  S  J  Q  I  E  J  C  E  L
M  G  C  C  G  K  B  R  N  T  G  E  O  M  E  T  R  I  C
J  E  B  A  A  Y  T  Y  T  T  Y  S  M  Y  E  O  F  F  B
R  I  B  Z  C  Q  P  P  Q  U  X  I  Z  A  D  L  E  E  R
S  C  X  C  E  W  X  K  H  O  Q  R  J  J  E  P  E  A  X
A  O  O  Q  D  D  E  L  G  N  A  U  M  Q  W  B  T  E  Y
```

Definitions

- three dimensional figure with only one base
- point that divides a segment into two congruent segments
- a polygon with 10 sides
- set of numbers that follows a pattern
- prediction that suggests what you expect will happen
- interest calculated only on the principal
- the name of the side opposite the right angle

- set of all points in a plane that are the same distance from a given point
- a polygon with six sides
- this figure is made of two rays with a common endpoint
- sequence in which you add the same number to the previous term
- sequence in which you multiply the previous term by the same number
- the principal plus interest
- distance around a circle
- segment that has both endpoints on the circle

- figures that have the same size and shape
- two angles whose sum is 90 degrees
- relationship that assigns exactly one output value for each input value
- the amount of money that you deposit or borrow
- interest paid on the original principal plus any interest that has been left in the account

Name _____ Class _____ Date _____

Practice 10-1

Graphing Points in Four Quadrants

Name the point with the given coordinates.

1. $(-2, 2)$ _____   2. $(8, 0)$ _____

3. $(4, -3)$ _____   4. $(-7, 3)$ _____

5. $(0, -5)$ _____   6. $(-8, -4)$ _____

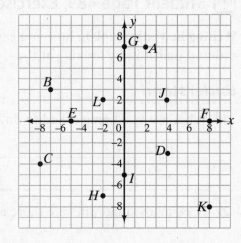

Write the coordinates of each point.

7. E _____   8. A _____

9. H _____   10. K _____

11. G _____   12. J _____

Identify the quadrant in which each point lies.

13. $(-4, 3)$ 14. $(7, 21)$ 15. $(5, -8)$ 16. $(-2, -7)$

_____   _____   _____   _____

17. Three vertices of a trapezoid are $(0, 6)$, $(-6, -1)$, and $(-6, -6)$. Find coordinates of a fourth vertex that would make this figure a proper trapezoid with one right angle.

   • On the grid at the right, graph the three vertices and draw the two sides.

   • Graph the fourth vertex of the trapezoid and draw the other two sides. What are the coordinates of the fourth vertex?

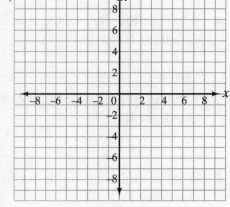

_____

Graph each polygon on the grid at the right. Use (0, 0) as one vertex and label all vertices.

18. a square with sides 5 units long

19. a square with sides 4 units long

20. a rectangle with horizontal length 5 units and vertical length 3 units

21. a rectangle with horizontal length 3 units and vertical length 6 units

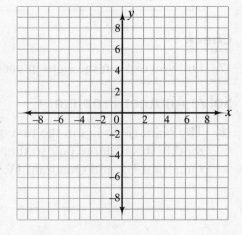

10-1 • Guided Problem Solving

GPS Student Page 489, Exercise 35:

Writing in Math Explain how you can tell which quadrant an ordered pair is in by looking at the signs of its *x*- and *y*-coordinates.

Understand

1. What are you being asked to do?

   _____

   _____

2. How many quadrants are there and how are they labeled?

   _____

Plan and Carry Out

3. What are the signs of the coordinates of ordered pairs in Quadrant I?

   _____

4. What are the signs of the coordinates of ordered pairs in Quadrant II?

   _____

5. What are the signs of the coordinates of ordered pairs in Quadrant III?

   _____

6. What are the signs of the coordinates of ordered pairs in Quadrant IV?

   _____

Check

7. Did you explain the signs in each quadrant? _____

Solve Another Problem

8. The point $(3, 5)$ lies in the first quadrant. Explain how to modify this ordered pair so that it would lie in Quadrant II, Quadrant III, and Quadrant IV.

   _____

   _____

Practice 10-2

Graphing Linear Equations

Determine whether each ordered pair is a solution of $y = x - 4$.

1. $(0, -4)$ _____   **2.** $(5, -1)$ _____   **3.** $(-3, -7)$ _____   **4.** $(-7, -3)$ _____

Find three solutions for each equation.

5. $y = x + 5$ _____

6. $y = -x + 7$ _____

7. $y = 2x - 1$ _____

Graph each linear equation.

8. $y = 3x - 1$ **9.** $y = -2x + 1$ **10.** $y = 2x - 4$

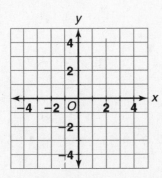 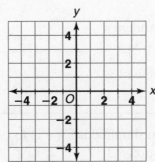 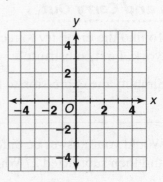

11. The graph of $y = -x$ passes through which quadrants?

_____

12. Use the graph below to determine the coordinates of the point that is a solution of the equations of lines p and q.

_____

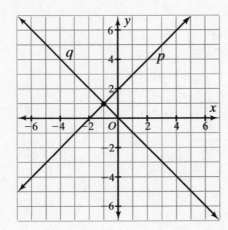

10-2 • Guided Problem Solving

GPS Student Page 494, Exercise 39:

Error Analysis A student says that $(-1, -5)$ is a solution of $y = -3x - 2$. What error do you think the student made?

Understand

1. Is $(-1, -5)$ a correct solution to the equation? How do you know this from just reading the question?

   _____

   _____

Plan and Carry Out

2. To find the error, try to recreate the student's work. First, substitute $x = -1$ into $-3x - 2$. _____

3. Simplify the expression to find the value of y.

   _____

4. Would your answer be different if you simplified $-3(-1)$ to -3 and then subtracted 2? What would you get?

   _____

5. What mistake do you think the student made?

   _____

   _____

Check

6. What if the student substituted -5 for y and then solved the equation? Solve the problem this way and identify an error the student could make to get $x = -1$.

   _____

   _____

Solve Another Problem

7. A student gives $(2, -9)$ as a solution to the equation $y = 2x - 5$. What error do you think the student made?

   _____

   _____

Name _____ Class _____ Date _____

Practice 10-3

Finding the Slope of a Line

Find the slope of each line.

1. _____

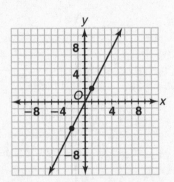

2. _____

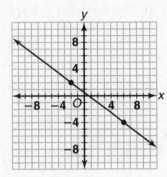

Use the coordinate plane to graph the given points. Find the slope of the line through the points.

3. $(-4, 6), (8, 4)$ _____

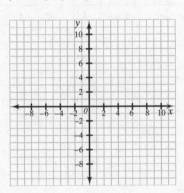

4. $(-1, 3), (4, 6)$ _____

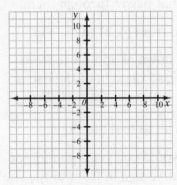

5. Up which slope would it be easiest to push a heavy cart: $\frac{1}{2}, \frac{1}{6}, 3$, or 5? _____

6. Which slope would probably give you the greatest speed down a hill when you are skiing: $\frac{1}{8}, \frac{1}{4}$, 1, or 2? _____

7. Which slope would be the most dangerous for a roofer trying to repair a roof: $\frac{1}{16}, \frac{1}{10}, \frac{1}{2}$, or $\frac{3}{2}$? _____

Draw a line with the given slope through the given point.

8. $P(5, 1)$, slope $= -\frac{1}{3}$

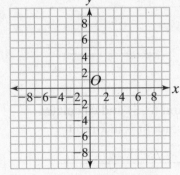

9. $K(-2, 4)$, slope $= 3$

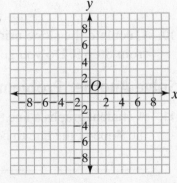

10-3 • Guided Problem Solving

GPS Student Page 501, Exercise 20:

Error Analysis Your classmate graphs a line through $(4, 2)$ and $(5, -1)$ and finds that the slope equals 3. Explain why your classmate is incorrect.

Understand

1. What are you being asked to do?

   _____

2. What is the formula for the slope of a line?

   _____

Plan and Carry Out

3. Graph the two points on a coordinate plane and draw the line that passes through them.

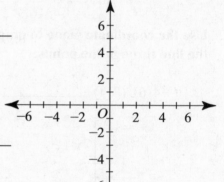

4. What is the run from $(4, 2)$ to $(5, -1)$? _____

5. The line slants down as you move from $(4, 2)$ to $(5, -1)$, so the sign of the rise is negative. What is the rise from $(4, 2)$ to $(5, -1)$? _____

6. Calculate rise/run to find the slope. _____

7. What answer would you get if you forgot to put the negative sign in front of the rise? _____

8. Why is your classmate incorrect? _____

   _____

Check

9. What are the rise and run if you calculate the rise and run by moving right to left, from $(5, -1)$ to $(4, 2)$?

   _____

10. Calculate the slope using the rise and run from Step 9. Do you get the same answer? _____

Solve Another Problem

11. A student graphs a line through points $(3, -1)$ and $(5, 3)$ and calculates the slope of the line to be -2. Explain why the student is incorrect.

   _____

   _____

Practice 10-4

Match each graph with one of the equations below.

1.

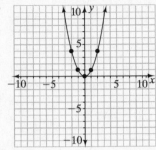

2.

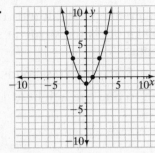

3.

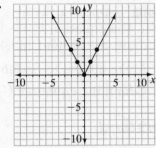

_____

4.

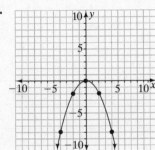

5.

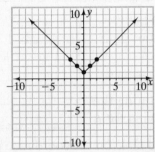

6.

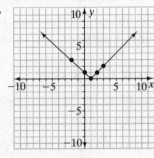

_____

A. $y = |x - 1|$ **B.** $y = x^2$ **C.** $y = -\frac{1}{2}x^2$

D. $y = |x| + 1$ **E.** $y = |2x|$ **F.** $y = x^2 - 1$

7. a. Complete the table below for the equation $y = x^2 + 2$.

x	−3	−2	−1	0	1	2	3
y							

b. Graph the ordered pairs and connect the points as smoothly as possible.

c. Describe how this graph is different from the graph of $y = x^2$.

_____

_____

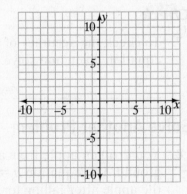

10-4 • Guided Problem Solving

GPS **Student Page 507, Exercise 30:**

Skydiving Suppose a skydiver leaps from a plane at an altitude of 12,000 ft. The equation $h = -16t^2 + 12,000$ models the skydiver's height above the ground, in feet, at t seconds.

   a. Make a table to find the height at 0, 5, 10, and 20 seconds.

   b. Graph the equation. Use the graph to find the height at 12 s.

Understand

1. What does the variable t in the equation represent? h?

   _____

2. Will the graph you draw for part (b) be
   a line, a parabola, or an absolute value? _____

Plan and Carry Out

3. Complete the table at right by subsituting the values of t into the equation and solving for h.

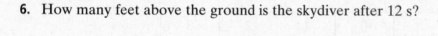

t	0	5	10	20
h				

4. Graph each (t, h) ordered pair from the table on the coordinate plane at the right. The t values are on the horizontal axis, and the h values are on the vertical axis. Connect the points with a smooth curve.

5. Find the point on the curve that corresponds to $t = 12$. What value of h does the graph pass through at that point?

   _____

6. How many feet above the ground is the skydiver after 12 s?

   _____

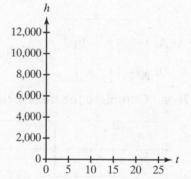

Check

7. To check the accuracy of your graph, substitute $t = 12$ into the equation given and solve. Is your answer for Step 6 reasonable?

   _____

Solve Another Problem

8. You drop an apple from a hot-air balloon that is 200 ft above the ground. The equation $h = 200 - 16t^2$ gives the height, in feet, of the apple after falling for t seconds. Use a graph to find the height of the apple after 2 seconds.

   _____

Practice 10-5

Use the graph at the right for Exercises 1–3.

1. Give the coordinates of point *A* after it has been translated down 3 units. _____

2. Give the coordinates of point *B* after it has been translated left 3 units. _____

3. What are the coordinates of point *N* after it is translated right 8 units and up 5 units? _____

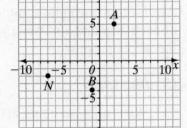

Graph each translation of *ABCD*.
Use arrow notation to show the translation.

4. *A* (2, 1), *B* (4, 5), *C* (7, 4), *D* (5, −1); right 2 units

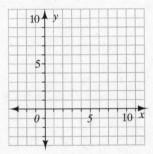

5. *A* (2, 1), *B* (4, 5), *C* (7, 4), *D* (5, −1); down 1 unit, left 2 units

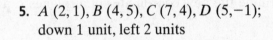
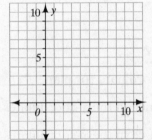

Write the rule for the translation shown in each graph.

6.

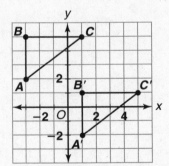

7.

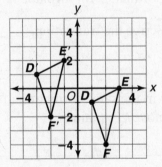

10-5 • Guided Problem Solving

GPS **Student Page 513, Exercise 22:**

Aviation Three airplanes are flying in a triangular formation. After 1 min, airplane P moves to P'. Give the new coordinates of each airplane and write a rule to describe the direction that the airplanes move.

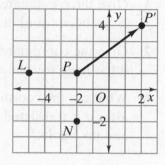

Understand

1. What are you being asked to do?

   _____

2. How does finding the new coordinates of airplane P help you to determine the new coordinates of airplanes L and N?

   _____

   _____

Plan and Carry Out

3. What is the new coordinate for plane P? _____

4. What is the difference in the x-coordinates of P and P'? _____

5. What is the difference in the y-coordinates of P and P'? _____

6. Use the differences found in steps 4 and 5 to find the new coordinates for airplane L. _____

7. Use the differences found in steps 4 and 5 to find the new coordinates for airplane N. _____

8. Write a rule to describe the translation. _____

Check

9. Are the airplanes in the same formation after the move as they were before the move? Explain.

   _____

   _____

Solve Another Problem

10. Three airplanes are flying in a triangular formation. If airplane P moves to P', find the new coordinates of the other two planes and write a rule to describe the move.

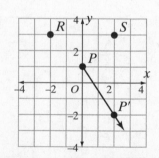

   _____

Practice 10-6

Line Symmetry and Reflections

Use the graph at the right for Exercises 1–3.

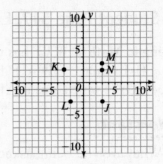

1. For which two points is the *x*-axis a line of reflection?

   _____

2. For which two points is the *y*-axis a line of reflection?

   _____

3. Points *L* and *J* are not reflections across the *y*-axis. Why not?

   _____

   _____

△ *A'B'C'* is a reflection of △ *ABC* over the *x*-axis. Draw
△ *A'B'C'* and complete each statement.

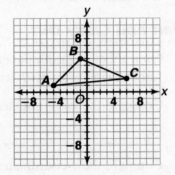

4. $A(-5, 1) \rightarrow A'(x, y)$ _____

5. $B(-1, 5) \rightarrow B'(x, y)$ _____

6. $C(6, 2) \rightarrow C'(x, y)$ _____

**Draw the lines of symmetry for each figure.
If there are no lines of symmetry, write *none*.**

7.

8.

9.

10.

**Graph each point and its reflection across the indicated axis. Write
the coordinates of the reflected point.**

11. $V(-3, 4)$ across the *y*-axis _____

12. $W(-4, -2)$ across the *x*-axis _____

13. $X(2, 2)$ across the *x*-axis _____

14. $Y(0, 3)$ across the *x*-axis _____

15. $Z(4, -6)$ across the *y*-axis _____

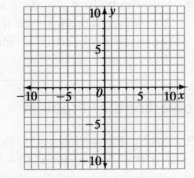

10-6 • Guided Problem Solving

GPS Student Page 517, Exercise 25:

Writing in Math $\triangle WXY$ has vertices $W(-4, -2)$, $X(4, 2)$, and $Y(1, -4)$. Its image $\triangle W'X'Y'$ has vertices $W'(-4, 2)$, $X'(4, -2)$, and $Y'(1, 4)$. Over which axis is $\triangle WXY$ reflected? Explain.

Understand

1. What are you being asked to do?

   _____

2. What is a good way to visualize the problem?

   _____

Plan and Carry Out

3. On a sheet of graph paper, graph triangles $\triangle WXY$ and $\triangle W'X'Y'$. Label each vertex with its coordinates.

4. Compare the x-coordinates of both triangles. What do you notice?

   _____

5. Compare the y-coordinates of both triangles. What do you notice?

   _____

   _____

6. If only the y-coordinates are changed to their opposites, which axis is an object reflected over? _____

7. Over which axis was $\triangle WXY$ reflected? _____

Check

8. Fold the picture you drew in Step 3 over the axis across which it is reflected. Check to see if the vertices of $\triangle WXY$ correspond to the vertices of $\triangle W'X'Y'$. Does your answer check?

   _____

Solve Another Problem

9. $\triangle ABC$ has vertices $A(1, 3)$, $B(-2, 2)$, and $C(-1, -4)$. Its image $\triangle A'B'C'$ has vertices $A'(-1, 3)$, $B'(2, 2)$, and $C'(1, -4)$. Over which axis was ABC reflected? Explain.

   _____

Practice 10-7

Rotational Symmetry and Rotations

Does the figure have rotational symmetry? Explain.

1.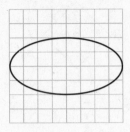

2.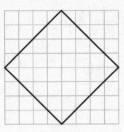

3.

4.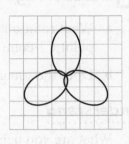

_____   _____   _____   _____

Draw the images of the figure after the given rotation about point _O_.

5. 90° rotation

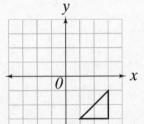

6. 180° rotation

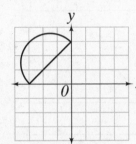

7. 270° rotation

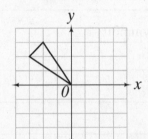

8. 180° rotation

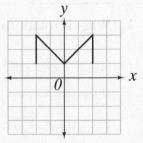

Figure II is the image of Figure I. Identify the transformation as a translation, a reflection, or a rotation.

9.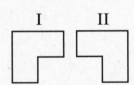

_____

10.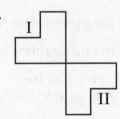

_____

11.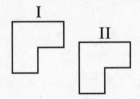

_____

12.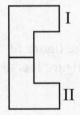

_____

10-7 • Guided Problem Solving

GPS **Student Page 522, Exercise 23:**

a. What rotation will move point A to point B? Point A to point C? Point A to point D?

b. Does the square have rotational symmetry? Explain.

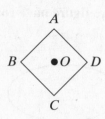

Understand

1. What are you being asked to do?

   _____

   _____

   _____

2. What is rotational symmetry?

   _____

   _____

   _____

Plan and Carry Out

3. How many degrees does the figure rotate from A to B? _____

4. How many degrees does the figure rotate from A to C? _____

5. How many degrees does the figure rotate from A to D? _____

6. Does the figure fit exactly on top of the
   original in the rotations in Steps 3–5? _____

7. According to your answers to Steps 6 and 7,
   does the square have rotational symmetry? _____

Check

8. Are the rotations that make the figure fit
   exactly on top of the original figure less than 360°? _____

Solve Another Problem

9. a. What rotation will move point A to point C? Point B to point D?

   _____

   b. Does the figure have rotational symmetry? Explain.

   _____

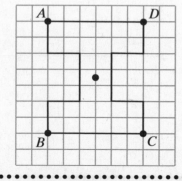

10A: Graphic Organizer

For use before Lesson 10-1

Study Skill As you learn new skills, practice them regularly. Each time you work a problem, it should seem easier than the time before. Keep a list of problems that you want to spend extra time practicing.

Write your answers.

1. What is the chapter title? _____

2. How many lessons are there in this chapter? _____

3. What is the topic of the Test-Taking Strategies page? _____

_____

4. Complete the graphic organizer below as you work through the chapter.
   • In the center, write the title of the chapter.
   • When you begin a lesson, write the lesson name in a rectangle.
   • When you complete a lesson, write a skill or key concept in a circle linked to that lesson block.
   • When you complete the chapter, use this graphic organizer to help you review.

10B: Reading Comprehension

Study Skill Go to class prepared. Always bring your textbook, notebook or paper, and a pencil, unless your teacher tells you otherwise.

Below is a coordinate map of the midwestern and eastern United States. The horizontal scale uses letters and the vertical scale uses numbers to identify various locations. Use the map to answer the questions below. Letters are typically written first, followed by numbers.

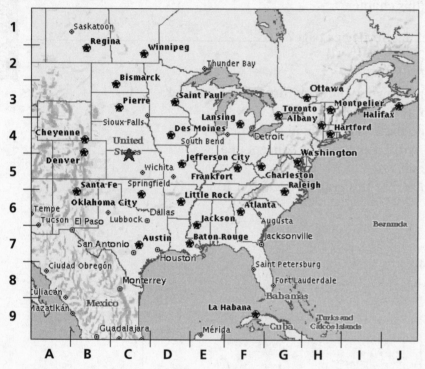

1. What are the coordinates for Tucson?

2. What are the coordinates for Montpelier?

3. Which state capital is located at D4?

4. Which cities are located at C7?

5. How would you identify the location of Bismarck?

6. What is the difference in the vertical coordinates for Atlanta and Saint Paul?

7. **High-Use Academic Words** In Exercise 5, what does it mean to identify?

    a. to come together to form a single unit   b. to show that you recognize something

10C: Reading/Writing Math Symbols

For use after Lesson 10-5

Study Skill Read aloud or recite when you are studying at home; reciting a rule or formula can help you to remember it and recall it for later use.

Write each mathematical statement in words.

1. $m\angle A = 47°$

_____

2. $M(-2, 0)$

_____

3. $y = 8x + 4$

_____

4. $P(3, 4) \rightarrow P'(5, 2)$

_____

5. $(x, y) \rightarrow (x - 2, y + 1)$

_____

_____

6. (x, y) for $x > 0$ and $y > 0$

_____

_____

7. $C(1, 2),$ slope $= \frac{1}{2}$

_____

_____

_____

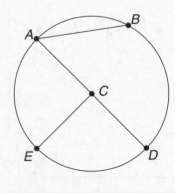

Use appropriate symbols to identify the parts of Circle C.

8. two chords _____

9. three radii _____

10. one diameter _____

11. three central angles _____

12. two semicircles _____

10D: Visual Vocabulary Practice

For use after Lesson 10-6

Study Skill When a math exercise is difficult, try to determine what makes it difficult. Is it a word that you don't understand? Are the numbers difficult to use?

Concept List

linear equation	slope	origin
coordinate plane	reflection	translation
nonlinear equation	x-coordinate	y-coordinate

Write the concept that best describes each exercise. Choose from the concept list above.

1.	2.	3.
$(0, 0)$	2 for the ordered pair $(4, 2)$	$y = 2x - 3$
_____	_____	_____

4.	5.	6.
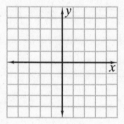	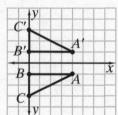	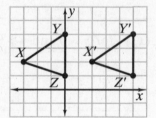
_____	_____	_____

7.	8.	9.
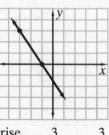 $\dfrac{\text{rise}}{\text{run}} = \dfrac{3}{-2} = -\dfrac{3}{2}$	$-\dfrac{1}{2}$ for the ordered pair $\left(-\dfrac{1}{2}, 8\right)$	$y = -\dfrac{1}{2}x^2 + 5$
_____	_____	_____

10E: Vocabulary Check

Study Skill Strengthen your vocabulary. Use these pages and add cues and summaries by applying the Cornell Notetaking style.

Write the definition for each word or term at the right. To check your work, fold the paper back along the dotted line to see the correct answers.

_____ line of symmetry

_____
_____

_____ transformations

_____
_____

_____ image

_____
_____

_____ quadrants

_____
_____

_____ rotation

_____
_____

10E: Vocabulary Check (continued)

For use after Lesson 10-7

Write the vocabulary word or term for each definition. To check your work, fold the paper forward along the dotted line to see the correct answers.

a line that divides a figure into mirror images

_____

a change in the position, shape, or size of a figure

_____

the result of a transformation of a point, line, or figure

_____

the four regions of the coordinate plane divided by the *x*- and *y*-axes

_____

a transformation that turns a figure about a fixed point

_____

10F: Vocabulary Review

For use with the Chapter Review

Study Skill Use a highlighter to mark material that is important in your notes or on teacher handouts. When you review for tests, pay special attention to this highlighted information.

Match the term in Column A with its definition in Column B.

Column A	Column B
1. transformation	A. transformation that creates symmetry
2. decagon	B. polygon with 10 sides
3. reflection	C. segment that has both endpoints on the circle
4. chord	D. quadrilateral with four congruent sides
5. rhombus	E. change of position, shape, or size of a figure
6. slope	F. quadrilateral with exactly one pair of parallel sides
7. trapezoid	G. ratio that describes the steepness of a line

Match the term in Column A with its definition in Column B.

Column A	Column B
8. complementary	H. two angles whose sum is 180 degrees
9. rotation	I. identifies the location of a point
10. hypotenuse	J. one side of a figure is the mirror image of the other side
11. translation	K. transformation that moves points the same distance and in the same direction
12. symmetry	L. two angles whose sum is 90 degrees
13. ordered pair	M. the longest side of a right triangle
14. supplementary	N. transformation that turns a figure about a fixed point
15. radius	O. segment with one endpoint at the center and the other endpoint on the circle

Vocabulary and Study Skills

Practice 11-1

Make a frequency table and a line plot for the data.

1. boxes of juice sold per day:

   26 21 26 24 27 23 24 22

   26 21 23 26 24 26 23

Ms. Makita made a line plot to show the scores her students got on a test. At the right is Ms. Makita's line plot.

2. What does each data item or ✗ represent?

   _____

3. How many more students scored 75 than scored 95?

   _____

4. How many students scored over 85? _____

5. What scores did the same number of students get?

   _____

Test Scores

```
✗           ✗
✗  ✗  ✗  ✗
✗  ✗  ✗  ✗        ✗
✗  ✗  ✗  ✗  ✗  ✗
✗  ✗  ✗  ✗  ✗  ✗
✗  ✗  ✗  ✗  ✗  ✗
75 80 85 90 95 100
```

Nathan asked 24 classmates to estimate the total number of hours (to the nearest quarter hour) they spend doing homework Monday through Thursday. The frequency table below shows their responses.

Hours Spent Doing Homework

Number of Hours	Frequency
1 – 1.75	1
2 – 2.75	1
3 – 3.75	2
4 – 4.75	6
5 – 5.75	8
6 – 6.75	3
7 – 7.75	2
8 – 8.75	1

6. Can you tell from the table how many students do homework for two hours or less? Explain.

   _____

7. How many more students do homework for at least 5 hours than do homework for less than 4 hours?

8. Make a histogram for the data. Use the intervals in the table.

11-1 • Guided Problem Solving

GPS **Student Page 535, Exercise 12:**

Books The line plot shows the number of books each bookstore customer bought. How many customers bought more than three books?

Number of Books Purchased

```
            X
    X       X
    X   X   X
    X   X   X           X
    X   X   X   X   X   X
    1   2   3   4   5   6
```

Understand

1. In the line plot, what do the numbers at the bottom represent?

   _____

2. In the line plot, what do the X's represent?

   _____

   _____

Plan and Carry Out

3. To find the number of customers who bought more than three books, in which columns do you have to look?

   _____

4. How many customers bought 4 books? _____

5. How many customers bought 5 books? _____

6. How many customers bought 6 books? _____

7. How many customers bought more than 3 books?

   _____

Check

8. Why do you not include the customers who bought 3 books?

   _____

   _____

Solve Another Problem

9. The line plot shows how many CDs each customer in a music store bought. How many customers bought two or fewer CDs?

   _____

Number of CDs Purchased

```
        X
        X
    X   X   X
    X   X   X   X   X
    0   1   2   3   4
```

Practice 11-2

Use the spreadsheet at the right for Exercises 1–4.

Tickets Sold to Concert Performances

	A	B	C
1	**Performance**	**Adult Tickets**	**Student Tickets**
2	**Thursday**	47	65
3	**Friday**	125	133
4	**Saturday**	143	92

1. What is the value in cell B3?

_____

2. Which cell shows 65 tickets sold?

_____

3. How many more adult tickets than student tickets were sold on Saturday?

_____

4. The concert producer thought she would have the greatest attendance on Saturday. Compare the data with her expectation.

_____

_____

Decide whether a double bar graph or a double line graph is more appropriate for the given data. Draw the graph.

5. students taking foreign language classes

Year	Boys	Girls
1990	45	60
1991	50	55
1992	70	60
1993	55	75

6. extracurricular sport activities

Sport	Boys	Girls
basketball	40	30
volleyball	30	40
soccer	40	25

11-2 • Guided Problem Solving

GPS Student Page 541, Exercise 23:

Writing in Math Describe how you would display measurements of a pet's growth over several years. What measurements would you use? How would you display them?

Understand

1. What ways of displaying data have you learned?

   _____

2. Which of these could you use to show the growth of an animal?

   _____

Plan and Carry Out

3. Which type of data display or graph provides the most detail about representing changes over time? _____

4. What kind of growth patterns or information about your pet would you want to know? _____

5. What units of measurement would you use in your graph to determine these growth patterns? What time units and limits would you use to analyze your data?

   _____

6. Explain your steps in constructing this data display.

   _____

Check

7. Follow the steps you wrote in Step 6. Does your data display clearly show units of measure and time to provide you with the information you wanted? Can you draw accurate conclusions about the growth of your pet over time from the display?

   _____

Solve Another Problem

8. Olivia wants to know which band that students in each of the four grades prefer. They must decide between a salsa band and a rock band. Describe how you would gather and display this information. What type of graph would be the best choice to represent this data? Explain.

   _____

Practice 11-3

The stem-and-leaf plot at the right shows the number of baskets scored by one of ten intramural teams last season. Use it for Exercises 1–4.

5	2	6	9
6	0	4	6
7	1	5	
8	4	8	

8|4 means 84

1. How many data items are there?

   _____

2. What is the least measurement given?

   _____

3. What is the greatest measurement given?

   _____

4. In how many games did the team score less than 70 baskets?

   _____

5. Draw a stem-and-leaf plot for the set of data.

   science test scores: 83   73   78   60   85

                          92   95   85   99   68

Use the stem-and-leaf plot from Exercise 5 to answer Exercises 6–8.

6. Find the mode of the test scores.

   _____

7. How many data items are in the set?

   _____

8. Find the mean of the test scores.

   _____

9. You have a spreadsheet showing how many DVDs people bought in 1998, 2000, and 2002. The spreadsheet also shows how many videocassettes were bought in 1998, 2000, and 2002. Which is the most effective data display choice: a double line graph or a stem-and-leaf plot? Explain your answer.

   _____

   _____

   _____

   _____

11-3 • Guided Problem Solving

GPS **Student Page 546, Exercise 8:**

Height How many males are 65 in. tall?

		Student Height (in.)	
	Female		**Male**
7 4 3 1 0 0	5	6 7	
8 5 4 1 0	6	2 3 5 5 6 7 9	
0	7	1 2 3 4 6	

Key: $61 \leftarrow 1 \mid 6 \mid 3 \rightarrow 63$

Understand

1. What data does the stem-and-leaf plot display?

   _____

2. What is the question asking you to find?

   _____

Plan and Carry Out

3. Circle the part of the stem-and-leaf plot that pertains to males.

4. According to the key, what place value do the numbers on the right have?

   _____

5. According to the key, what place value do the numbers between the stems have?

   _____

6. Underline the row that has a 6 in the tens place.

7. Circle the fives in the row you underlined in Step 6.

8. Count the number of fives you circled in the male half of the stem-and-leaf plot. How many males are 65 in. tall?

   _____

Check

9. Write out the heights of all of the males in the stem-and-leaf plot. Count the number of males who are 65 in. tall.

   _____

Solve Another Problem

10. In the stem-and-leaf plot at the right, how many female students scored 91 on their test?

    _____

		Test Scores	
	Female		**Male**
	0	5	
	7	6	1 3
	9 4	7	6 8
	9 6 1 1	8	2 8 8 9 9
3 1 1 1 1 0	9	2 2 9	

Key: $79 \leftarrow 9 \mid 7 \mid 3 \rightarrow 73$

Practice 11-4

You want to survey students in your school about their exercise habits. Tell whether the situations described in Exercises 1 and 2 are likely to give a random sample of the population. Explain.

1. You select every tenth student on an alphabetical list of the students in your school. You survey the selected students in their first-period classes.

_____

_____

2. At lunchtime you stand by a vending machine. You survey every student who buys something from the vending machine.

_____

_____

Is each question *biased* or *fair*? Rewrite biased questions as fair questions.

3. Do you think bike helmets should be mandatory for all bike riders?

_____

4. Do you prefer the natural beauty of hardwood floors in your home?

_____

5. Do you exercise regularly?

_____

6. Do you eat at least the recommended number of servings of fruits and vegetables to ensure a healthy and long life?

_____

7. Do you prefer the look and feel of thick lush carpeting in your living room?

_____

8. Do you take a daily multiple vitamin to supplement your diet?

_____

9. Do you read the newspaper to be informed about world events?

_____

10. Do you feel that the TV news is a sensational portrayal of life's problems?

_____

Name _____ Class _____ Date _____

11-4 • Guided Problem Solving

Parks Suppose you are gathering information about visitors to Yosemite National Park. You survey every tenth person entering the park. Would you get a random sample of visitors? Explain.

Understand

1. What is a random sample?

_____

_____

2. What are you being asked to do?

_____

_____

Plan and Carry Out

3. What is the population you are surveying?

_____

4. Does every person in the population have an equal chance of being surveyed? _____

5. Is this a random sample? Why or why not? _____

_____

Check

6. How else could you randomly survey the people at Yosemite National Park?

_____

_____

Solve Another Problem

7. You want to survey the people at the local pool about the food served in the snack shack. You decide to walk around the kiddy pool and survey parents. Is this a random sample? Why or why not?

_____

_____

Practice 11-5

Estimating Population Size

Workers at a state park caught, tagged, and set free the species shown at the right. Later that same year, the workers caught the number of animals shown in the table below and counted the tagged animals. Use a proportion to estimate the park population of each species.

Tagged Animals	
Bears	12
Squirrels	50
Raccoons	23
Rabbits	42
Trout	46
Skunks	21

	Caught	Counted Tagged	Estimated Population
1. Bears	30	9	
2. Squirrels	1,102	28	
3. Raccoons	412	10	
4. Rabbits	210	2	
5. Trout	318	25	
6. Skunks	45	6	

A park ranger tags 100 animals. Use a proportion to estimate the total population for each sample.

7. 23 out of 100 animals are tagged

_____

8. 12 out of 75 animals are tagged

_____

9. 8 out of 116 animals are tagged

_____

10. 5 out of 63 animals are tagged

_____

11. 4 out of 83 animals are tagged

_____

12. 3 out of 121 animals are tagged

_____

13. 83 out of 125 animals are tagged

_____

14. 7 out of 165 animals are tagged

_____

Use a proportion to estimate each animal population.

15. Total ducks counted: 1,100
Marked ducks counted: 257
Total marked ducks: 960

_____

16. Total alligators counted: 310
Marked alligators counted: 16
Total marked alligators: 90

_____

Name _____ Class _____ Date _____

11-5 • Guided Problem Solving

GPS **Student Page 556, Exercise 19:**

Sharks A biologist is studying the shark populaton off the Florida coast. He captures, tags, and sets free 38 sharks. A week later, 8 out of 25 sharks captured have tags. He uses the proportion $\frac{25}{8} = \frac{38}{x}$ to estimate that the population is about 12.

    a. Error Analysis Find the error in the biologist's proportion.

    b. Estimate the shark population.

Understand

1. What are you being asked to do?

_____

Plan and Carry Out

2. If x represents all the sharks off the coast of Florida, write the ratio of the sharks the biologist originally tagged to the number of all the sharks off the coast of Florida. _____

3. How many sharks did the biologist capture the second time? How many were tagged? _____

4. Write a ratio comparing the sharks the biologist found tagged and the number that were captured the second time. _____

5. Set the ratios from Steps 2 and 4 equal to form the correct proportion. _____

6. What is wrong with the biologist's proportion? _____

7. Solve this proportion to find the correct estimate. _____

Check

8. Explain why the biologist should have known the estimate was wrong.

_____

_____

Solve Another Problem

9. A ranger traps, tags, and releases 32 jackrabbits. Later she captures 12 jackrabbits, of which 4 are tagged. The ranger estimates that there are 96 jackrabbits in the area. Write a proportion and check the ranger's estimate. Is she correct?

_____

Practice 11-6

**The table below shows the number of students
enrolled in swimming classes for 2001 to 2003.**

1. Use the data to create a double line graph
   that emphasizes the increase in the number
   of students enrolled in summer swim classes.

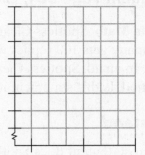

Swim Class Enrollment		
	Boys	**Girls**
2001	375	360
2002	400	395
2003	410	420

2. Use the data again to create a second double
   line graph that does not emphasize the increase
   in the number of students enrolled in the
   summer swim classes.

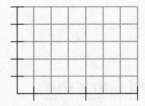

3. Which graph could be used to request additional reserved
   times for swim classes at the pool?

   _____

   _____

**Vince has the following scores on chapter tests in his math class. Use
this data in Exercises 4–6.**

   95   89   83   90   83

4. Find the mean, median, and mode of his test scores.

   _____

5. Should Vince describe his tests using the mean, the median, or
   the mode to show his ability to do well in math?

   _____

   _____

6. Should his teacher use the mean, the median, or the mode to
   encourage Vince to check his work carefully on the next test?

   _____

   _____

11-6 • Guided Problem Solving

GPS **Student Page 564, Exercise 19:**

Writing in Math Spotless Cleaners sends out 200 customer surveys. The company gets 100 replies with 97 customers saying they are satisfied. In an ad, Spotless Cleaners says that 97% of its customers are satisfied. Is this statement misleading? Explain.

Understand

1. What statement does Spotless Cleaners make?

   _____

2. What are you being asked to do?

   _____

   _____

Plan and Carry Out

3. How many surveys did Spotless Cleaners send out? _____

4. How many replies did Spotless Cleaners get back? _____

5. Did Spotless Cleaners represent all of
   the surveys they sent out in their ad? _____

6. How many surveys did Spotless
   Cleaners not report? _____

7. Is this statement misleading? Why? _____

   _____

Check

8. Using the correct sample size, 200, what
   percentage of customers does the data represent? _____

Solve Another Problem

9. Students can receive either Advanced, Proficient, or Basic on the state standardized test. The local newspaper reports that only 30% of the students passed the state standardized test at the proficient level. How does this statement mislead its readers?

   _____

   _____

   _____

Practice 11-7

Tell what trend you would expect to see in scatter plots comparing the sets of data in Exercises 1–4. Explain your reasoning.

1. a person's height and the person's shoe size

_____

_____

2. the age of a child and amount of weekly allowance that the child receives

_____

_____

3. the distance one lives from school and the length of the school day

_____

_____

4. the average number of hours a child sleeps and the age of the child

_____

_____

5. Make a scatter plot of the following data. Does the scatter plot show any trend? If so, what?

_____

Number of Hours of Practice	Number of Successful Free Throws out of 10
6	3
7	5
8	6
9	6
10	7
11	7
12	6
13	7

Describe the trend in each scatter plot.

6.

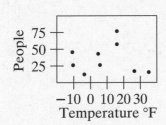

7.

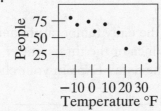

8.

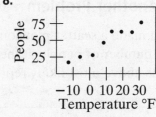

_____   _____   _____

11-7 • Guided Problem Solving

GPS **Student Page 570, Exercise 16:**

Carmella made a scatter plot comparing the daily temperature and the number of people at a beach. Which of the three scatter plots most likely represents the data? Explain your choice.

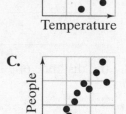

Understand

1. What two variables do the scatter plots relate?

_____

2. What are you asked to do?

_____

_____

Plan and Carry Out

3. What does the scatter plot in choice A indicate?

_____

4. What does the scatter plot in choice B indicate?

_____

_____

5. What does the scatter plot in choice C indicate?

_____

6. Which of the three choices
   most likely represents the data? _____

Check

7. Explain your answer to Step 6.

_____

_____

Solve Another Problem

8. You made a scatter plot comparing the daily temperature and the number of people at the mall. Which of the three scatter plots above most likely represents the data? Explain your choice.

_____

_____

11A: Graphic Organizer

For use before Lesson 11-1

Study Skill As your teacher presents new material in the chapter, keep a paper and pencil handy to write down notes and questions. If you miss class, borrow a classmate's notes so you will not fall behind.

Write your answers.

1. What is the chapter title? _____

2. How many lessons are there in this chapter? _____

3. What is the topic of the Test-Taking Strategies page? _____

4. Complete the graphic organizer below as you work through the chapter.
   • In the center, write the title of the chapter.
   • When you begin a lesson, write the lesson name in a rectangle.
   • When you complete a lesson, write a skill or key concept in a circle linked to that lesson block.
   • When you complete the chapter, use this graphic organizer to help you review.

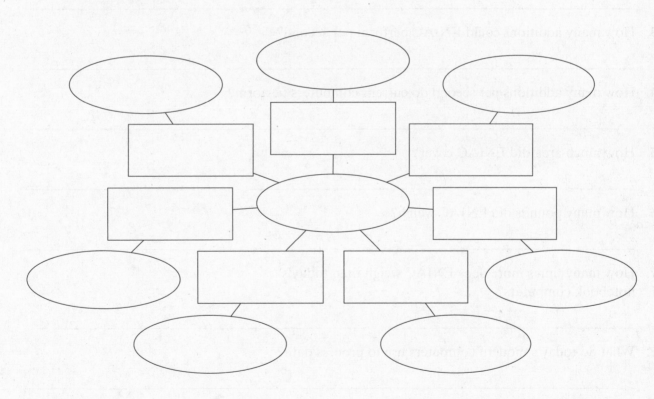

11B: Reading Comprehension

For use after Lesson 11-3

Study Skill Take short breaks between assignments.

Read the paragraph and answer the questions.

In 1945, the first electronic computer was built. ENIAC, which stands for Electronic Numerical Integrator and Calculator, was able to do 5,000 additions per second. Current computers are capable of doing 100,000 times as many additions per second. ENIAC weighed approximately 30 tons and had a length of 40 feet and a width of 45 feet. Present-day computer notebooks weigh about 3 pounds. Unlike modern computers, which use microprocessors composed of thousands or millions of transistors, ENIAC used vacuum tubes to process data. It had about 18,000 tubes, each the size of a small light bulb.

1. What does the acronym ENIAC stand for?

   _____

2. How many years ago was ENIAC built?

   _____

3. How many additions could ENIAC perform per second?

   _____

4. How many additions per second do current computers perform?

   _____

5. How much area did ENIAC cover?

   _____

6 How many pounds did ENIAC weigh?

   _____

7. How many times more does ENIAC weigh than today's notebook computers?

   _____

8. What do today's modern computers use to process data?

   _____

9. **High-Use Academic Words** In Exercise 1, what does the word *acronym* mean?

   a. a certain way in which something appears

   b. a word formed from the first letters of several other words

11C: Reading/Writing Math Symbols   For use after Lesson 11-4

Study Skill Make a realistic study schedule. Plan ahead when your teacher assigns a long-term project.

Some mathematical symbols have multiple meanings. Explain the meaning of the bar (−) in each of the following.

1. $2.\overline{3}$

_____

2. $11 - 15$

_____

3. $\overline{GH}$

_____

4. $3 + (-7)$

_____

5. $\frac{1}{5}$

_____

The bar (−) takes on different meanings when used with other symbols. Explain the meaning of each symbol below.

6. $=$ _____

7. $\leq$ _____

8. $\cong$ _____

9. $\stackrel{?}{=}$ _____

10. $\neq$ _____

When they are vertical, the bars also take on different meanings. Explain the meaning of these symbols.

11. $|\quad|$, as in $|-3| = 3$

_____

12. $\|$, as in $m \parallel n$

_____

11D: Visual Vocabulary Practice

For use after Lesson 11-7

Study Skill When interpreting an illustration, notice the information that is given and also notice what is not given. Do not make assumptions.

Concept List

biased question	double bar graph	histogram
frequency table	line plot	population
sample	no trend	negative trend

Write the concept that best describes each exercise. Choose from the concept list above.

1.
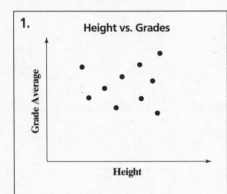
Height vs. Grades

_____

2. Number of Sports Played by Students

Sports	Tally	Frequency
0	卌	5
1				2
2					3
3	卌 ||	7

_____

3. Sandy conducted a survey at her college. She chose a random sample from all freshmen and asked how much time they study each week. The freshmen class represents this for the survey.

_____

4.
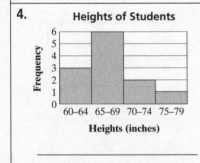
Heights of Students

_____

5.
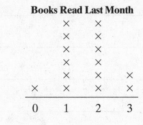
Books Read Last Month

_____

6.
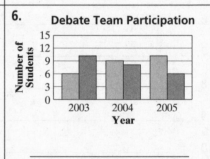
Debate Team Participation

_____

7. "Do you prefer lovable dogs or lazy cats?"

_____

8.
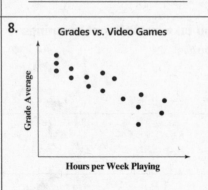
Grades vs. Video Games

_____

9. Derrick conducted a survey using the customers at a local ice cream shop. Derrick chose every 5th and 8th customer entering the shop to represent this.

_____

11E: Vocabulary Check

Study Skill Strengthen your vocabulary. Use these pages and add cues and summaries by applying the Cornell Notetaking style.

Write the definition for each word or term at the right. To check your work, fold the paper back along the dotted line to see the correct answers.

_____ biased question

_____

_____

_____ legend

_____

_____

_____ positive trend

_____

_____ cell

_____

_____

_____ random sample

_____

_____

Vocabulary and Study Skills

11E: Vocabulary Check (continued)

Write the vocabulary word or term for each definition. To check your work, fold the paper forward along the dotted line to see the correct answers.

a question that makes an unjustified assumption or makes one answer appear better than the other

_____

something that identifies data that are compared

_____

when one set of values increases, the other tends to increase

_____

a box where a row and a column meet

_____

a sample where each member of the population has an equal chance of being selected

_____

11F: Vocabulary Review

For use with the Chapter Review

Study Skill Take notes while you study. Use a highlighter to emphasize important material in your notes.

Circle the term that correctly completes each sentence.

1. A flip that creates symmetry is a (*translation, reflection*).

2. The first number in an ordered pair is the (*x, y*) coordinate.

3. Lines in a coordinate plane that are parallel to the *y*-axis are (*horizontal, vertical*).

4. A (*line plot, frequency table*) uses a number line with "x" marks to represent each data item.

5. You can use a (*bar, circle*) graph to easily compare amounts.

6. The (*mean, median*) is the middle number in a data set when the values are written in order from least to greatest.

7. The (*mode, range*) of a data set is the difference between the greatest and least data values.

8. A (*line graph, scatter plot*) can be used to investigate the relationship between two sets of data.

9. A sequence is (*arithmetic, geometric*) if each term is found by adding the same number to the previous term.

10. (*Principal, Interest*) is the amount of money borrowed or deposited.

11. The (*area, surface area*) of a prism is the sum of the areas of the faces.

12. (*Circumference, Area*) is the distance around a circle.

13. The opposite of squaring a number is finding its (*square root, perfect square*).

14. The (*slope, bisector*) of a line segment is a line, segment, or ray, that goes through the midpoint of the segment.

Practice 12-1

Probability

You spin a spinner numbered 1 through 10. Each outcome is equally
likely. Find the probabilities below as a fraction, decimal, and percent.

1. $P(9)$

2. $P(\text{even})$

3. $P(\text{number greater than 0})$

4. $P(\text{multiple of 4})$

_____ _____ _____ _____

There are eight blue marbles, nine orange marbles, and six yellow
marbles in a bag. You draw one marble at random. Find each
probability.

5. $P(\text{blue marble})$ _____

6. $P(\text{yellow marble})$ _____

7. What marble could you add or remove so
that the probability of drawing a blue marble is $\frac{1}{3}$?

_____

A box contains 12 slips of paper as shown.
Each slip of paper is equally likely to be drawn.
Find each probability.

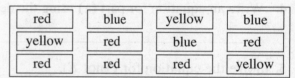

red	blue	yellow	blue
yellow	red	blue	red
red	red	red	yellow

8. $P(\text{red})$

9. $P(\text{blue})$

10. $P(\text{yellow})$

_____ _____ _____

11. $P(\text{red or blue})$

12. $P(\text{red or yellow})$

13. $P(\text{blue or yellow})$

_____ _____ _____

14. $P(\text{not red})$

15. $P(\text{not blue})$

16. $P(\text{not yellow})$

_____ _____ _____

You select a letter randomly from a bag containing the letters
S, P, I, N, N, E, and R. Find the odds in favor of each outcome.

17. selecting an N

18. selecting an S

_____ _____

12-1 • Guided Problem Solving

GPS Student Page 583, Exercise 32:

a. Suppose $P(E) = 0.3$. Find $P(\text{not } E)$.

b. Suppose $P(\text{not } E) = 65\%$. Find $P(E)$.

Understand

1. What is the relationship between E and not E?

_____

2. What is the sum of the probability of an event
   and the probability of the event's complement? _____

3. What is the difference between part a and part b?

_____

_____

Plan and Carry Out

4. Write an equation for part (a) using the definition of a complement.

_____

5. Solve the equation for $P(\text{not } E)$. _____

6. Write 65% as a decimal. _____

7. Write an equation for part (b) using the definition of a complement.

_____

8. Solve the equation for $P(E)$. _____

Check

9. How could you use a sum to check your answers?

_____

_____

Solve Another Problem

10. Suppose $P(E) = \frac{4}{5}$. Find $P(\text{not } E)$.

_____

_____

Practice 12-2

Suppose you observe the color of socks worn by students in your class: 12 have white, 4 have black, 3 have blue, and 1 has red. Find each experimental probability as a fraction in simplest form.

1. P(white) _____   **2.** P(red) _____   **3.** P(blue) _____

4. P(black) _____   **5.** P(yellow) _____   **6.** P(black or red) _____

Use the data in the table at the right for Exercises 7–12. Find each experimental probability as a percent.

Favorite Snack Survey Results

Snack	Number of Students
Fruit	8
Granola	2
Pretzels	3
Chips	7
Carrots	5

7. P(fruit) _____   **8.** P(granola) _____

9. P(pretzels) _____   **10.** P(carrots) _____

11. P(not fruit) _____   **12.** P(granola or chips) _____

13. Do an experiment to find the probability that a word chosen randomly in a book is the word *the*. How many words did you look at to find P(the)? What is P(the)?

_____

14. Suppose the following is the result of tossing a coin 5 times:

heads, tails, heads, tails, heads

What is the experimental probability for heads?

_____

Solve.

15. The probability that a twelve-year-old has a brother or sister is 25%. Suppose you survey 300 twelve-year-olds. About how many do you think will have a brother or sister? _____

16. a. A quality control inspector found flaws in 13 out of 150 sweaters. Find the probability that a sweater has a flaw. Round to the nearest tenth of a percent. _____

   b. Suppose the company produces 500 sweaters a day. How many will not have flaws? _____

   c. Suppose the company produces 600 sweaters a day. How many will have flaws? _____

12-2 • Guided Problem Solving

GPS Student Page 588, Exercise 14:

a. **Science** The probability that a male human is colorblind is 8%. Suppose you interview 1,000 males. About how many would you expect to be colorblind?

b. **Reasoning** Will you always get the same number? Explain.

Understand

1. What does it mean to be colorblind?

   _____

2. What are you being asked to do in part (a)?

   _____

   _____

Plan and Carry Out

3. Find 8% of 1,000. _____

4. How many males out of 1,000 would you expect to be colorblind?

   _____

5. Will you always get exactly this number? Explain.

   _____

   _____

   _____

Check

6. How could you find the answer another way?

   _____

Solve Another Problem

7. The probability of a person being left-handed is about 11%. Suppose you interview 500 people. About how many would you expect to be left-handed?

   _____

Name _____ Class _____ Date _____

Practice 12-3

Make a table to show the sample space and find the number of outcomes. Then find the probability.

1. A theater uses a letter to show which row a seat is in, and a number to show the column. If there are eight rows and ten columns, what is the probability that you select a seat at random that is in column 1? _____

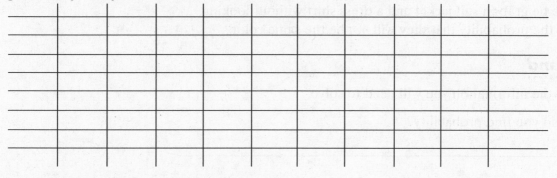

Make a tree diagram. Then find the probability.

2. A coin is tossed three times.
   a. Make a tree diagram that shows all the possible outcomes of how the coin will land.
   b. Find the probability that the coin will land heads up all three times or tails up all three times.

   _____

Use the counting principle.

3. A pizza company makes pizza in three different sizes: small, medium, and large. There are four possible toppings: pepperoni, sausage, green pepper, and mushroom. How many different kinds of pizza with one topping are available? _____

4. You can choose from three types of sandwiches for lunch and three types of juice. How many possible lunch combinations of sandwich and juice can you have? _____

Susan has red, blue, and yellow sweaters. Joanne has green, red, and white sweaters. Diane's sweaters are red, blue, and mauve. Each girl has only one sweater of each color and will pick a sweater to wear at random. Find each probability.

5. *P*(each girl chooses a different color)   6. *P*(each girl chooses the same color)

   _____   _____

7. *P*(two girls choose the same color, and the third chooses a different color)   8. *P*(each girl chooses a red sweater)

   _____   _____

12-3 • Guided Problem Solving

GPS **Student Page 595, Exercise 23:**

a. **Clothes** Ardell has four suit jackets (white, blue, green, and tan) and four dress shirts in the same colors. How many different jacket/shirt outfits does Ardell have?

b. Suppose he grabs a suit jacket and a dress shirt without looking. What is the probability that they will *not* be the same color?

Understand

1. Circle the information you will need to solve.

2. How do you find probability?

_____

_____

Plan and Carry Out

3. How many different suit jackets are there? _____

4. How many different dress shirts are there? _____

5. Using the counting principle, how many different jacket/shirt outfits does Ardell have? _____

6. How many same color jacket/shirt outfits does Ardell have? _____

7. How many different color jacket/shirt outfits does Ardell have? _____

8. What is the probability that they will *not* be the same color? _____

Check

9. How else could you find the total number of jacket/shirt outfits?

_____

Solve Another Problem

10. a. Joseph has three pairs of shoes (white, brown, and black) and four pairs of socks (white, brown, black, and blue). How many sock/shoe pairs are there?

    b. If Joseph selects a pair of shoes and a pair of socks without looking, what is the probability they will be the same color?

_____

Practice 12-4 **Compound Events**

Each letter in the word MASSACHUSETTS is written on a card. The cards are placed in a basket. Find each probability.

1. What is the probability of selecting two S's if the first card is replaced before selecting the second card?

_____

2. What is the probability of selecting two S's if the first card is not replaced before selecting the second card?

_____

You roll a fair number cube. Find each probability.

3. $P(3, \text{then } 5)$

_____

4. $P(2, \text{then } 2)$

_____

5. $P(5, \text{then } 4, \text{then } 6)$

_____

6. $P(6, \text{then } 0)$

_____

Four girls and eight boys are running for president or vice president of the Student Council. Find each probability.

7. Find the probability that two boys are elected.

_____

8. Find the probability that two girls are elected.

_____

9. Find the probability that the president is a boy and the vice president is a girl.

_____

10. Find the probability that the president is a girl and the vice president is a boy.

_____

A box contains ten balls, numbered 1 through 10. Marisha draws a ball. She records its number and then returns it to the bag. Then Penney draws a ball. Find each probability.

11. $P(9, \text{then } 3)$

_____

12. $P(\text{even, then odd})$

_____

13. $P(\text{odd, then } 2)$

_____

14. $P(\text{the sum of the numbers is } 25)$

_____

15. $P(\text{prime, then composite})$

_____

16. $P(\text{a factor of } 8, \text{then a multiple of } 2)$

_____

12-4 • Guided Problem Solving

GPS **Student Page 602, Exercise 26:**

Events with no outcomes in common are called *disjoint events* or *mutually exclusive events*. To find the probability of mutually exclusive events, add the probabilities of the individual events. Suppose you select a number from 21 to 30 at random. What is the probability of selecting a number that is even or prime?

Understand

1. What are disjoint or mutually exclusive events?

   _____

2. What are you being asked to do?

   _____

   _____

3. Why are selecting an even and selecting a prime number between 21 and 30 disjoint events?

   _____

Plan and Carry Out

4. How many numbers are there from 21 to 30? (Remember to include 21 and 30.) _____

5. List all the even numbers between 21 and 30. How many are there? _____

6. What is the probability of choosing an even number between 21 and 30? _____

7. List all the prime numbers between 21 and 30. How many are there? _____

8. What is the probability of choosing a prime number between 21 and 30? _____

9. What is the probability of choosing an even or prime number between 21 and 30? _____

Check

10. Write your answer as a fraction, decimal, and percent. _____

Solve Another Problem

11. Suppose you roll a number cube. What is the probability that you roll a number less than 3 or a number greater than or equal to 5?

_____

Guided Problem Solving

Practice 12-5

Find the number of permutations of each group of letters.

1. C, H, A, I, R   **2.** L, I, G, H, T, S   **3.** C, O, M, P, U, T, E, R

_____   _____   _____

Write the number of permutations in factorial form. Then simplify.

4. S, P, A, C, E

_____

5. P, L, A, N

_____

6. S, A, M, P, L, E

_____

Find the number of three-letter permutations of the letters.

7. A, P, Q, M   **8.** L, S, U, V, R   **9.** M, B, T, O, D, K

_____   _____   _____

Find the value of each factorial expression.

10. 9!   **11.** 7!   **12.** 6!

_____   _____   _____

Solve.

13. Suppose that first-, second-, and third-place winners of a
contest are to be selected from eight students who entered.
In how many ways can the winners be chosen?   _____

14. Antonio has nine different sweat shirts that he can wear for his
job doing yardwork. He has three pairs of jeans and two pairs
of sweat pants. How many different outfits can Antonio wear
for the yardwork?   _____

15. Ramona has a combination lock for her bicycle. She knows the
numbers are 20, 41, and 6, but she can't remember the order.
How many different arrangements are possible?   _____

16. Travis is planting 5 rosebushes along a fence. Each rosebush has
a different flower color: red, yellow, pink, peach, and white. If he
wants to plant 3 rosebushes in between white and yellow rosebushes, in how many ways can he plant the 5 rosebushes?   _____

12-5 • Guided Problem Solving

GPS **Student Page 609, Exercise 34:**

Tourism The owner of a tour boat business has 15 employees. There are three different jobs—driving the boat, checking the boat for safety, and managing the money. In how many different ways can the jobs be assigned to three different people?

Understand

1. Circle the information you will need to solve.

2. What are you being asked to do?

_____

_____

3. What is a permutation?

_____

_____

Plan and Carry Out

4. How many people can be assigned
   to do the first job, driving the boat? _____

5. After the driver has been chosen, how many people can be assigned to do the second job, checking the boat for safety?

   _____

6. After the manager has been chosen, how many people can be assigned to do the third job, managing the money?

   _____

7. Using the counting principle, in how many different ways can the jobs be assigned? _____

Check

8. Explain why you do not use 15! in this exercise.

   _____

   _____

Solve Another Problem

9. There are four offices open in the student government: president, vice-president, treasurer, and secretary. If 18 students run in the election, how many ways can the offices be filled?

_____

Practice 12-6

Combinations

Find the number of combinations.

1. Choose 3 people from 4.

   _____

2. Choose 4 people from 6.

   _____

Use the numbers 3, 5, 8, 10, 12, 15, 20. Make a list of all the combinations.

3. 2 even numbers

   _____

4. 3 odd numbers

   _____

5. 1 even, 1 odd

   _____

   _____

6. any 2 numbers

   _____

   _____

   _____

7. You just bought five new books to read. You want to take two of them with you on vacation. In how many ways can you choose two books to take?   _____

Charmayne is organizing a track meet. There are 4 runners in her class. Each runner must compete one-on-one against each of the other runners in her class.

8. How many races must Charmayne schedule? _____

9. Must Charmayne schedule permutations or combinations? _____

A committee for the end-of-year party is composed of 4 eighth graders and 3 seventh graders. A three-member subcommittee is formed.

10. How many different combinations of eighth graders could there be if there are 3 eighth graders on the subcommittee?

    _____

11. How many different combinations of seventh graders could there be if the subcommittee consists of 3 seventh graders?

    _____

12-6 • Guided Problem Solving

GPS Student Page 612, Exercise 22:

Music You have 5 different CDs to play. Your CD player can hold 3 CDs. How many different combinations of 3 CDs can you select?

Understand

1. Circle the information you will need to solve.

2. What are you being asked to do?

   _____

   _____

3. What is a combination?

   _____

   _____

   _____

Plan and Carry Out

4. What is the formula you can use to find the number of combinations?

   _____

   _____

5. Find the total number of permutations for the 5 CDs.

   _____

6. Find the total number of permutations for the 3 spaces in your CD player. _____

7. Find the number of combinations. _____

8. How many different combinations of 3 CDs can you select?

   _____

Check

9. If you make an organized list of all the possible permutations, how many duplicate groups would you have to eliminate to find the number of combinations? _____

Solve Another Problem

10. You are allowed to take two different elective classes. There are eight different classes you can choose from. How many different combinations of two electives are there?

    _____

    _____

12A: Graphic Organizer

Study Skill Try to read new lessons before your teacher presents them in class. Important information is sometimes printed in **boldface** type or highlighted inside a box or with color. Pay special attention to this information.

Write your answers.

1. What is the chapter title? _____

2. How many lessons are there in this chapter? _____

3. What is the topic of the Test-Taking Strategies page? _____

4. Complete the graphic organizer below as you work through the chapter.
   • In the center, write the title of the chapter.
   • When you begin a lesson, write the lesson name in a rectangle.
   • When you complete a lesson, write a skill or key concept in a circle linked to that lesson block.
   • When you complete the chapter, use this graphic organizer to help you review.

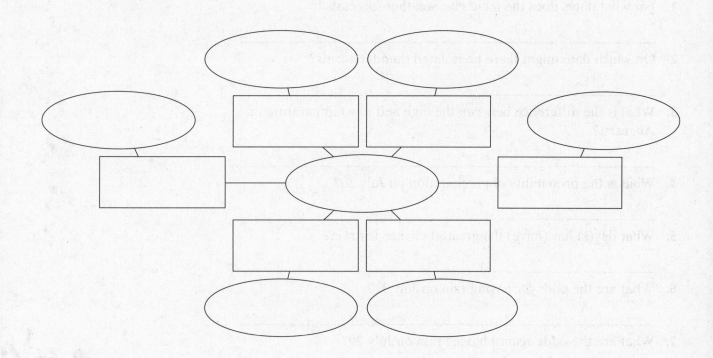

12B: Reading Comprehension

Study Skill When you complete a math exercise, always make sure your answer makes sense.

Below is an 8-day forecast of weather conditions. Use the table to answer the questions.

Date	Weather Prediction	High/Low Temp °F	% Chance of Precipitation
July 26 evening	Isolated T-Storms	67°	30%
July 27	PM T-Storms	87° / 71°	40%
July 28	Partly Cloudy	91° / 71°	20%
July 29	Scattered T-Storms	90° / 64°	40%
July 30	Partly Cloudy	87° / 65°	20%
July 31	Partly Cloudy	87° / 60°	20%
Aug 01	Partly Cloudy	83° / 59°	20%
Aug 02	Partly Cloudy	87° / 60°	0%

1. For what dates does the table give weather forecasts?

   _____

2. On which date might there be isolated thunderstorms?

   _____

3. What is the difference between the high and low temperature on August 1?

   _____

4. What is the probability of precipitation on July 30?

   _____

5. What day(s) has (have) the greatest chance for rain?

   _____

6. What are the odds *for* having rain on July 31?

   _____

7. What are the odds *against* having rain on July 29?

   _____

8. **High-Use Academic Words** What is an *exercise,* as mentioned in the study skill?

   a. something done to develop a skill   b. a group or set alike in some way

12C: Reading/Writing Math Symbols **For use after Lesson 12-5**

Study Skill Write assignments down; do not rely only on your memory.

Write the meaning of each mathematical expression.

1. $P(A)$ _____

2. $P(\text{not } A)$ _____

3. $P(A, \text{then } B)$ _____

_____

4. $5!$ _____

5. $n!$ _____

6. $_nP_r$ _____

7. $_nC_r$ _____

_____

8. $_9C_4$ _____

_____

Write each statement using appropriate mathematical symbols.

9. the probability of event C occurring

_____

10. the probability of rolling an odd number on a number cube

_____

11. the probability of event D, and then event E occurring

_____

12. $7 \cdot 6 \cdot 5 \cdot 4 \cdot 3 \cdot 2 \cdot 1$

_____

13. the number of ways 10 items can be chosen 5 at a time where order does not matter

_____

14. the number of ways 6 items can be chosen 3 at a time where order matters

_____

12D: Visual Vocabulary Practice

For use after Lesson 12-6

High-Use Academic Words

Study Skill Mathematics is like learning a foreign language. You have to know the vocabulary before you can speak the language correctly.

Concept List

counting principle	complement	independent events
combinations	permutations	dependent events
outcome	factorial	sample space

Write the concept that best describes each exercise. Choose from the concept list above.

1. $7!$ $= 7 \times 6 \times 5 \times 4 \times 3 \times 2 \times 1$ $= 5,040$ _____	**2.** $\boxed{\text{A B C}}$ AB AC BC _____	**3.** A jar contains 2 red marbles, 1 blue marble, and 1 green marble. You draw one marble and record the color. This is represented by the set {red, blue, and green}. _____
4. $P(A, \text{then } B) = P(A) \times P(B)$ for these events _____	**5.** If you flip a coin, then flipping heads is an example of this. _____	**6.** Pedro draws a card from a standard 52-card deck. He then rolls a six-sided number cube. The total number of possible outcomes is $52 \times 6 = 312$. _____
7. $\boxed{\text{A B C}}$ AB BA AC CA BC CB _____	**8.** $P(A, \text{then } B) =$ $P(A) \times P(B \text{ after } A)$ for these events _____	**9.** Renee rolls a six-sided number cube. If an event represents rolling an even number, then this is represented by the set {1, 3, 5}. _____

12E: Vocabulary Check

Study Skill Strengthen your vocabulary. Use these pages and add cues and summaries by applying the Cornell Notetaking style.

Write the definition for each word or term at the right. To check your work, fold the paper back along the dotted line to see the correct answers.

_____   combination

_____

_____

_____   permutation

_____

_____   event

_____

_____   theoretical probability

_____

_____   experimental probability

_____

12E: Vocabulary Check (continued) For use after Lesson 12-6

Write the vocabulary word or term for each definition. To check your work, fold the paper forward along the dotted line to see the correct answers.

a grouping of objects in which the order of objects does not matter

_____

an arrangement of objects in a particular order

_____

a collection of possible outcomes

_____

the ratio of the number of favorable outcomes to the number of possible outcomes

_____

the ratio of the number of times an event occurs to the total number of trials

_____

12F: Vocabulary Review Puzzle

For use with the Chapter Review

Study Skill When using a word bank, read the words first. Then answer the questions.

Complete the crossword puzzle. Use the words from the following list.

parallelogram	conjecture	decagon	equation	mode
combination	symmetry	variable	discount	prime
independent	permutation	dependent	outcome	slope

DOWN

1. prediction that suggests what you expect will happen

2. difference between the original price and the sale price

3. letter that stands for a number

5. ratio that describes the steepness of a line

6. arrangement of objects in a particular order

7. number that occurs most often in a data set

9. grouping of objects in which order does not matter

10. mathematical statement with an equal sign

12. polygon with ten sides

13. whole number with only two factors, itself and the number one

ACROSS

2. Events are _____ if the occurrence of one event affects the probability of the occurrence of another event.

4. A figure has _____ if one side of the figure is the mirror image of the other side.

6. four-sided figure with two sets of parallel lines

8. possible result of an action

11. Events are _____ if the occurrence of one event does not affect the probability of the occurrence of another event.